Microsoft®
WORD 97
VISUAL BASIC®

Step by Step

Other titles in the *Step by Step* series:

Microsoft Access 97 Step by Step

Microsoft Access 97/ Visual Basic Step by Step

Microsoft Excel 97 Step by Step

Microsoft Excel 97 Step by Step, Advanced Topics

Microsoft Excel 97/ Visual Basic Step by Step

Microsoft FrontPage 97 Step by Step

Microsoft Internet Explorer 3.0 Step by Step

Microsoft Office 97 Integration Step by Step

Microsoft Outlook 97 Step by Step

Microsoft PowerPoint 97 Step by Step

Microsoft Team Manager 97 Step by Step

Microsoft Visual Basic 5 Step by Step

Microsoft Windows 95 Step by Step

Microsoft Windows NT Workstation version 4.0 Step by Step

Microsoft Word 97 Step by Step

Microsoft Word 97 Step by Step, Advanced Topics

Step by Step books are also available for the Microsoft Office 95 programs.

Microsoft®
WORD 97
VISUAL BASIC®
Step by Step

PUBLISHED BY
Microsoft Press
A Division of Microsoft Corporation
One Microsoft Way
Redmond, Washington 98052-6399

Library of Congress Cataloging-in-Publication Data Pending

Printed and bound in the United States of America.

1 2 3 4 5 6 7 8 9   WCWC   2 1 0 9 8 7

Distributed to the book trade in Canada by Macmillan of Canada, a division of Canada Publishing
Corporation.

A CIP catalogue record for this book is available from the British Library.

Microsoft Press books are available through booksellers and distributors worldwide. For further
information about international editions, contact your local Microsoft Corporation office. Or contact
Microsoft Press International directly at fax (206) 936-7329.

For WASSER*Studio*
Project Manager: Marcelle Amelia
Print Production Manager: Mary C. Gutierrez
Desktop Publishing Lead: Kim Tapia
Desktop Publisher: Arlene Rubin
Copy Editor: Tresy Kilbourne
Technical Editor: Robert Bageant

For Microsoft Press
Acquisitions Editor: Casey D. Doyle
Project Editors: Stuart J. Stuple and Saul Candib

About the Authors

Michael Halvorson worked for Microsoft Corporation from 1985 to 1993, where he was employed as a technical editor, an acquisitions editor, and a localization manager. He received a B.A. in Computer Science from Pacific Lutheran University and an M.A. in History from the University of Washington. Michael is currently pursuing a doctorate in late-medieval European history, with an emphasis in popular piety during the German Reformation.

Michael is the author of *Learn Visual Basic Now* and *Microsoft Visual Basic 5 Step by Step*, and is coauthor (with Michael Young) of *Running Microsoft Office 97*, all published by Microsoft Press. You can reach him electronically by mailing Mike_Halvorson@msn.com.

Chris Kinata (chris@halcyon.com) first learned BASIC in 1967, remembers the installation of the first Internet terminal at USC in 1971, and in perverse moments (always after midnight, past a deadline, with a flaky beta), reminisces about programming with punch cards. He has designed biofeedback devices, converted brain waves into computer art shown in real art galleries, and was in Peru looking for UFOs before Shirley MacLaine. He was employee #720 at Microsoft, worked for 5 years as Senior Technical Editor, Special Projects Editor, and Word Guru. In 1989 he bailed out to home-school his kids in glorious Ballard, USA, and is author or co-author of *Working with Word*, *Complete Guide to Microsoft Excel Macros*, and *Running Microsoft Excel*. He loves children, dreaming, archery, and playing Magic.

Acknowledgments

Each computer book is a truly collaborative effort, and this book is no exception. The authors would like to thank Casey Doyle, acquisitions editor, for starting the project and working with us on the early outline; Stuart Stuple, project editor, for expertly managing the scheduling details at Microsoft Press; and Laura Sackerman, series consultant, for her help with matters related to design and series consistency.

At Wasser, Inc., we would like to thank Marcelle Amelia and Mary Gutierrez, project managers, for skillfully routing all project materials and finding us when we were elusive; Kim Tapia, principal desktop publisher, for expertly handling graphics and artwork; and Arlene Rubin, desktop publisher, for her exacting efforts with type, layout, and design. Our editors deserve a special measure of praise: thanks to Tresy Kilbourne, for refining the pedagogical content and smoothing out our prose, and to Robert Bageant, for testing the macros and applying his software development expertise to the step-by-step exercises.

Finally, we would like to thank Martin Sawicki, program manager in the Desktop Applications Division at Microsoft, for providing us with early guidance and support materials related to macro programming in Word Visual Basic.

Table of Contents

Run a macro, see "Running a macro," page 7 (Lesson 1)

Manage macro modules and Word objects, see "The Project Explorer," page 15 (Lesson 1)

Edit a macro in the Code window, see "Editing a Macro with Visual Basic," page 9 (Lesson 1)

Set object properties, see "The Properties Window," page 17 (Lesson 1)

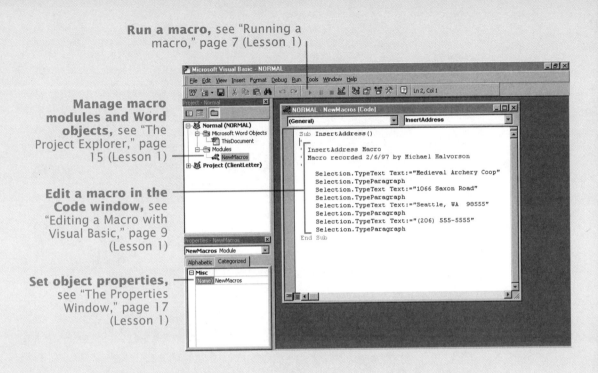

Create custom menus for your macros, see "Creating Custom Menus," page 93 (Lesson 4)

Create macro toolbars, see "Creating Custom Toolbars," page 87 (Lesson 4)

Build tables automatically, see "Using a Loop to Manage Tables," page 67 (Lesson 3)

Create a macro that automatically renumbers graphics, see "Renumbering Graphics in a Chapter," page 77 (Lesson 3)

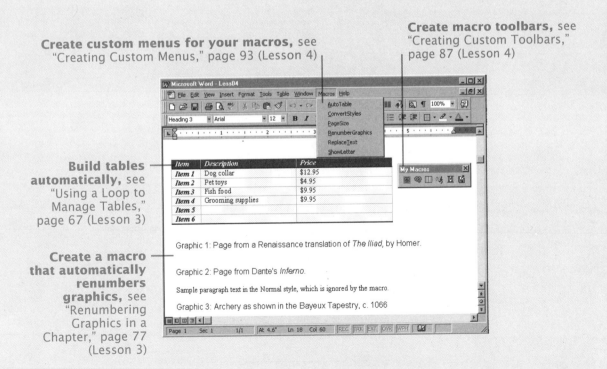

Open custom dialog boxes in your macros, see "Getting Started with UserForms," page 108 (Lesson 5)

Create invoices and other forms directly from dialog boxes, see "The InvoiceMaker Macro," page 122 (Lesson 5)

Use option buttons, check boxes, lists, and other features, see "Controls for Gathering Input," page 121 (Lesson 5)

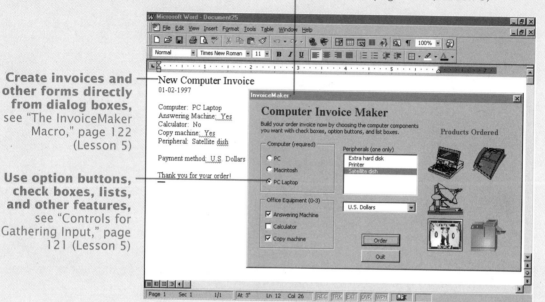

Manage the text in a Word document, see "Displaying Paragraphs with the TextBox Control," page 117 (Lesson 5)

Process UserForm input, see "Examine the CheckBox Code and ListBox Code," page 126 (Lesson 5)

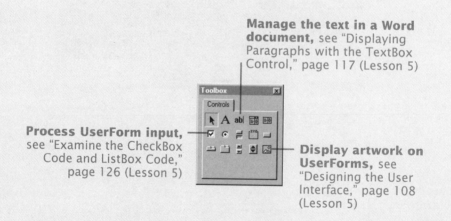

Display artwork on UserForms, see "Designing the User Interface," page 108 (Lesson 5)

Create a custom toolbar for document navigation, see "Navigating Using the Browser Buttons," page 174 (Lesson 8)

Assemble one master document from dozens of component files on the Internet, see "Assembling a Large Document from Many Files," page 227 (Lesson 10)

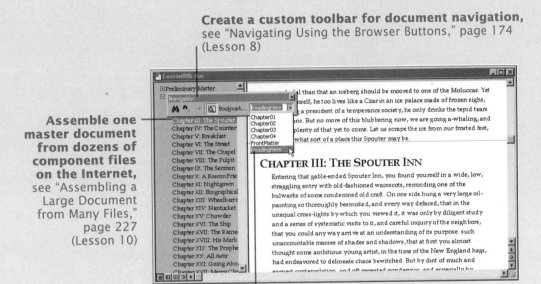

Display the active bookmarks in a document, see "Navigating Using Bookmarks," page 178 (Lesson 8)

Format summary information in concise tables, see "Create the FormatStyleTableDoc procedure," page 200 (Lesson 9)

Determine which styles are active, see "Detecting Whether a Style Is in Use in a Document," page 202 (Lesson 9)

Effectively manage the styles in your Word documents, see "Working with Style Sheets," page 196 (Lesson 9)

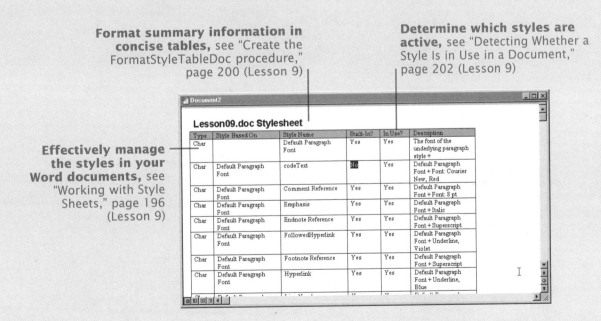

*Quick*Look Guide

Automatically convert Word tables to Excel pivot tables,
see "Using Excel's PivotTable Feature," page 256 (Lesson 11)

Sales Table in Word

Sales Rep	Region	Month	Sale	Description
Anderson, Rhea	South	February	$700	Advance orders, front list
Anderson, Rhea	South	February	$1,400	Educational kits
Anderson, Rhea	South	January	$750	Educational kits
Blickle, Peter	West	February	$600	Advance orders, front list
Blickle, Peter	West	January	$1,100	Misc. backlist books
Blickle, Peter	West	January	$500	Misc. backlist books
Cashel, Seamus	Midwest	January	$1,200	Advance orders, front list
Cashel, Seamus	Midwest	January	$1000	Educational kits
Cashel, Seamus	Midwest	February	$450	Misc. backlist orders
Greif, Jacob	East	January	$1,000	Advance orders, front list
Greif, Jacob	East	January	$250	Advance orders, front list
Greif, Jacob	East	February	$800	Misc. backlist orders

Pivot Table in Excel

	A	B	C	D	E	F
1	Sum of Sale	Sales Rep				
2	Month	Anderson, Rhea	Blickle, Peter	Cashel, Seamus	Greif, Jacob	Grand Total
3	January	750	1600	2200	1250	5800
4	February	2100	600	450	800	3950
5	Grand Total	2850	2200	2650	2050	9750
6						

Create variables in your macro code to manage information,
see "Declaring Variables," page 35 (Lesson 2)

```
Less11 - NewMacros [Code]                              _ □ ×
(General)                          ▼    PivotTable              ▼
  Sub PivotTable()
  '
  ' PivotTable Macro
  ' Macro created 02/05/97 by Michael Halvorson
  ' Note: This macro requires Excel 97.

  Dim x1 As Object
  Dim oTable, myRange, aCell, r, c

  If Selection.Information(wdWithInTable) = True Then
      Set oTable = Selection.Tables(1)
      Set x1 = CreateObject("Excel.Sheet") 'start Excel
      x1.Application.Visible = True        'show Excel
      r = 0                                'initialize row count
      Do  'copy each table cell from Word to Excel
```

Use Excel commands from a Word macro, see
"Automating Excel from Word," page 250 (Lesson 11)

Finding Your Best Starting Point

Microsoft Word 97 includes a new programming language called Visual Basic for Applications that you can use to quickly and efficiently build tools that will streamline your word processing, manage complex documents, automate Internet connections, and much more. With *Microsoft Word 97/Visual Basic Step by Step*, you'll quickly learn how to use Visual Basic for Applications to write your own time-saving macros. Once you learn how to use Visual Basic, you can use your new skills to supercharge word processing activities in your workgroup, publish and manage electronic documents on the Web, and integrate Word's functionality with other Microsoft Office applications, such as Microsoft Excel and Microsoft Access.

 IMPORTANT This book is designed for use with Microsoft Word 97 for the Windows 95 and Windows NT version 4.0 operating systems. Microsoft Word 97 is not included with this book—you must purchase it separately and install it before you can complete the lessons. (Microsoft Word is also part of Microsoft Office.) To find out what software you're running, you can check the product package or you can start the software, click the Help menu at the top of the screen, and click About Microsoft Word. If your software is not compatible with this book, a Step by Step book for your software is probably available. Many of the Step by Step titles are listed on the second page of this book. If the book you want isn't listed, please visit our World Wide Web site at http://www.microsoft.com/mspress/ or call 1-800-MSPRESS for more information.

Finding Your Best Starting Point in This Book

This book is designed for readers learning Word Visual Basic for the first time, for readers with previous WordBasic macro experience, and for experienced Visual Basic programmers who want to write Visual Basic macros in Word. Use the following table to find your best starting point in this book.

If you are	Follow these steps
New...	
to Word Visual Basic and programming	**1** Install the practice files as described in "Installing and Using the Practice Files."
	2 Practice recording, editing, and running a simple macro in Lesson 1.
	3 Learn fundamental and advanced programming skills by reading Lessons 2 through 11 sequentially.

If you are	Follow these steps
Switching...	
to Word Visual Basic from WordBasic	**1** Install the practice files as described in "Installing and Using the Practice Files."
	2 Skim the lessons in Part 1, and then work through the lessons in Parts 2 and 3 sequentially.
	3 For information about converting WordBasic macros to Visual Basic, search for "WordBasic, converting macros to Visual Basic" in the Microsoft Word Visual Basic online Help.
to Word Visual Basic from the Microsoft Visual Basic compiler or from another version of Visual Basic for Applications	**1** Install the practice files as described in "Installing and Using the Practice Files."
	2 Complete Lesson 1, skim through Lessons 2 through 6, and then work through Lessons 7 through 11 sequentially.
	3 For specific information about using Word's features programmatically from a Visual Basic application, see Lesson 11.

If you are	Follow these steps

Referencing...

this book after working
through the lessons

1 Use the index to locate information about specific topics, and use the table of contents and the *Quick*Look Guide to locate information about general topics.

2 Read the Lesson Summary at the end of each lesson for a brief review of the major tasks in the lesson. The Lesson Summary topics are listed in the same order as they are presented in the lesson.

Corrections, Comments, and Help

Every effort has been made to ensure the accuracy of this book and the contents of the practice files disc. Microsoft Press provides corrections and additional content for its books through the World Wide Web at

http://www.microsoft.com/mspress/support/

If you have comments, questions, or ideas regarding this book or the practice files disc, please send them to Microsoft Press.

Send e-mail to

mspinput@microsoft.com

Or send postal mail to

Microsoft Press

Attn: Step by Step Series Editor

One Microsoft Way

Redmond, WA 98052-6399

Please note that support for Word 97/Visual Basic is not offered through the above addresses. For help using Visual Basic for Applications, you can call Microsoft Word AnswerPoint at (206) 462-9673 on weekdays between 6 A.M. and 6 P.M. Pacific time.

Visit Our World Wide Web Site

We also invite you to visit the Microsoft Press World Wide Web site. You can visit Microsoft Press at the following location:

http://www.microsoft.com/mspress/

You'll find descriptions for the complete line of Microsoft Press books (including others by Michael Halvorson and Chris Kinata), information about ordering titles, notices of special features and events, additional content for Microsoft Press books, and much more.

You can also find out the latest in software developments and news from Microsoft Corporation by visiting the following World Wide Web site:

http://www.microsoft.com/

Get online and check it out!

Installing
and Using the
Practice Files

The disc inside the back cover of this book contains practice files that you'll use as you complete the exercises in this course. For example, when you're learning how to create UserForms with Word's Visual Basic Editor, you'll open one of the practice files—a graphical order-entry system named InvoiceMaker—and then add features to it with controls in the Visual Basic toolbox. By using the practice files, you won't waste time creating the samples used in the lessons—instead, you can concentrate on learning how to master Visual Basic programming techniques. With the files and the step-by-step instructions in the lessons, you'll also learn by doing, which is an easy and effective way to acquire and remember new skills.

IMPORTANT Before you break the seal on the practice disc package, be sure that this book matches your version of the software. This book is designed for use with Microsoft Word 97 for the Windows 95 and Windows NT version 4.0 operating systems. (Microsoft Word 97 is sold separately, and as part of the Microsoft Office 97 software suite.) To find out what software you're running, you can check the product package or you can start the software, click the Help menu at the top of the screen, and then click About Microsoft Word. If your program is not compatible with this book, a Step by Step book matching your software may be available. Many of the Step by Step titles are listed on the second page of this book. If the book you want isn't listed, please visit our World Wide Web site at http://www.microsoft.com/mspress/ or call 1-800-MSPRESS for more information.

Install the practice files on your computer

Follow these steps to install the practice files on your computer's hard disk so that you can use them with the exercises in this book.

In Windows 95, you will be prompted for a user name and password when starting Windows 95 if your computer is configured for user profiles.

If you don't know your user name or password, contact your system administrator for assistance.

Close

1 If your computer isn't on, turn it on now.

2 If you're using Windows NT, press CTRL+ALT+DEL to display a dialog box asking for your user name and password. If you are using Windows 95, you will see this dialog box only if your computer is connected to a network or configured for user profiles.

3 If the dialog box appears, type your user name and password in the appropriate boxes, and then click OK. If you see the Welcome dialog box, click the Close button.

4 Remove the disc from the package inside the back cover of this book.

5 Insert the disc in your CD-ROM drive.

6 On the taskbar at the bottom of your screen, click the Start button, and then click Run.

The Run dialog box appears.

Click Start... ...and then click Run.

7 In the Open box, type **d:setup**. Don't add spaces as you type. (If your CD-ROM drive is associated with a different drive letter, such as e, type that letter in place of the d.)

8 Click OK, and then follow the directions on the screen.

The setup program window appears with recommended options preselected for you. For best results in using the practice files with this book, accept these preselected settings. (If you change the installation location, you will need to manually adjust the pathnames in a few macros to locate essential components, such as Word documents and artwork, when you use them.)

Microsoft
Press
Welcome

9 When the files have been installed, remove the disc from your CD-ROM drive and replace it in the package inside the back cover of the book.

A folder called \WordVB is now on your hard disk, and the practice files are in that folder.

NOTE In addition to installing the practice files, the Setup program created a shortcut to the Microsoft Press World Wide Web site on your Desktop. If your computer is set up to connect to the Internet, you can double-click the shortcut to visit the Microsoft Press Web site. You can also connect to the Web site directly at http://www.microsoft.com/mspress/.

Using the Practice Files

Each lesson in this book explains when and how to use any practice files for that lesson. When it's time to use a practice file, the book will list instructions for how to open the file. The lessons are built around scenarios that simulate real programming projects, so you can easily apply the skills you learn to your own work.

For those of you who like to know all the details, here's a list of the Word macros included on the practice disc. For your convenience, each lesson includes one Word document containing all the macros developed in that lesson. You can experiment with the macros in a lesson by opening the lesson documents listed below, and then pressing ALT+F8 to display the Macros dialog box.

Lesson	Project	Description
1 (Less01.doc)	InsertAddress	Inserts a business address in a Word document.
2 (Less02.doc)	CenterHeading	Formats the selected text with shading, border formatting, and center alignment.
	CopyParagraph	Copies the first paragraph in the active document to a new document.
	DisplayUser	Uses the MsgBox function and the UserName property to display the registered owner of the current copy of Word.
	InsertHead	Simplifies adding headings by prompting the user for the text, and then applying custom formatting.

Using the Practice Files, *continued*

Lesson	Project	Description
	SalesTax	Computes the cost of the selected value with sales tax. (Demonstrates how to use variables, formulas, and currency formatting in program code.)
3 (Less03.doc)	AutoTable	Demonstrates For...Next loops; inserts a table with column headings at the insertion points, and applies an AutoFormat color scheme to it.
	ConvertStyles	Demonstrates If...Then...Else structures; converts Heading 1, Heading 2, and Heading 3 styles to formatted text in the Normal style.
	PageSize	Demonstrates Select Case structures; displays the current document type as identified by Page Setup.
	RenumberGraphics	Demonstrates the Do loop; automatically renumbers graphics in a chapter that are formatted with the Heading 3 style.
	ReplaceText	Demonstrates the With statement and the Find method; runs an automatic search and replace throughout the document.
	ShowLetter	Demonstrates the For Each loop; opens the Sample.doc file if it is not already open.
4 (Less04.doc)	ChangePageSize	Identifies the current document type, and uses the Page Size dialog box to change it, if necessary.
	DimWindowMenu	Disables (and enables) the Window menu, demonstrating how to control the menu bar with program code.
	FormatText	Uses the Dialogs object to configure the Font dialog box with 24-point Times New Roman type.
	OpenMacros	Opens the MyMacros toolbar, a custom toolbar containing all the macros developed in Lesson 3.

Lesson	Project	Description
5 (Less05.doc)	InvoiceMaker	Demonstrates a graphical ordering system; uses toolbox controls to prompt the user for the ultimate computer system, and then creates an invoice.
	MusicTrivia	Runs a simple UserForm demonstrating Label, CommandButton, and Image controls.
	ParaScan	Demonstrates an editing utility that displays each paragraph in the active document with a custom dialog box, and then allows the user to format the paragraph or delete it.
6 (Less06.doc)	Document_Close	Opens a Log file (Less06.log) and records the current time and date when the Less06.doc document is closed.
	RuntimeError	Generates a run-time error when you create a table. (See Lesson 6 for information about writing a error handler to solve this problem.)
7 (Less07.doc)	MyCounter	Presents a dialog box listing each instance of the Character, Word, and Sentence collection objects in the current selection.
	WordSelectorForward	Cycles forward through the Word objects in the current selection.
	WordSelectorBackward	Cycles backward through the Word objects in the current selection.
	SentSelectorForward	Cycles forward through the Sentence objects in the current selection.
	SentSelectorBackward	Cycles backward through the Sentence objects in the current selection.
8 (Less08.doc)	AddBookmarkCombo	Creates a Bookmark combo box that lists the bookmarks defined in the active document.
	BookmarkChoice	Processes the selection of an item from the Bookmarks combo box and selects the associated bookmark.

Using the Practice Files, *continued*

Lesson	Project	Description
	App_DocumentChange	An application-level event handler that updates the Bookmarks combo box when a document is activated.
	Register_Event_Handler	Connects the App_DocumentChange handler with the Word application so that the handler will process document change events.
	DateTimeStamp	Inserts the current date and time at the insertion point.
	LogProgress	Creates a table that records statistics for the active document at specified intervals.
9 (Less09.doc)	StyleMapper	Main procedure for a system of macros that creates a table listing the style sheet for the active document.
	GetStyleArray	Reads style sheet information into an array.
	CreateStyleTableDoc	Creates a document to hold the style sheet information.
	FormatStyleTableDoc	Formats the style sheet table.
	StyleReallyInUse	Function that returns True if the specified style is really used in a document.
	TestStyleReallyInUse	Tests the StyleReallyInUse function.
	WriteLine	Writes a line of text, formatted in the specified style.
	ModulesToWordDoc	Reads macros in each module of the active document, creates a new code listing document, and lists macros in the document.
	FormatStyles	Redefines the Normal style in the code listing document.
	FormatDoc	Formats the code listing document.
	FormatHeader	Formats the header of the code listing document.

Lesson	Project	Description
10 (Less10.doc)	GetASCII	Displays a dialog box listing the character, ASCII code, and Unicode values for the selected character.
	TrueTitleCase	Converts the selected text into true title case.
	CombineFiles	Main procedure for combining a series of files into a single document.
	SetupWorkDir	Requests the user to locate the source directory for the files to assemble.
	ReadFileList	Reads the list of filenames in the source directory into an array.
	WriteFileListToDoc	Inserts the list of filenames into the Less10.doc practice file.
	CopyFilesToWorkDir	Copies the list of files into a working directory, and corrects filename extensions.
	SortFileList	Sorts the array containing the list of filenames.
	AppendFiles	Creates a new document, and appends each file in the list to the document.
11 (Less11.doc)	ExcelPMT	Uses Automation to start Microsoft Excel 97, then determines a loan payment with the Excel Pmt function. (Requires Excel 97.)
	PivotTable	Uses Automation to copy a table from Word to Excel, and then summarizes the table with the Excel PivotTable wizard. (Requires Excel 97.)
	RunPresentation	Uses Automation to start Microsoft PowerPoint 97 and run a presentation containing "curious PowerPoint facts." (Requires PowerPoint 97.)
	Spelling.vbp	A Visual Basic 5.0 program that uses Automation to call Microsoft Word and check the grammar and spelling in a paragraph. (Requires Visual Basic 5.0 compiler.)

Uninstalling the Practice Files

Use the following steps to delete the practice files added to your hard drive by the Word 97/Visual Basic Step by Step installation program.

1   Click Start, point to Settings, and then click Control Panel.

2   Double-click the Add/Remove Programs icon.

3   Select Microsoft Word 97/Visual Basic Step by Step from the list, and then click Add/Remove.

A confirmation message appears.

4   Click Yes.

5   Click OK to close the Add/Remove Programs Properties dialog box.

The practice files are uninstalled.

6   Close the Control Panel window.

Need Help with the Practice Files?

Every effort has been made to ensure the accuracy of this book and the contents of the practice files disc. If you do encounter a problem, Microsoft Press provides corrections for its books through the World Wide Web at

http://www.microsoft.com/mspress/support/

We also invite you to visit our main Web page at

http://www.microsoft.com/mspress/

You'll find descriptions for all of our books, information about ordering titles, notices of special features and events, additional content for Microsoft Press books, and much more.

Conventions and Features Used in This Book

Before you start the lessons, you can save time by understanding how instructions, keys to press, and so on are shown in the book. Please take a moment to read the following list, which also points out helpful features of the book that you might want to use.

Typographic Conventions Used in This Book

- Hands-on exercises for you to follow are given in numbered lists of steps (1, 2, and so on). An arrowhead bullet (▶) indicates an exercise that has only one step.

- Text that you are to type appears in **bold**.

- A plus sign (+) between two key names means that you must press those keys together. For example, "Press ALT+TAB" means that you hold down the ALT key while you press the TAB key.

- Program code is formatted monospace (`monospace`) and indented when set on a line by itself, to help you type in the Visual Basic Editor.

Supplementary Features

The following icons identify the different types of supplementary material:

	Notes labeled	Alert you to
	Note	Additional information about Word Visual Basic
	Tip	Alternatives for a step or programming practice
	Important	Essential information that you should check before continuing with the lesson

Other Features of This Book

- You can learn special programming techniques, background information, or program features by reading the shaded boxes that appear throughout the lessons. These shaded boxes often highlight difficult terminology or suggest future areas for exploration.

- You can learn about options or techniques that build on what you just learned by trying the optional "One Step Further" exercise at the end of many lessons.

- You can get a quick reminder of how to perform the tasks you learned by reading the Lesson Summary at the end of a lesson.

- You can quickly determine what online Help topics are available by referring to the Help topics listed at the end of each lesson. The Help system provides a complete online reference to both Microsoft Word and the Visual Basic Editor. To learn more about online Help, see Lesson 1.

Part
1

Visual Basic Fundamentals

Creating Your First Macro

Estimated time

40 min.

In this lesson you will learn how to:

- Record and run a Visual Basic macro.
- Edit a macro with Visual Basic.
- Use commands and tools in the Visual Basic Editor.

This book explores Visual Basic for Applications, the powerful new macro language included in Microsoft Word 97. With Visual Basic, you can create a wide variety of word processing utilities and productivity applications, including customized business forms, mail merge tools, Hypertext Markup Language (HTML) and Internet utilities, search and replace macros, and time-saving desktop publishing tools. In this step-by-step instruction book, you'll learn both the fundamental skills necessary to create macros, and the powerful programming techniques that will push Word to its limits.

In this lesson, you'll take your first steps with Visual Basic. First, you'll learn how to record a macro and run it inside Word. The macro you'll build inserts a custom mailing address in a document when you press ALT+A—a simple beginning, but one that will give you valuable experience with Visual Basic tools and terminology. Next, you'll learn how to edit and customize the macro by using the Visual Basic Code window, a special text editor designed especially for Word macros. Finally, you'll learn how to manage your macros with the commands and tools in the Visual Basic Editor, a special part of Word that appears when you work with macros.

Recording a Macro with Word

A *macro* is a named set of instructions that tells Word to perform an action for you. In Word 97, you can record new macros by using the Record New Macro command, or you can type macros from scratch in the Visual Basic Editor. In both cases, macros are written in a special programming language called Visual Basic for Applications. The core features of this programming language are also included in Microsoft Excel, Microsoft Access, Microsoft Project, Microsoft PowerPoint, and Microsoft Visual Basic, so once you learn how to create macros in Word, you'll have many of the programming skills you need to create useful macros in other applications.

Planning a Macro

Before you create a macro in Word, you should spend some time thinking generally about how your macro will be used. First, you should consider who will run your macro, and the different operating conditions your users will encounter when they use the macro. Since most word processing macros streamline text editing and document management tasks, you should aim to create general purpose tools that work well for a variety of document types.

In addition, you should make sure that Word doesn't already provide a built-in solution for your text processing tasks before you write the macro. For example, if you routinely boldface a heading, increase the point size, and apply border formatting, you could record a macro to automatically format the headings for you. But it would actually be faster for you to use the Style command on the Format menu to apply a heading style that accomplishes the same formatting effect. In other words, don't use macros unless the commands that you want to record are involved enough to justify a macro.

This word to the wise doesn't mean you shouldn't use macros to automate your document management. Actually, we're arguing just the opposite. But before you get started, it makes sense to be comfortable with the majority of Word's features, so you know how and when to use macros to their greatest effect. Word's Visual Basic macro language is sophisticated enough for many advanced tasks, such as creating a custom file converter or controlling FTP access to a variety of Web sites on the Internet (we'll get to this in Part 3). However, the best macros are often the ones that automate just four or five simple Word commands. And although you can create macros from scratch with Visual Basic (see Lesson 2), the best way to learn about macros is recording and editing them.

Recording a Macro

Let's start with a simple example. Imagine that you want to insert a standard mailing address for your company into a variety of Word documents. Rather than type the text from scratch each time, you decide to create a macro that inserts the text automatically when you press the key combination ALT+A. Complete the following steps to record the macro with the Record New Macro command.

Use the Record New Macro command

[handwritten: actions which will be stored in the]

1   Open the document in which you want to record the macro, or create a new one. *[handwritten: D:\ggmacros\glesson1.doc]*

[handwritten: Not the same as the above document]

By default, your macro will be stored in the Normal document template (Normal.dot), so it will be available to all your Word documents.

2   From the Tools menu, click Macro, and then click Record New Macro to open the Record Macro dialog box.

Your screen should look like the following:

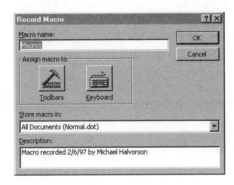

3   In the Macro Name text box, type **InsertAddress**, the name of your macro.

4   Click Keyboard in the Record Macro dialog box to display the Customize Keyboard dialog box. This is the place where you specify the shortcut key that will run your macro.

TIP   To run your macro with a menu command or toolbar button, click Toolbars in the Record Macro dialog box and specify a custom menu command or toolbar button for the macro. (For more information, see One Step Further at the end of this lesson.)

[handwritten: 28.6.13 ✓]

When you're finished recording your macro, you can run it by pressing ALT+A.

5 Press ALT+A to assign the shortcut key ALT+A to your macro, and then verify that the Save Changes In drop-down list box is set to Normal.

Your screen should look similar to the one below:

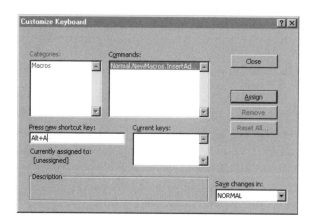

6 In the Customize Keyboard dialog box, click Assign, and then click Close to accept your keyboard shortcut and start recording the macro.

Word displays the Stop Recording toolbar, and changes the mouse pointer to a recording icon. From this point on, any key you press or any command that you execute in Word will be "taped" by the macro recorder.

 TIP The Stop Recording toolbar contains two useful toolbar buttons, Stop Recording and Pause/Resume Recording. When you're finished recording your macro, click Stop Recording and Word will stop saving your commands and close the macro. If you want to pause the recording temporarily, click Pause Recording, modify your document as needed, and then click the Resume Recording button when you're ready to continue.

---

7 Type the following address (or one of your own) in the active Word document and then press ENTER:

**Medieval Archery Coop
1066 Saxon Road
Seattle, WA 98555
(206) 555-5555**

8 Click Stop Recording to end your macro.

That's all there is to it! Now that you've recorded your first macro, let's run it in your Word document to verify that it displays the address correctly.

*Stop
Recording*

28.6.13

Running a Macro

To give you flexibility in automating your work, Word provides you with five methods for running your macros. You can:

- Double-click the macro name in the Macros dialog box.
- Press a macro shortcut key (if one has been assigned).
- Click the macro from a menu (if you added the macro name to a menu).
- Click a custom macro button on a toolbar (if you assigned the macro to a toolbar button).
- Start the Visual Basic Editor, and run the macro inside it.

In the following exercises, you will run the InsertAddress macro with the Macros dialog box and with the ALT+A shortcut key.

Run a macro with the Macros dialog box

To run a macro with the Macros dialog box, follow these steps:

1 Press ENTER to add a blank line to your document.

2 From the Tools menu, click Macro, and then click Macros.

You'll see the following dialog box:

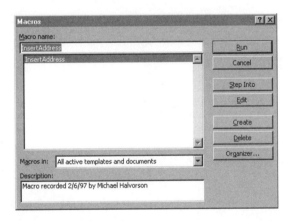

The Macros dialog box is a comprehensive tool for managing macros. With the Macros dialog box, you can run, debug (that is, step into), edit, record (create), delete, and organize macros.

TIP Since the Macros dialog box is so useful, you may want to memorize the keyboard shortcut for opening it: ALT+F8).

28.6.13 √

3 Specify the location of the macro you want to run in the Macros In drop-down list box.

By default, the macros in all your active (open) templates and documents are listed, but you can also list the macros in a specific template or document by picking a name from the Macros In list box.

4 Finally, double-click the macro you want to run in the Macros list box.

If you double-click the InsertAddress macro, the company address text will be inserted into the current document, as shown in the following illustration:

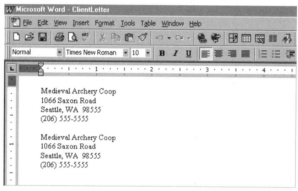

Run a macro with a shortcut key

If you assigned a shortcut key to your macro when you created it, you can also run it in Word by pressing the designated shortcut key. To run the InsertAddress macro with the ALT+A shortcut key, follow these steps:

1 Press ENTER to add a blank line to your document.

2 Press ALT+A to run the InsertAddress macro.

Word runs the macro and inserts your company address in the current document. That's all there is to it!

TIP After you run a macro, the Undo command on Word's Edit menu works a little differently than you might expect. Rather than undoing the entire macro, the Undo command only reverses the last command executed in the macro. If your macro contains several commands or keyboard operations, such as the InsertAddress macro does, you can only reverse the steps performed by the macro actions by clicking the Undo drop-down list on Word's Standard toolbar, and then selecting all the commands in the macro. As you'll see in the next section, Word stores each Visual Basic command separately in your macro.

Editing a Macro with Visual Basic

In Word 97, you can edit your recorded macros and create new macros from scratch by using the Visual Basic Editor, a special Office 97 utility with its own windows, menus, and programming tools. In this section, you'll learn how to use the Visual Basic Editor to edit the InsertAddress macro. Feel free to experiment a little in this section—the skills you learn will come in handy each time you work with macros.

Edit the InsertAddress macro

To edit your InsertAddress macro with the Visual Basic Editor, follow these steps:

1   From the Tools menu, click Macro, and then click Macros.

You'll see the Macros dialog box, with the InsertAddress macro listed in the list box.

2   Click Edit in the Macros dialog box.

The Visual Basic Editor appears.

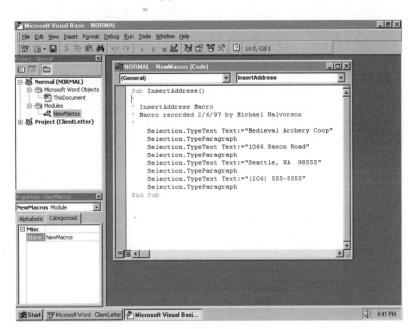

28.6.13 ✓

The Visual Basic Editor includes a variety of programming tools to help you write, edit, test, and manage your Word macros. We'll describe the most important programming tools a little later in the lesson. For now, concentrate on the large text editing window in the middle of the screen, called the Code window.

The Code window displays the contents of your Word macro in a programming language called Visual Basic. Each program statement in this macro follows a particular programming rule, and the trick to learning macro programming with Word is understanding the *syntax* principles and program logic behind each of the Visual Basic statements.

The macro is stored in a special program code container called a *subroutine*, which itself is part of the more comprehensive container called a *module*. This particular subroutine is called InsertAddress, and it is delimited by the Sub and End Sub statements, respectively. Within the body of the subroutine you'll see descriptive comments, which appear in green type, and the Visual Basic program statements that do the work of the macro, which appear in black type. In this macro, the Sub and End Sub statements appear in blue type, because they are special reserved words in the Visual Basic programming language, called *keywords*.

 TIP *Syntax* is the technical term for the exact spelling, order, and spacing of words, keywords, and punctuation in a macro.

In the following exercise, you'll use the Code window to add a descriptive comment to the macro, and edit the business phone number.

Use the Code window

1   Press the DOWN ARROW key three times, and then press the RIGHT ARROW key once to move the insertion point after the fourth single quotation mark in the macro. (You can also use the mouse to move the insertion point, if you prefer.)

2   Press SPACEBAR once, type **My first macro**, and press ENTER.

Visual Basic inserts your new comment and displays it in green type. Comments are for documentation purposes only, and are not used by the macro when it runs. We recommend you use comments as informal notes about how your macro works if you plan to share your macro with friends and work associates. (They're especially useful when you write

10

complicated program statements.) Your Code window should look like this:

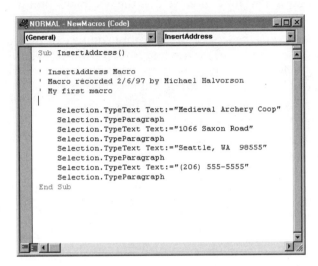

3 Now move the insertion point to the program statement containing the phone number you entered when recording the macro, and change the last four digits to **1234**.

Your Code window should look like this:

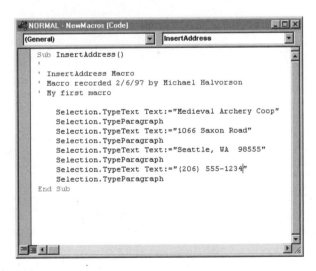

Selection is an object that identifies the insertion point in a document.

This simple edit will change the output of your macro the next time you run it. Although we're not focusing on the exact details of the Visual Basic program statements right now, you may find it interesting to know what the words "Selection" and "TypeText" are doing in the program code. Selection is an

28.6.13

object, or component, of the current document or application that can be controlled by your program. The Selection object designates a particular location in your document for action—either the text block that is highlighted, or the current insertion point.

TypeText is a method that inserts text.

TypeText is a *method*, or command, that can be executed using the specified object. When the TypeText method is used with the Selection object, Word inserts the text specified at the current insertion point—exactly what your InsertAddress macro does when you run it!

You're finished editing the InsertAddress macro for now. In the next two exercises, you'll run the macro again and save your changes to disk.

Using the Visual Basic Programming Tools

The Visual Basic Editor contains a number of useful programming tools to help you construct and manage your macros. In this section, you'll learn how to use the most important programming tools and how to organize them with a technique called *docking*. As you work through the book, you'll gain additional experience with the tools by constructing practical, working macros.

The essential Visual Basic tools include:

- The menu bar
- Toolbars
- The Project Explorer
- The Properties window
- The online Help system

The Menu Bar

The menu bar in the Visual Basic Editor contains commands that are specifically designed to edit and manage your macros. Unlike the last version of Word, which contained no special programming menus or commands, Word 97 accesses a comprehensive collection of menus and commands specifically designed for Visual Basic programming. The following table describes the purpose of each menu:

Menu name	Purpose
File	Save macros, import and export useful routines, remove macros, and print the contents of the Code window.
Edit	Edit and search for text in the Code window, format code, and display information about available properties, methods, and constants.
View	Display the various tools in the development environment.

28-6.13 √

Menu name	Purpose
Insert	Extend your macro with new objects and features. Specify a new code procedure, a custom dialog box (UserForm), a module, or a supporting file.
Format	Format the objects and text in a custom UserForm dialog box.
Debug	Detect and fix bugs (defects) in your macros.
Run	Execute your macros. A special command, Break, is useful for debugging.
Tools	Customize your macro with references to other object libraries and controls, text formatting options in the Code window, and property settings. The Macros command is identical to the Macros command on Word's Tools menu.
Window	Adjust the size and orientation of windows in the development environment, and switch between open documents.
Help	Display online Help and connect to frequently used Visual Basic Web sites.

Use the menu bar

Now try using the Run Sub/UserForm command on the Run menu to verify the edits you made to your macro. (Word should insert your address with an updated phone number.)

1 From the Run menu, click Run Sub/UserForm.

   Word runs your macro again in the current, open document. Since the InsertAddress macro has no visible user interface, you won't see it run in the Visual Basic Editor. You'll need to restore your Word document again to see the results.

2 Click the Microsoft Word program icon on the Windows taskbar.

   Windows returns to Word and displays the current, open document.

3 Verify that the InsertAddress macro correctly displayed your address text.

   If you've followed all the exercises in this lesson, you should see four addresses, and the last one should have a new phone number.

28.6.13 ✓

13

4 When you're ready to return to Visual Basic, click the Microsoft Visual Basic program icon on the Windows taskbar.

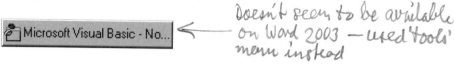

Doesn't seem to be available on Word 2003 — used 'tools' menu instead

Run the macro again if you like, and take some time to experiment with other menus and commands.

The Toolbars

The Visual Basic toolbars provide rapid access to the most common commands and procedures in the Visual Basic Editor. As a Word user, you've probably had plenty of practice using the Word toolbars to run commands. The process is the same in the Visual Basic Editor. To learn more about a toolbar button, hold the mouse over the button until a descriptive ToolTip appears that describes the button's purpose. To execute a command associated with a toolbar button, simply click the button and watch the command run.

By default, only the Standard toolbar appears, but you can add special purpose Visual Basic toolbars by clicking Toolbars from the View menu.

The following illustration shows the purpose of the buttons and controls on the Standard toolbar:

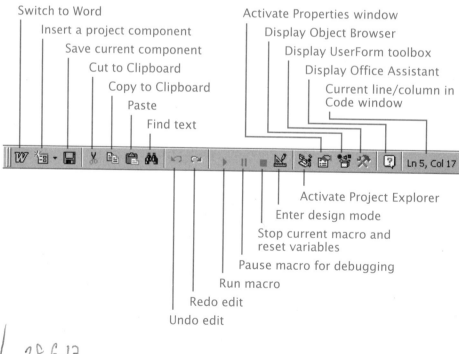

28.6.13

Use the toolbar to save your macro

In this exercise, you will use the Save button on the toolbar to save your macro edits to the Normal document template (Normal.dot). Since a version of the InsertAddress macro is already located in Normal.dot, the save process is only one step.

Save

> ➤ Click the Save button on the Standard toolbar.
>
> Visual Basic saves your macro edits to Normal.dot.

 TIP The Save button on the Standard toolbar saves changes to the component that is currently highlighted in the Project Explorer. (See below.) To see the name of the file that Visual Basic will use when it saves, hold the mouse pointer over the Save button until the ToolTip appears, which identifies the current filename.

The Project Explorer

Project Explorer

The Visual Basic Project Explorer is an organizational tool that displays a hierarchical list of the projects currently open in Word, and any of their supporting components. Using the Project Explorer, you can add or delete components from a project, compare elements and reorganize them, and display items of interest. If the Project Explorer is not visible, you can display it by clicking Project Explorer from the View menu, or by clicking the Project Explorer toolbar button.

When you first start using the Project Explorer, you might find its assortment of folders and components a bit confusing. Stick with it. The Project Explorer is actually a very useful programming tool, and its secrets can be readily comprehended. Each project name corresponds to a document or template that is currently open in Word. In the following illustration of the Project Explorer, the Normal.dot template and the ClientLetter.doc document files are shown with their supporting component files. (If you've been following the exercises to this point, these are also the files you'll see on your own computer screen.) You'll see additional projects in your Project window if you have other documents open, or if Microsoft Outlook is running and Word is your e-mail editor.

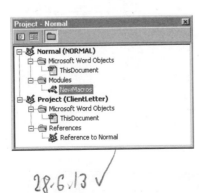

 28·6·13 ✓

With Visual Basic, you can customize several different components of a Word document or template. As we demonstrated earlier in the lesson, you can record a macro and store it in a module that becomes part of the document or template. However, you can also add one or more of the following items to your project:

- Word objects, such as additional Word documents
- Standard modules, which contain macros and other useful program code
- Custom dialog boxes, called UserForms
- Class modules, which define objects and the methods and properties used to control them
- References to commands and objects in other Windows applications

The Project Explorer keeps track of all these different components and provides access to them via two special buttons: View Code and View Object. To switch from one component to the next, you click the project you want to work with, click the folder you want to open, and then click the component you want to view. If the component contains program code such as a module or a UserForm, you can examine it by clicking the View Code button. If the component contains a user interface (such as a Word document or a UserForm), you can examine it by clicking the View Object button.

In the next exercise, you'll use the Project Explorer to examine the user interface for the sample document you currently have open in Word. (In our example, the sample file is named ClientLetter.doc.)

Use the Project Explorer

Project Explorer

1   Click the Project Explorer button on the toolbar.

The Project window is highlighted in the programming environment. (If the window was not open, it will appear now.) You'll see a Project Explorer window that looks like this:

View code ——— 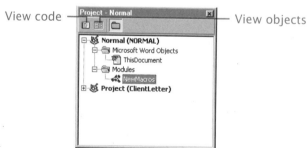 ——— View objects

handwritten note: I've used 'Glessont' instead of 'ClientLetter'

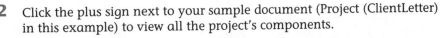

2 Click the plus sign next to your sample document (Project (ClientLetter) in this example) to view all the project's components.

You'll see a folder named Microsoft Word Objects and a folder named References.

3 Double-click the Microsoft Word Objects folder to open it, and then select the object named ThisDocument. Each project you work with that is based on a Word document or template will have a ThisDocument entry, which you can use to customize how your Word file opens and closes.

NOTE To learn how to use the ThisDocument object to run macros when your documents open and close, see Lesson 6.

4 To view the sample document's user interface, click View Object in the Project Explorer. Word minimizes the Visual Basic Editor, and displays the sample document (ClientLetter).

View Object

5 When you're finished viewing the sample document, click the Microsoft Visual Basic button on the Windows taskbar to return to Visual Basic.

6 Click the NewMacros module in the Normal project to switch back to the project that contains your InsertAddress macro.

7 Click View Code in the Project Explorer to display the program code for your macro in the Code window.

View Code

The Properties Window

The Properties window lets you change the customizable attributes or property settings for Word objects at design time.

The Properties window lets you change the characteristics, or *property settings,* of the Word objects, modules, and UserForms in your projects. A property setting is a quality of one of the components in your project. For example, the Name property of the module in the Normal project that contains your InsertAddress macro is currently NewMacros. (Whenever you record a macro and place it in the Normal template, Word automatically places it in the NewMacros module.) If you'd like to change the name of this module to reflect its new contents, you can change it in the Properties window.

Inside the Properties window you'll find an object drop-down list box, which you can use to switch between objects in the project component that is active. This list box is especially useful when the component you're working with contains multiple objects, such as a UserForm dialog box.

17

The main part of the Properties window contains two tabs, each of which displays a properties list, which contains property settings that you can modify while your macro is being built (a phase programmers call *design time*). In the Properties window, you can view property settings alphabetically or by category by clicking between the two tabs. As you'll learn in the next lesson, properties can also be set while your macro is running (that is, at *run time*) if you modify property settings appropriately with program code.

Take a moment now to change the Name property setting for the NewMacros module in the Normal template. By changing this setting from NewMacros to InsertAddress, you can clearly identify the contents of your address macro later, and your NewMacros module won't become too unwieldy. (You can keep all your macros in the NewMacros module if you like, but we recommend you save at least some of them in separate modules.)

Change the Name property

1 Verify that the NewMacros module is selected in the Normal project.
2 Click the Properties Window button on the toolbar.

Properties Window

The Properties window is highlighted in the programming environment. (If the Properties window was not open, it will appear now.)

The Properties window lists only one property for the NewMacros module, the Name property. Later you'll work with objects that contain dozens of property settings, but for now you get off easy.

3 Double-click the NewMacros name in the Properties window and press DELETE to erase the current property setting.
4 Type **InsertAddress**, and then press ENTER.

The setting of the Name property is changed from NewMacros to InsertAddress, and the new name appears in the Properties window and in the Modules folder in the Project Explorer.

The Help System

The Visual Basic development environment comes with its own Help system that describes how to use the Visual Basic tools and how to write Word macros. To get the complete Help system, you need to specify Word Visual Basic Help in Word's Help category when you run Setup. (The Word Visual Basic Help files are about 6.5 megabytes (MB) in size, so they are not included in the standard installation of Word 97 or Office 97.) If you didn't specifically include these files, run Setup again now to install the necessary material.

After you install Visual Basic Help, you can access it in several ways.

To get Help information	Do this
From the Office Assistant	From the Help menu, click Microsoft Visual Basic Help.
About a conceptual topic	From the Help menu, click Contents And Index, click the Contents tab, and double-click the topic that interests you.
About a specific programming tool, property, or language element	From the Help menu, click Contents And Index, click the Index tab, and type the word you're looking for in the text box.
While working in a window or a dialog box	Press F1, or click the Help button in the dialog box.
From a Microsoft Web site	From the Help menu, click Microsoft On The Web, and then click one of the Visual Basic home pages that appear.

 TIP If you installed Office 97 on your computer, your system will probably contain many separate Help files about Visual Basic programming. If you want to search only the Microsoft Word Visual Basic Help files, click Contents And Index from the Help menu, click the Contents tab, open the Microsoft Word Visual Basic Reference topic, and then double-click the Word Visual Basic shortcut icon that appears. The Help dialog box that appears will contain only Word documentation.

You can use the following steps to get help on a specific topic in Visual Basic. This practice exercise instructs you to search for information about the Properties window, but you can substitute your own topic.

24.8-13 ✓

Get Help on a specific topic

The Help menu is your door to the Visual Basic Help system.

1 From the Help menu, click Contents And Index.

2 Click the Index tab, and then type **properties window** (or another search topic) in the text box.

As you type the words *properties window*, Help topics beginning with "p," then "pr," and so on appear in the list box until your screen looks like the illustration below.

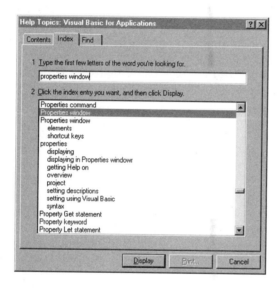

3 Double-click the second Properties window topic in the list box, and then double-click the Properties Window entry in the Topics Found dialog box.

Word displays information about the Visual Basic Properties window. If all the information doesn't fit in your window, the window will have scroll bars that you can use to see the rest of the text.

4 Click See Also, which is near the top of the window and underlined in green.

The Topics Found dialog box opens. Double-click the second topic to learn about keyboard shortcuts active in the Properties window.

5 When you're finished, click the Close button on the Help window's title bar to exit the Help system.

The Visual Basic Help system is a useful resource for learning about the Visual Basic Editor and many topics related to writing Word macros. Be sure to use it if you have a question.

Moving, Docking, and Resizing Tools

Use docking to organize your windows and tools.

With several programming tools on the screen, the Visual Basic Editor can become a pretty busy place. To give you complete control over the shape and size of the elements in the Editor, Word allows you to move, dock, and resize each of the programming tools.

To move a window, the toolbox, or the toolbar, you simply click the title bar and drag the object to a new location. If you align one window to the edge of another window, it will attach itself to the window, or *dock*. Dockable windows are advantageous because they always remain visible; they won't become hidden behind other windows.

If you want to see more of a docked window, simply drag one of its borders to see more content. If you get tired of docking and want your tools to overlap each other, click Options from the Tools menu, click the Docking tab, and then remove the check mark from each tool you want to stand on its own.

As you work through the following lessons, practice moving, docking, and resizing the different tools in the Visual Basic Editor until you feel comfortable with them.

Closing Visual Basic

When you're finished working on a Visual Basic macro, you have two options: You can minimize the Visual Basic Editor and return to Word, or you can close Visual Basic and return to Word. Unless you plan to edit another macro soon, there is no reason to leave Visual Basic running. If you need it again, it's simple to start it again using the Macros dialog box.

Minimize Visual Basic and return to Word

➤ Click the Minimize button on the Visual Basic title bar.

Visual Basic appears as a button on the Windows taskbar, and Word reappears in a window.

Quit Visual Basic and return to Word

➤ Click the Close button on the Visual Basic title bar.

Visual Basic quits, and Word reappears in a window.

 TIP The keyboard shortcut for quitting Visual Basic and returning to Word is ALT+Q.

One Step Further: Assigning Macros to a Toolbar

Here's one last trick to further customize your macro. If you plan on using InsertAddress often, you can assign it to a toolbar or a menu to access it more quickly. Word 97 lets you completely customize the look and content of your menus and toolbars. Follow these steps:

Add InsertAddress to a toolbar or menu

1 From the View menu, click Toolbars, and then click Customize.

Word displays the Customize dialog box which contains three tabs.

2 Click the Commands tab, and use the scroll bar in the Categories list box to find the Macros category. Click Macros.

A list of the active macros in Normal.dot appears in the Commands list box. If you created the InsertAddress macro and renamed the NewMacros module, you'll see an entry named Normal.InsertAddress.InsertAddress.

3 Drag the InsertAddress macro to the toolbar or menu you would like to place it on.

As you drag the macro, a tiny insertion pointer appears to help you position the item. When you release the mouse button, the macro appears as a new command or button. Your screen should look like this:

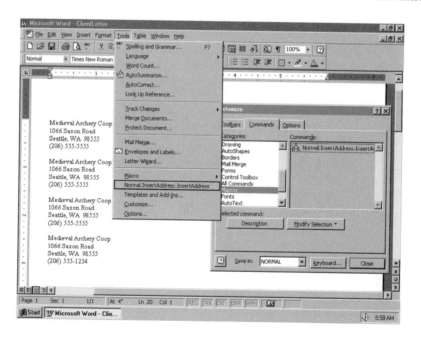

4 If you want to remove one or more buttons or commands (including the InsertAddress macro), simply drag them off the toolbars or menus while the Customize dialog box is open.

5 When you're finished, click the Close button.

Just like that, your macro has become part of Word's user interface!

If you want to continue to the next lesson

➤ Keep Word running, and turn to Lesson 2.

If you want to quit Word for now

➤ From Word's File menu, click Exit. If you see a Save dialog box, click Yes.

Lesson Summary

To	Do this	Button
Record a macro	From the Word Tools menu, click Macro, and then click Record New Macro.	
Run a macro	From the Word Tools menu, click Macro, click Macros, and then double-click the name of the macro.	
Edit a macro	From the Word Tools menu, click Macro, click Macros, and then click the macro and click Edit.	
Open the Project Explorer	From the Visual Basic View menu, click Project Explorer.	
Examine an object's program code	Select the object in the Project Explorer, and click View Code.	
Examine an object's user interface	Select the object in the Project Explorer, and click View Object.	
Open the Properties window	From the Visual Basic View menu, click Properties Window.	
Get Help with Visual Basic	Click a command from the Visual Basic Help menu.	

Lesson Summary, *continued*

To	Do this	Button
Move or dock a window or programming tool	Point to the window or tool on the title bar and drag it to a new location.	
Add a macro command to a menu or toolbar	From the Word View menu, click Toolbars, and then click Customize.	

For online information about	**From the Visual Basic Help menu, click Contents And Index, click the Index tab, and then**	
Editing macros and using the Code window	Search for "code window"	
Using the toolbar	Search for "toolbars, standard"	
Using the Project Explorer	Search for "project explorer"	
Setting properties	Search for "properties window"	

Preview of the Next Lesson

In the next lesson, "Variables, Operators, and Functions," you'll learn more about the programmable objects, properties, and methods in Word, and how to use variables, operators, and functions in mathematical equations.

Variables, Operators, and Functions

Estimated time
40 min.

In this lesson you will learn how to:

- Create program statements that use Word constants.
- Use variables to store data in your macros.
- Use Visual Basic functions to manage input and output.
- Use mathematical operators to create formulas.

In this lesson, you'll learn more about the Visual Basic program statements that collectively constitute a macro. You'll learn how to use special values called constants to run Word commands, and how to use storage containers called variables to store data temporarily in your macro. You'll also learn how to use Visual Basic functions to transfer information back and forth between Word documents, and how to use mathematical operators to perform tasks such as addition and multiplication. With this essential grounding in program syntax, you'll be ready to tackle more sophisticated text processing tasks.

Start the lesson

➤ Start Word, and open a new, blank document. As you work through Lesson 2, you'll create five new macros in this document, and you'll save them to disk under the name **MyLess02.doc**.

The Anatomy of a Visual Basic Program Statement

As you learned in Lesson 1, a line of code in a Word macro is called a *program statement*. A program statement is any combination of Visual Basic keywords, objects, properties, methods, functions, operators, and symbols that collectively create a valid instruction recognized by Word's macro interpreter. A complete program statement can be a simple keyword such as

```
Beep
```

which sounds a note from your computer's speaker, or it can be a combination of elements, such as the following program statement in Word, which uses the TypeText method of the Selection object to insert the text *St. Cuthbert* into the current document:

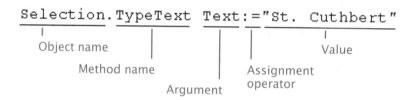

The rules of construction that must be used when you build a program statement are called statement *syntax*. Word Visual Basic shares many of its syntax rules with earlier versions of the Basic programming language and with other Microsoft Office Macro languages. The trick to writing good program statements is learning the syntax of the most useful language elements and then using those elements correctly to manage Word's features through programming constructs called objects, properties, and methods.

What Is an Object?

Objects are the fundamental building blocks of Visual Basic; nearly everything you do in Visual Basic involves modifying objects. When you write Visual Basic macros for Word, your first task is to learn about the objects Word uses to represent its commands and features. For example, the current Word document is stored in the Document object, and within each document is a Paragraph object corresponding to each paragraph.

A *collection* is an object that contains several other objects, usually of the same type. For example, the Documents collection contains all the documents that are currently open in Word, and the Paragraphs collection contains all the paragraphs in the current document or selection. By using properties and methods, you can modify a single object or an entire collection of objects.

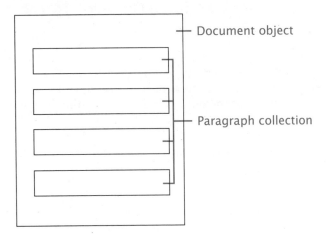

Document object

Paragraph collection

What Are Properties and Methods?

Properties and methods are special keywords you use to manipulate Visual Basic objects. Using a bicycle metaphor, properties are attributes such as the color or style of a bicycle (mountain bike, touring, or tandem), and methods are the actions a bicycle can perform (pedaling, jumping, or coasting). Here are some more specific examples.

Properties are attributes

A *property* is an attribute of an object or an aspect of its behavior. For example, the properties of a document include its name, its content, its save status, and the windows currently open to view it. To change the characteristics of an object, you change the values of its properties.

Here's how it works. To set the value of a property, follow the reference to one or more objects with a period, the property name, an equal sign, and the new property value. For example, this program statement uses the SplitSpecial property to open a separate pane in the active window to display all the footnotes in a document:

```
ActiveWindow.View.SplitSpecial = wdPaneFootnotes
```

In this case both ActiveWindow and View are objects (the View object is contained in the ActiveWindow object). SplitSpecial is a property that can be assigned one of 18 values associated with split windows. In this example, the value assigned to SplitSpecial is a constant named wdPaneFootnotes, a special value used to identify footnotes in Word's object library. (You'll learn more about constants in the next section.)

Methods perform actions

A *method* is an action that an object can perform. For example, you can use the Save method to save all the open documents in Word with the following program statement:

```
Documents.Save
```

In most cases, methods are actions and properties are characteristics. Using a method causes something to happen to an object, while using a property returns information about the object or causes a quality of the object to change.

How Can I Learn More About Word's Object Model?

Each lesson in this book explores a new feature of Word's object model, so you'll be getting lots of practice using objects, properties, and methods to streamline your word processing tasks. However, you can also learn about Word's object model on your own by using these features:

Word's interactive object chart   If you use the Index tab to search for "object hierarchy" in the Microsoft Word Visual Basic online Help, Word will display an interactive chart you can use to explore the programmable objects in Word. (Run Help from the Visual Basic Editor, and be sure to open the Microsoft Word Visual Basic topic on the Contents tab first.) When you click an object in the chart, Word displays an online Help file that describes how you use the object in Visual Basic code.

Object Browser   The Visual Basic Editor includes a tool called the Object Browser that lets you display the properties and methods associated with all the objects in your system, including those supported by Microsoft Word. You'll learn more about using the Object Browser in Lesson 7.

Microsoft Word Visual Basic online Help   Word lists each object, property, and method in its online Help file. You can access these Help topics by clicking Contents And Index from the Visual Basic Editor Help menu, and then double-clicking the Microsoft Word Visual Basic Reference topic. You can also press F1 while in the Object Browser or the Code window.

Code window "auto list"   When you type the name of a Word object followed by a period in the Code window, the Visual Basic Editor automatically lists all the properties and methods that you can use with the object. For example, if you type *ActiveDocument* and a period, a drop-down list of all the methods and properties associated with the ActiveDocument object appears. To specify one of the elements in your program code, simply double-click the desired method or property, and the element is appended to the statement.

In the following lessons, you'll learn more about using Word's objects, properties, and methods in program statements. First, you'll learn how to assign values to properties with Word constants.

Using Word Constants

A common characteristic of many Word macros is a program statement that changes the structure of a document or a command option in the word processor itself. For example, you might change the line spacing in a particular paragraph to double space, or you might change Word's document view to Page Layout view. To make such a change using a Visual Basic macro, you need to use a *constant* in your program statement, a special value supplied by Word to adjust settings in the word processor.

True to its name, a constant is a named value that doesn't change while your macro runs. It replaces a number or word in your macro with a coded label that can be easily remembered. You can create your own constants to store information, as you'll learn later in the lesson, but the most useful constants are special values called *intrinsic constants* that Word and other Windows applications define in object libraries for your use.

For example, to change Word's document view to Page Layout view, you could use the wdPageView constant, as shown in the following program statement:

```
ActiveWindow.View.Type = wdPageView
```

This example contains the following elements:

- The ActiveWindow object, which represents the current, open window in Word.

- The View property, which returns an object representing the active view in the active window.

- The Type property, which sets the document view type for the window. (Options include Normal, Online Layout, Page Layout, Master, or Outline.)

- The wdPageView Word constant, which sets the view to Page Layout view. (Other useful constants include wdNormalView, wdOnlineView, wdMasterView, and wdOutlineView.)

NOTE   The letters *wd* at the beginning of the wdPageView constant identify it as an intrinsic constant in the Microsoft Word object library. The Word object library is a special file declaring objects, properties, methods, and constants that is automatically included in Word macros. Constants in the Word object library actually represent down-to-earth numbers; for example, wdPageView represents the number 3. But when you write Word macros, you'll find the constant names much easier to remember.

Other Office applications have their own constant prefixes and object libraries, including *xl* (Microsoft Excel object library), *ac* (Microsoft Access object library), and *vb* (Visual Basic for Applications object library).

Creating Custom Formatting with Constants

Take a moment now to try a simple example with Word constants. In this exercise, you'll create a macro, called CenterHeading, that uses Word constants to format selected text in a document with shading, border formatting, and center alignment. You'll also learn how to type in a new macro from scratch with the Visual Basic Editor, a technique you'll use often in this book.

 TIP If you installed the sample files, the CenterHeading macro is located in the Less02 document in the \WordVB\Less02 folder on your hard disk. You can either load and run the macro on your own, or type it in now from scratch.

Create the CenterHeading macro

To create the CenterHeading macro, follow these steps:

1 Start Word and open a new, blank document.

   In this exercise, you'll create the CenterHeading macro in a new document file, not in the Normal.dot template.

2 From the Tools menu, click Macro, and then click Macros.

   Word opens the Macros dialog box, the place where you create and run Visual Basic macros.

3 Type **CenterHeading** in the Name text box, and then click the Macros In drop-down list box and select your new, blank document in the list. (In this example, the new document is named Document6.)

4 Click Create.

   Word starts the Visual Basic Editor, and opens a new macro procedure named CenterHeading in the Code window. When you create a new macro from scratch, you use the Code window to type in the program statements that make up the macro. You enter your code between the Sub and End Sub statements, which mark the beginning and end of the macro, respectively.

5 Begin creating your macro now by typing the object name **Selection** followed by a period.

   When you type a period after an object name that is recognized by the Visual Basic Editor, a drop-down list box appears with a list of the objects, properties, and methods that are compatible with the object name you typed. Each of the program statements in this macro will begin with the Selection object, because you are formatting selected text in your Word document.

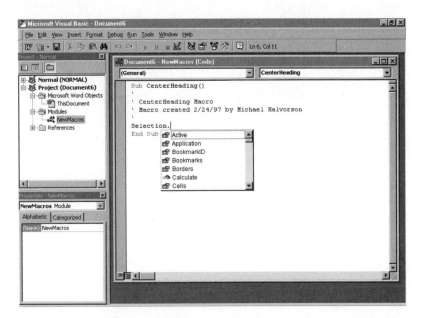

6 Scroll down the drop-down list, double-click the Shading property, and then type a period to open a second drop-down list.

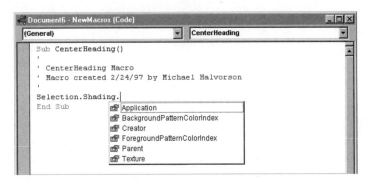

7 Double-click the Texture property in the list box to build a program statement that adjusts the shading formatting of the selected text in your document.

The Visual Basic Editor displays the expression *Selection.Shading.Texture* in the Code window.

8 Now finish your program statement by typing an equals sign (=), double-clicking the wdTexture10Percent constant in the drop-down list box, and pressing ENTER.

Congratulations! You've completed your first program statement, a command that adds 10% background shading to the selected text in your Word document.

9 Now complete your macro by entering the following three program statements. You can either use the drop-down lists to pick objects, properties, and constants (as you did above), or you can type the program statements directly into the Code window.

```
Selection.Borders(wdBorderBottom).LineStyle = wdLineStyleSingle
Selection.Borders(wdBorderBottom).LineWidth = wdLineWidth150pt
Selection.ParagraphFormat.Alignment = wdAlignParagraphCenter
```

When you run the macro, the first two program statements that use the Borders property will format the selected paragraph with a single underline border that is 1.5 points wide. Notice that two Word constants are used in each program statement: a constant that identifies which border is being formatted (wdBorderBottom), and a constant that selects the formatting options you have chosen (wdLineStyleSingle and wdLineWidth150pt). The final program statement uses the

ParagraphFormat property to set the paragraph alignment of the selected paragraph to center alignment.

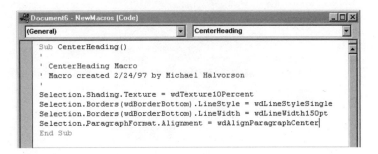

```
Document6 - NewMacros (Code)
(General)                                      CenterHeading

Sub CenterHeading()
'
' CenterHeading Macro
' Macro created 2/24/97 by Michael Halvorson
'
Selection.Shading.Texture = wdTexture10Percent
Selection.Borders(wdBorderBottom).LineStyle = wdLineStyleSingle
Selection.Borders(wdBorderBottom).LineWidth = wdLineWidth150pt
Selection.ParagraphFormat.Alignment = wdAlignParagraphCenter
End Sub
```

Run the CenterHeading macro

Now run the CenterHeading macro in your Word document to create the custom formatting effect. Follow these steps:

View Microsoft Word

1 Click the View Microsoft Word button on the Visual Basic Editor toolbar.

Word displays the blank document containing the CenterHeading macro.

2 Type **Table of Contents** and press ENTER to create some text you can use to test your macro.

3 Select the entire line or paragraph you typed, and change the point size to 16 points. (Your macro will function perfectly at any point size, but a medium-sized font looks best for a heading.)

> **NOTE** The CenterHeading macro is designed for formatting paragraphs only. (You need to select everything you typed, including the end-of-paragraph mark.) If you select only a few words or characters in a line, you'll get different results than shown here.

4 From the Tools menu, click Macro, and then click Macros.

5 Click the CenterHeading macro if it is not already selected, and then click Run.

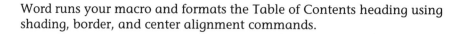

Word runs your macro and formats the Table of Contents heading using shading, border, and center alignment commands.

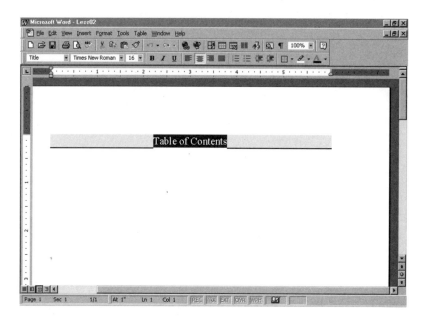

That's it! You've entered your first formatting macro from scratch. You can now customize the CenterHeading macro by returning to the Visual Basic Editor and selecting different formatting constants in the Code window, or you can assign the macro to a menu or toolbar for easy access.

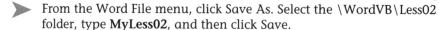

TIP Assigning the macro to a menu or toolbar will make it easier to use. For more information, see Lesson 1, "One Step Further: Assigning Macros to a Toolbar."

Before you move on, however, save your Word document to preserve the macro you just created.

From the Word File menu, click Save As. Select the \WordVB\Less02 folder, type **MyLess02**, and then click Save.

Declaring Variables

In the last section, you learned how to use unchanging values called constants to specify formatting options in your macros. In this section, you will learn how to create temporary storage containers called *variables* to store information that is updated periodically as your macro runs. Variables are useful because they let you assign a short, easy-to-remember name to a piece of data you plan to work with. Variables can hold the following types of information:

- Numbers or words you assign to your macro when you create it, such as an age or important date
- Special values that are entered by the user when the macro runs, such as a name or heading title
- Information from a Word document, such as words, paragraphs, tables, or footnotes
- The result of a specific calculation, such as the amount of sales tax that is due on a purchase

We'll cover the process of declaring and using variables in the next few sections.

Making Reservations for Variables: The Dim Statement

Dim reserves space for a variable.

Before you use a variable, you need to make a reservation for, or *dimension,* it in your macro. This is accomplished by placing the Dim keyword and the name of the variable at the beginning of your macro. Such an action reserves room in memory for the variable when the macro runs, and it lets Visual Basic know what type of data it should expect to see later.

For example, the following statement creates space for a variable named FullName in a macro:

```
Dim FullName
```

Working with Specific Data Types

By default, Word creates variables in a general purpose format or *type* called Variant. However, you can also fine-tune your variables by identifying the exact type of information you want to store. For example, the following Dim statement creates a variable named Years that can hold any whole number between -32,768 and +32,767 (the default range for integer variables):

```
Dim Years As Integer
```

Visual Basic lets you identify the variable type in advance so that you can control how much memory your macro uses. This might not seem like a big deal now, but when you start using several dozen variables in your macros (or collections of variables called arrays), the amount of memory consumed by variables can add up.

The following table lists the fundamental data types you can use in your macro if you choose to use a specific data type when you declare a variable.

 TIP Variable storage size is measured in bytes—the amount of storage space required to store 8 bits (approximately 1 character).

Data type	Size	Range
Byte	1 byte	0 through 255
Integer	2 bytes	-32,768 through 32,767
Long	4 bytes	-2,147,483,648 through 2,147,483,647
Single	4 bytes	-3.402823E38 through 3.402823E38
Double	8 bytes	-1.79769313486232E308 through 1.79769313486232E308
Currency	8 bytes	-922337203685477.5808 through 922337203685477.5807
String	1 byte per character	0 through 65,400 characters
Boolean	2 bytes	True or False
Date	8 bytes	January 1, 100, through December 31, 9999
Variant	16 bytes (with numbers); 22 bytes + 1 byte per character (with strings)	All data type ranges

Putting Variables to Work

You store data in a variable by using the assignment operator (=).

After you declare a variable, you are free to assign information to it in your code. For example, the following program statement assigns the string *Clare of Assisi* to the FullName variable.

```
FullName = "Clare of Assisi"
```

After this assignment, the FullName variable can be used in place of *Clare of Assisi* in your code. For example, the assignment statement

```
Selection.TypeText Text:=FullName
```

would insert *Clare of Assisi* into the current document using the TypeText method of the Selection object.

TIP   If you'd like Visual Basic to verify that you've properly dimensioned all your variables, place the Option Explicit statement at the top of your macro. You can also do this automatically for each new macro by clicking Options from the Tools menu, clicking the Editor tab, and selecting the Require Variable Declaration check box. When you use Option Explicit in this way, Visual Basic generates an error message whenever it finds a variable that has not been explicitly declared in the code. (The likely reason for such a message would be a spelling error in the variable name.)

Using Visual Basic Functions

An excellent use for a variable is to hold information input from the user. One way to manage this input is to use special Visual Basic keywords called *functions* that perform useful work and then return important values to the macro. In this section, you'll learn how to use the InputBox and MsgBox functions to manage input and output in a Word document, and how to use arguments to pass information to a function.

Using a Variable to Store Input

The InputBox function is designed as a simple way to receive input from the user and store it temporarily in a variable. In the following example, you'll enhance the CenterHeading macro by adding a dialog box that prompts the user for the name of a new heading. You'll also learn how to make a procedure call in a macro.

TIP   The following macro, called InsertHead, is located in the \WordVB\Less02.doc file. You can either load and run the macro on your own, or type it in now from scratch.

37

Insert a new head with InputBox

1   From the Word Tools menu, click Macro, and then click Macros.

Word opens the Macros dialog box. If the MyLess02.doc file is not listed as the active document in the Macros In list box, select it now. (We place all the macros completed in each lesson together in their own file to help you organize them.)

2   Type **InsertHead** in the Name text box, and then click Create.

Word starts the Visual Basic Editor and opens a new macro procedure named InsertHead in the Code window.

3   Type the following program statements to declare two variables and use the InputBox function:

```
Dim Prompt, Heading
Prompt = "Please enter your heading title."
Heading = InputBox$(Prompt)
Selection.Font.Size = 16
Selection.TypeText Text:=Heading
```

This time you're declaring two variables by using the Dim statement: Prompt and Heading. The second line in the event procedure assigns a group of characters, or *text string,* to the Prompt variable. This message will be used as a text argument for the InputBox function. (An *argument* is a value or expression passed to a sub procedure or a function.)

The next line *calls* (or runs) the InputBox function and assigns the result—the text string the user enters—to the Heading variable. InputBox is a special Visual Basic function that displays a dialog box on the screen and prompts the user for input. In addition to a prompt string, the InputBox function supports other arguments you may want to use occasionally. Consult the Visual Basic online Help for details.

After InputBox has returned a text string to the macro, the fourth statement in the procedure changes the font size to 16 points (suitable for a heading), and the fifth statement inserts the text in your document using the TypeText method.

Now you'll use the commands in the CenterHeading macro to add some formatting interest to your new head. But rather than type the CenterHeading statements again in your macro, you can accomplish the same effect by simply adding the name of the CenterHeading procedure to the bottom of your routine.

4   Below the Selection statement, type **CenterHeading** and press ENTER.

Adding the name of another procedure to your macro is known as "calling a procedure." When the Visual Basic interpreter encounters this particular statement, it will run the CenterHeading macro in the InsertHead macro.

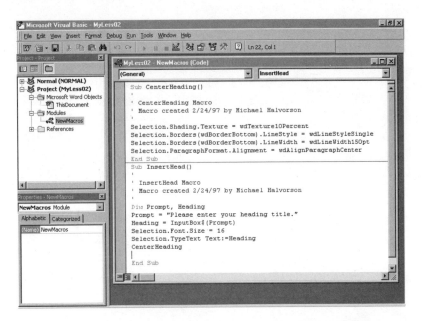

NOTE To call one procedure from another procedure, the procedures must be located in the same module, or the procedure that is called needs to be declared in a module that is part of the current project or the Normal.dot template. Otherwise Visual Basic won't be able to find the procedure name you specify.

Run the InsertHead macro

Now run the InsertHead macro in your Word document to try out the InputBox function and your two variables.

View Microsoft Word

1 Click the View Microsoft Word button on the Visual Basic Editor toolbar.

Word displays the MyLess02 document you created earlier in the lesson.

2 From the Tools menu, click Macro, and then click Macros.

3 Click the InsertHead macro if it is not already selected, and then click Run.

Word runs your macro and displays an InputBox with the prompt string you specified.

4   Type **Spanish Ports on the Costa del Sol** and press ENTER.

The InputBox function returns your heading to the macro, and places it in the Heading variable. The program then uses the variable and the CenterHeading procedure to apply some custom formatting.

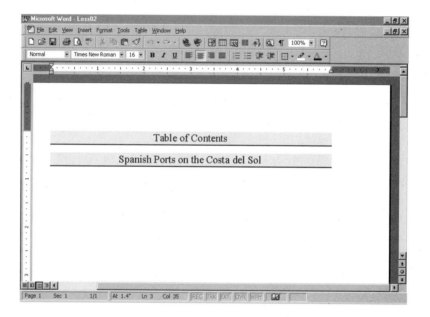

You can use the dialog box created by the InputBox function in your programs any time you want to prompt the user for information. It provides a nice complement to the more sophisticated dialog boxes called UserForms, which you'll learn about in Lesson 5. In the next exercise, you'll learn how to use a similar function to display text in a dialog box.

Click the Save button on Word's Standard toolbar to save the InsertHead macro to disk in the MyLess02.doc file.

What Are Arguments?

As you learned using InputBox, Visual Basic functions often use one or more arguments to define their activities. For example, the InputBox function used the Prompt variable as an argument to display dialog box instructions for the user. When a function uses one or more arguments, the arguments are separated by commas, and the whole group of arguments is enclosed in parentheses. The following statement shows a function call that has two arguments:

```
Heading = InputBox$(Prompt, Title)
```
    | | └──┬──┘
Variable   Arguments
name
            Method name

Using a Variable for Output

The MsgBox function uses text strings to display output in a dialog box. It supports a number of optional arguments.

You can display the contents of a variable by assigning the variable to a method (such as the TypeText method of the Selection object) or by passing the variable as an argument to a dialog box function. One useful dialog box function for displaying output is the MsgBox function. Like InputBox, MsgBox takes one or more arguments as input, and the results of the function call can be assigned to a variable.

The syntax for the MsgBox function is:

ButtonClicked = MsgBox(*Message, ButtonStyle, Title*)

The following items are important:

- *ButtonClicked* represents a variable that receives the result of the function. It indicates which button was clicked in the dialog box.

- *Message* is the text to be displayed on the screen.

- *ButtonStyle* is a constant that determines the number and style of the buttons in the dialog box. Options include vbOKOnly, VbOKCancel, VbAbortRetryIgnore, VbYesNoCancel, VbYesNo, and VbRetryCancel.

- *Title* is the text displayed in the message box title bar.

 TIP In Visual Basic syntax listings, items in italic type are placeholders for variables or other values in your program code. By convention, programmers use italic to highlight the parts of program syntax that you need to customize with your own instructions. (You'll also see the convention in the Visual Basic online Help.)

If you're just displaying a message in MsgBox, the assignment operator (=), the *ButtonClicked* variable, and the *ButtonStyle* argument are optional. You won't be using these in the following exercise; for more information about them, see Lesson 4 or search for "MsgBox" in the Visual Basic online Help.

In the following exercise, you'll use a MsgBox function to display the user name associated with your copy of Word. This name is stored on the User Information tab in the Options dialog box, and can be modified with the Options command on the Word Tools menu. Word places the registered user name in comments and revision annotations, so it's a good idea to check this setting periodically with a macro.

TIP   The following macro, called DisplayUser, is located in the \WordVB\Less02.doc file. You can either load and run the macro on your own, or type it in now from scratch.

Display the registered user with MsgBox

Often you'll find it handy to display a status message about a document with a macro. Follow these steps to create a macro that displays information about the registered user.

1   From the Word Tools menu, click Macro, and then click Macros.

Specify the MyLess02.doc file in the Macros In list box if it is not already selected.

2   Type **DisplayUser** in the Name text box, and then click Create.

Word starts the Visual Basic Editor and opens a new macro procedure named DisplayUser in the Code window.

3   Type the following program statements to declare one variable and use the InputBox function:

```
Dim DialogTitle As String
DialogTitle = "The current user name is"
MsgBox (Application.UserName), , DialogTitle
```

The first statement declares a variable of type String to hold some descriptive text for the MsgBox function. (Since the variable will only hold text, we're declaring it as a String to save a little memory.) The second statement assigns a text value to the string variable. The third statement displays a message box on the screen, and places the contents of the DialogTitle variable in the title bar. The UserName property of the Application object is then placed inside the message box. (When no *ButtonClicked* variable is used with MsgBox, the parentheses go around only the first argument.)

> **TIP** You can also use the UserName property to set the user name in Word. For example, to change the user name to Chris Kinata, type **Application.UserName = "Chris Kinata".**

Run the DisplayUser macro

Now run the DisplayUser macro in your Word document to try out the MsgBox function.

View Microsoft Word

1 Click the View Microsoft Word button on the Visual Basic Editor toolbar.

Word displays the MyLess02 document.

2 From the Tools menu, click Macro, and then click Macros.

3 Click the DisplayUser macro if it is not already selected, and then click Run.

Word runs your macro and displays the active user name for your copy of Word.

If the user name is not correct, change it now via the Options command on the Tools menu, or write a macro to do it!

4 Click the Save button on Word's Standard toolbar to save the DisplayUser macro to disk in the MyLess02.doc file.

Processing Text with Object Variables

Another use for variables is to hold portions of your document while your macro runs. For example, you might use a variable to hold a copy of a paragraph temporarily while you rearrange the paragraph's contents or move it to a new location. However, since documents and their contents are represented by objects in Visual Basic, you'll need to create a special container called an *object variable* when you want to reference an object in Word.

To declare an object variable in Visual Basic, use the following syntax:

```
Dim ObjectVar As Object
```

In the Dim statement, *ObjectVar* is name of the variable you'll assign the object to later in your program code. For example, to create an object variable to hold text, you might use the following Dim statement:

```
Dim myText as Object
```

43

After you dimension an object variable, you can use it to reference a Word object by creating a Set statement, following this syntax:

```
Set ObjectVar = ObjectName
```

The Set statement assigns an object to an object variable.

In the Set statement, *ObjectVar* is the name of your object variable, and *ObjectName* is an expression that returns a Word object. For example, to assign a Range object containing the text from the first paragraph in the active document to the myText object variable, you might use the following Set statement:

```
Set myText = ActiveDocument.Paragraphs(1).Range
```

After you assign an object to the object variable, you can use the variable just as you would the object. Thus, object variables save you typing time because the object variable names are usually shorter than the full object names. We'll use this method to work with Word objects often in this book.

 TIP The following macro, called CopyParagraph, is located in the \WordVB\Less02.doc file. You can either load and run the macro on your own, or type it in now from scratch.

Use an object variable to copy text

One practical use for an object variable is to hold a range reference when you copy text from one location to another. Follow these steps to create a macro that copies the first paragraph of the active document to a new document.

1   From the Word Tools menu, click Macro, and then click Macros.

    Specify the MyLess02.doc file in the Macros In list box if it is not already selected.

2   Type **CopyParagraph** in the Name text box, and then click Create.

    Word starts the Visual Basic Editor and opens a new macro procedure named CopyParagraph in the Code window.

3   Type the following program statements:

```
Dim myText As Object
Set myText = ActiveDocument.Paragraphs(1).Range
Documents.Add
Selection.InsertAfter myText
```

The first statement declares a variable, myText, of type Object to hold the reference to a Range object. The second statement then assigns a Range object representing the first paragraph in the active document to myText. The object expression contains a collection index (1), which specifies the first paragraph in the Paragraphs collection. (The second paragraph has an index of 2, the third paragraph an index of 3, and so on.)

NOTE The Range object contains the text of the first paragraph only, not the formatting. If you also want to copy the formatting of the paragraph, create a second object variable and use the Duplicate property of the Range object to copy the formatting.

Next, the Add method adds a new document to the Documents collection, and the InsertAfter method inserts the current value of the myText object variable into the new Word document.

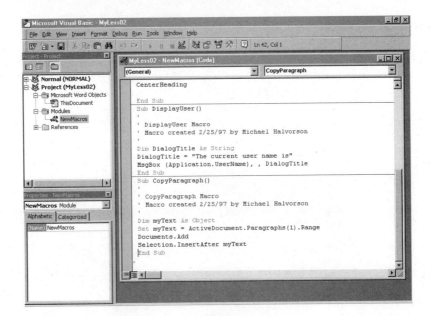

Run the CopyParagraph macro

Now run the CopyParagraph macro in your Word document.

View Microsoft Word

1   Click the View Microsoft Word button on the Visual Basic Editor toolbar.

    Word displays the MyLess02 document. If you've been following the exercises so far in this lesson, your document will contain two headings: *Table of Contents* and *Spanish Ports on the Costa del Sol*. The CopyParagraph macro should copy the first heading, *Table of Contents*, to a new document.

2   From the Tools menu, click Macro, and then click Macros.

3   Click the CopyParagraph macro if it is not already selected, and then click Run.

    Word runs your macro and creates a new document containing the *Table of Contents* paragraph (the text only, not the formatting).

45

4 After you have verified the operation of your macro, close the new document and discard your changes. (You won't need to save the new document in this lesson.)

5 Make MyLess02 the active document, and then click the Save button on Word's Standard toolbar to save the CopyParagraph macro to disk.

Constants: Variables That Don't Change

Earlier in the lesson, you practiced using Word's intrinsic constants to adjust settings in the word processor. You can also create constants for your own use in modules and procedures as an alternative to variables. If a variable in your program contains a value that never changes (such as π, a fixed mathematical entity), you might consider storing the value as a constant instead of as a variable. Constants operate a lot like variables, but you can't modify their values while a macro is running. They are declared with the Const keyword, as shown in the following example:

```
Const Pi = 3.14159265
```

The statement above creates a constant called Pi that can be used in place of the value of π in the program code.

To create a constant available to all the macros in a particular module, you can place the constant in the Declarations section of the module. For example:

```
Public Const Pi = 3.14159265
```

The Declarations section is at the top of a module, and is reserved for items that will have a public or "global" scope in the program. Public declarations can include variables, constants, functions, and sub procedures. (You'll learn more about public declarations later.)

Constants are very useful in program code, especially in mathematical formulas, such as Area = πr^2. The next section describes how you can use operators, constants, and variables to write similar formulas.

Building Formulas

Visual Basic operators hold together a formula.

A *formula* is a statement that combines numbers, variables, operators, and key-words, or some of these elements, to create a new value. Visual Basic contains several language elements designed for use in formulas. In this section, you'll practice working with mathematical operators, the symbols used to tie together the parts of a formula. With a few exceptions, the mathematical symbols you'll use are the ones you use in everyday life, and their operations are fairly intuitive.

Visual Basic provides the following mathematical operators:

Operator	Mathematical operation	Example
+	Addition	Sum = 15.95 + 22.50
-	Subtraction	Balance = 100 - 75
*	Multiplication	Product = 88 * 2
/	Division	Ratio = 6 / 5
\	Integer (whole number) division	FullDinners = 8 \ 3
Mod	Remainder division	Scraps = 8 Mod 3
^	Exponentiation (raising to a power)	AreaOfSquare = 5 ^ 2
&	String concatenation (joining words together)	FullName = "Bob" & "James"

Computing Formulas in Your Documents

Periodically, you may want to total numbers in a document or perform some sort of numeric calculation. The following exercise demonstrates how you can compute the sales tax for a dollar amount that is selected in the active document.

Compute the sales tax for an item

Word includes a formula feature that lets you total numbers in a table and perform other simple calculations. However, it doesn't contain a command that lets you make numeric computations on the fly with a selected number. In this exercise, you'll build a macro that computes the total cost of an item including sales tax.

1 From the Word Tools menu, click Macro, and then click Macros. Specify the MyLess02.doc file in the Macros In list box if it is not already selected.

2 Type **SalesTax** in the Name text box, and then click Create.

Word starts the Visual Basic Editor and opens a new macro procedure named SalesTax in the Code window.

3 Type the following program statements:

```
Const TaxRate = 1.081
Dim CostOfItem, TotalCost
CostOfItem = Selection.Text
TotalCost = CostOfItem * TaxRate
MsgBox Format(TotalCost, "$#,##0.00"), , "Total Cost with Tax"
```

The Const statement creates a constant that holds the current sales tax rate (in this example, a wintry 8.1%). You should change this rate to the current sales tax figure in your area. The Dim statement declares two variables of the Variant type, CostOfItem and TotalCost. Variant is a good choice in this case because the exact format of the numbers in your Word document will be unknown. (They could be large or small, integers or floating point value, and so on.)

The third statement in the macro uses the Text property of the Selection object to return the currently selected text to the CostOfItem variable. The fourth statement then uses a formula and the multiplication operator to compute the total cost of the item plus sales tax. Finally, the MsgBox function displays the total with the help of the Format function, so that the total appears with the proper currency formatting.

 TIP The Format function can display the results of a calculation in a variety of formats, including percent, integer, date, string, and other custom formats. For more information, search for "Format function" in the Visual Basic online Help.

Run the SalesTax macro

Now run the SalesTax macro in your Word document.

1 Click the View Microsoft Word button on the Visual Basic Editor toolbar.

Word displays the MyLess02 document.

*View Microsoft
Word*

2 The SalesTax macro requires that you select a number in your document, so clear some room and type the following test values (one per line) so that you can evaluate the macro:
10
$1,000.00
five bucks

3 Select *10* as the first test number.

4 Run the SalesTax macro by using the Macros dialog box.

Word immediately displays a message box containing the total cost of a $10 item with an 8.1% sales tax.

5 Click OK to close the dialog box, and then select *$1,000.00* and run the macro again. (You should verify that the macro can handle currency formatting.)

Fortunately, you are using Variant variables in you macro, which can handle the switch between floating point and currency formatting.

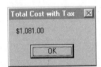

6 Click OK, and then select *five bucks* and run the macro.

7 This time, Visual Basic generates a run-time error that stops the macro and displays a dialog box explaining the problem. *Type mismatch* means that the value selected in the document (*five bucks*) cannot be multiplied by the value in the TaxRate constant (1.081). Unfortunately, this macro will only work with numbers, not text.

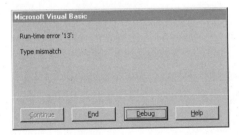

8 Click Debug.

Visual Basic highlights the program statement that caused the run-time error in the Code window.

9 Click the Reset button on the Visual Basic toolbar to stop the program.

Reset

49

View Microsoft Word

Save

10 Click the View Microsoft Word button on the Visual Basic toolbar to return to Word, and then click the Save button on Word's Standard toolbar to save the SalesTax macro to disk.

You're done working with macros in this lesson.

Copying Macros to the Normal Template

This lesson contains five macros, each located in the NewMacros module in the Less02 document. If you'd like to copy these macros to the Normal.dot template (so that you can use them without the Less02.doc file open), complete these steps:

1 Open the Macros dialog box and click Organizer.

2 Verify that the Less02 document is open in the left text box, and then select the NewMacros module in it.

3 Click Rename and change the name of the NewMacros module to **Less02**. (You can't copy one NewMacros module over another.)

4 Verify that the Normal template is open in the right text box, and then click Copy to copy the Less02 module into the Normal template.

5 When you're finished copying macros, click the Close button.

One Step Further: Using Operator Precedence

Always keep the operator order of evaluation in mind when you are building mathematical formulas.

In the last exercise, you experimented with using variables, constants, and a mathematical operator to create a formula. Visual Basic lets you mix as many mathematical operators as you like in a formula, as long as each numeric variable and expression is separated from another by one operator. For example, this is an acceptable Visual Basic formula:

```
Total = 10 + 15 * 2 / 4 ^ 2
```

The formula processes several values and assigns the result to a variable named Total. But how is such an expression evaluated by Visual Basic? In other words, which mathematical operators does Visual Basic use first when solving the formula? You might not have noticed, but the order of evaluation matters a great deal in this example.

Visual Basic solves this dilemma by establishing a specific *order of precedence* for mathematical operations. This list of rules tells Visual Basic which operators to use first when evaluating an expression that contains more than one operator.

The following table shows the order in which operators will be evaluated. (Operators on the same level in this table are evaluated from left to right as they appear in an expression.)

Operator(s)	Order of precedence
( )	Expressions between parentheses are always evaluated first.
^	Exponentiation (raising a number to a power) is second.
-	Negation (creating a negative number) is third.
* /	Multiplication and division are fourth.
\	Integer division is fifth.
Mod	Remainder division is sixth.
+ -	Addition and subtraction are last.

Given the order of precedence in the above table, the expression

```
Total = 10 + 15 * 2 / 4 ^ 2
```

would be evaluated by Visual Basic in the following steps. (Boldface type is used to show the order of evaluation):

```
Total = 10 + 15 * 2 / 4 ^ 2
Total = 10 + 15 * 2 / 16
Total = 10 + 30 / 16
Total = 10 + 1.875
Total = 11.875
```

Using Parentheses in a Formula

Parentheses clarify and influence the order of evaluation.

You can use one or more pairs of parentheses in a formula to clarify the order of precedence. For example, Visual Basic would calculate the formula

```
Number = (8 - 5 * 3) ^ 2
```

by determining the value between the parentheses (–7) before doing the exponentiation—even though exponentiation has a higher order of precedence than subtraction and multiplication do. You can further refine the calculation by placing nested parentheses in the formula. For example, the formula

```
Number = ((8 - 5) * 3) ^ 2
```

directs Visual Basic to calculate the difference in the inner set of parentheses first, and then calculate the product in the outer parentheses, and then perform the exponentiation. The results produced by the two formulas are different: the first formula evaluates to 49 and the second to 81. Parentheses can change the result of a mathematical operation, in addition to making it easier to read.

If you want to continue to the next lesson

➤ Keep Word running, and turn to Lesson 3.

If you want to quit Word for now

➤ From the File menu, click Exit. If you see a Save dialog box, click Yes.

Lesson Summary

To	Do this

Declare a variable	Type **Dim** followed by the variable name at the top of your macro. (You can also specify a data type; the variant type is the default.) For example:
	
	```Dim Heading 'Variant type```
	```Dim Name As String 'String type```

Change the value of a variable	Assign a new value with the assignment operator (=). For example: ```Country = "Japan"```

Declare and use an object variable	Use the Dim and the Object keywords to declare the variable, and then use the Set keyword to assign an object reference to the variable. For example:
	
	```Dim myText As Object```
	```Set myText = _```
	``` ActiveDocument.Paragraphs(1).Range```

Get input with a dialog box	Use the InputBox function, and assign the result to a variable. For example: ```UserName = InputBox("What is your name?")```

Display output in a dialog box	Use the MsgBox function. (The string to be displayed in the dialog box can be stored in a variable.) For example:
	
	```Forecast = "Rain, mainly on the plain."```
	```MsgBox(Forecast),, "Spain Weather Report"```

Create a constant	Use the Const keyword followed by the constant name, the assignment operator (=), and the fixed value. For example: ```Const JackBennysAge = 39```

To	Do this
Create a formula	Link together numeric variables or values with one of the seven mathematical operators, and then assign the result to a variable or property. For example: `Result = 1 ^ 2 * 3 \ 4   'this equals 0`
Combine text strings	Use the string concatenation operator (&). For example: `Msg = "Hello" & ", " & "world!"`
Use a mathematical function	Add the function and any necessary arguments to a formula. For example: `Hypotenuse = Sqr(x ^ 2 + y ^ 2)`

Control the evaluation order in a formula	Use parentheses in the formula. For example:
	
	`Result = 1 + 2 ^ 3 \ 4        'this _`
	`    equals 3`
	`Result = (1 + 2) ^ ( 3 \ 4)   'this _`
	`    equals 1`

For online information about	From the Visual Basic Help menu, click Contents And Index, click the Index tab, and then
Word's intrinsic constants	Search for "intrinsic constants"
Declaring variables	Search for "variables, declaring"
Using object variables	Search for "objects, creating"
Using the InputBox function	Search for "InputBox"
Using the MsgBox function	Search for "MsgBox"
Operators and precedence	Search for the operator you want to examine

Preview of the Next Lesson

In the next lesson, "Using Decision Structures and Loops," you'll learn how to control the execution of program statements in your macros. You'll learn how to use the If...Then and Select Case statements, and how to execute different blocks of code depending on different conditions in your macro. You'll also learn how to loop through object collections efficiently with repeating statements called With statements and For...Each loops.

Using Decision Structures and Loops

Estimated time
50 min.

In this lesson you will learn how to:

- Use an If...Then statement to convert heading styles to formatted text.
- Use a Select Case statement to display the paper size for the current document.
- Use a For...Next loop to process information in a table.
- Use a For...Each loop to search the Documents collection for a particular document.
- Use a With statement to replace one word with another throughout a document.
- Write a Do loop to automatically number graphics in a chapter.

In the last lesson, you learned how to write Microsoft Word macros from scratch by using several essential keywords in the Visual Basic for Applications programming language. In this lesson, you'll learn how to add logic and efficiency to your macros by writing conditional expressions, decision structures, and loops that manage the information in your documents. These skills will allow you to write macros that format selected text, display settings in the word processor, work with collections, manage tables, and find and replace text strings.

Writing Conditional Expressions

Conditional expressions ask true-or-false questions.

One of the most useful tools for processing information in a macro is a *conditional expression*. A conditional expression is a part of a complete program statement that asks a true-or-false question about a property, a variable, or another piece of data in a macro. For example, the conditional expression

```
NumberOfWords < 100
```

evaluates to True if the NumberOfWords variable contains a value that is less than 100, and it evaluates to False if NumberOfWords contains a value that is greater than or equal to 100. You can use the following comparison operators in a conditional expression.

Comparison operator	Meaning
=	Equal to
< >	Not equal to
>	Greater than
<	Less than
> =	Greater than or equal to
< =	Less than or equal to

NOTE Expressions that can be evaluated as True or False are also known as Boolean expressions, and the True or False result can be assigned to a Boolean variable or property. You can assign Boolean values to certain object properties, variant variables, or Boolean variables that have been created by using the Dim statement and the As Boolean keywords.

The following table shows some conditional expressions and their results. In the next exercise, you'll work with the operators shown in the table.

Conditional expression	Result
10 < > 20	True (10 is not equal to 20)
Pages < 20	True if Pages is less than 20; otherwise, False
Application.UserName = "Hugh Victor"	True if the registered user name for your copy of Word is Hugh Victor; otherwise, False
Selection.Text = CityName	True if the selected text in your document matches the contents of the CityName variable; otherwise, False

Writing If...Then Decision Structures

If...Then decision structures let you add logic to your programs.

Conditional expressions can control the order in which statements are executed when they are used in a special block of statements known as a *decision structure*. An If...Then decision structure lets you evaluate a condition in the macro and take a course of action based on the result. In its simplest form, an If...Then decision structure is written on a single line, in the form

```
If condition Then statement
```

where the *condition* placeholder represents a conditional expression and *statement* represents a valid Visual Basic program statement. For example,

```
If Application.UserName = "Hugh Victor" Then MsgBox "Welcome, Hugh!"
```

is an If...Then decision structure that uses the conditional expression

```
Application.UserName = "Hugh Victor"
```

to determine whether the macro should display the message "Welcome, Hugh!" in a message box on the screen. If the UserName property of the Application object contains a name that matches "Hugh Victor," Visual Basic displays the message box; otherwise, it skips the MsgBox statement and executes the next line in the macro. Conditional expressions always result in a True or False value, never in a "maybe."

Testing Several Conditions in an If...Then Decision Structure

ElseIf and Else clauses let you ask additional questions in an If...Then structure.

Visual Basic also supports an If...Then decision structure that allows you to include several conditional expressions. This block of statements can be several lines long and contains the important keywords ElseIf, Else, and End If.

```
If condition1 Then
     statements executed if condition1 is True
ElseIf condition2 Then
     statements executed if condition2 is True
[Additional ElseIf clauses and statements can be placed here]
Else
     statements executed if none of the conditions is True
End If
```

In this structure, *condition1* is evaluated first. If this conditional expression is True, the block of statements below it is executed, one statement at a time. (You can include one or more program statements.) If the first condition is not True, the second conditional expression (*condition2*) is evaluated. If the second condition is True, the second block of statements is executed. (You can add additional ElseIf conditions and statements if you have more conditions to evaluate.) Finally, if none of the conditional expressions is True, the statements below the Else keyword are executed. The whole structure is closed at the bottom with the End If keywords.

The following code shows how a multiline If...Then structure could be used to determine the amount of tax due in a hypothetical progressive tax return, under which increasing amounts of income are taxed at higher marginal tax rates. If you were to run this routine in Word, it would prompt you for an adjusted income amount, and then display the amount of tax you owe.

Multiline If...Then structures are perfect for calculating values that fall in different ranges, such as numbers in a tax return.

```
Dim AdjustedIncome, TaxDue
AdjustedIncome = InputBox ("Please enter adjusted income.")
If AdjustedIncome <= 22750 Then          '15% tax bracket
    TaxDue = AdjustedIncome * 0.15
ElseIf AdjustedIncome <= 55100 Then      '28% tax bracket
    TaxDue = 3412 + ((AdjustedIncome - 22750) * 0.28)
ElseIf AdjustedIncome <= 115000 Then     '31% tax bracket
    TaxDue = 12470 + ((AdjustedIncome - 55100) * 0.31)
ElseIf AdjustedIncome <= 250000 Then     '36% tax bracket
    TaxDue = 31039 + ((AdjustedIncome - 115000) * 0.36)
Else                                     '39.6% tax bracket
    TaxDue = 79639 + ((AdjustedIncome - 250000) * 0.396)
End If
MsgBox TaxDue, , "You owe this much tax:"
```

In this decision structure, the variable AdjustedIncome is tested at the first income level and subsequent income levels until one of the conditional expressions evaluates to True and an income tax is determined for the taxpayer. This simple decision structure is quite useful. It could be used to compute the tax owed by any taxpayer in a progressive tax system (such as the one in the United States), provided the tax rates are complete and up to date and the value in the AdjustedIncome variable is correct. If the tax rates change, it is a simple matter to update the conditional expressions.

 IMPORTANT The order of the conditional expressions in your If...Then and ElseIf clauses is critical. If you reversed the order of the conditional expressions in the tax computation example—that is, if you listed rates in the structure from highest to lowest—taxpayers in the 15 percent, 28 percent, and 31 percent tax brackets would be placed in the 36 percent tax bracket because they all would have an income that is less than or equal to 250,000. (Visual Basic stops at the first conditional expression that is True, even if others are also True.) Since all the conditional expressions in this example test the same variable, they need to be listed in ascending order to get the taxpayers to fall out at the right spots. Moral: When you use two or more conditional expressions, watch their order carefully.

In the next exercise, you'll use an If...Then decision structure to convert a selected heading style to formatted text in the Normal style. This macro is useful if you want to reduce the amount of space a document takes up, or if you routinely convert one heading style to another.

TIP If you installed the sample files, the ConvertStyles macro is located in the Less03 document in the \WordVB\Less03 folder on your hard disk. You can either load and run the macro on your own, or type it in now from scratch.

Use an If...Then decision structure to convert styles

Word's Normal template includes three default formatting styles for headings: Heading 1, Heading 2, and Heading 3. The following steps show you how to convert these styles to all caps, underline, and italic formatting, respectively.

1 Start Word and open a new, blank document.

In this exercise, you'll create the ConvertStyles macro in a new document file. When you're finished, you'll save the document as MyLess02.doc.

2 From the Word Tools menu, click Macro, and then click Macros.

Word opens the Macros dialog box, the place where you create and run Visual Basic macros.

3 Type **ConvertStyles** in the Name text box, and then click the Macros In drop-down list and select your new, blank document in the list. (In this example, the new document is named Document1.)

4 Click Create.

Word starts the Visual Basic Editor, and opens a new macro procedure named ConvertStyles in the Code window.

5 Type the following program statements:

By convention, statements below If...Then, ElseIf, and Else clauses are indented.

```
If Selection.Type = wdSelectionIP Then
    MsgBox "No text selected."
ElseIf Selection.FormattedText.Style = "Heading 1" Then
    Selection.FormattedText.Style = wdStyleNormal
    Selection.Font.AllCaps = True
ElseIf Selection.FormattedText.Style = "Heading 2" Then
    Selection.FormattedText.Style = wdStyleNormal
    Selection.Font.Underline = True
ElseIf Selection.FormattedText.Style = "Heading 3" Then
    Selection.FormattedText.Style = wdStyleNormal
    Selection.Font.Italic = True
End If
```

This macro consists entirely of an If...Then decision structure, with one If statement and three ElseIf clauses. The first If statement uses the Type property of the Selection object to check if there is selected text in the document that can be evaluated by the macro. If so, the structure determines which heading style is active, converts the head back to the Normal style, and applies some simple text formatting to preserve the meaning of the heads. (Heading 1 becomes all caps, Heading 2 is underlined, and Heading 3 is formatted as italic.)

By modifying the style and formatting constants used in this example, you could easily modify the macro to convert other styles or apply other formatting options.

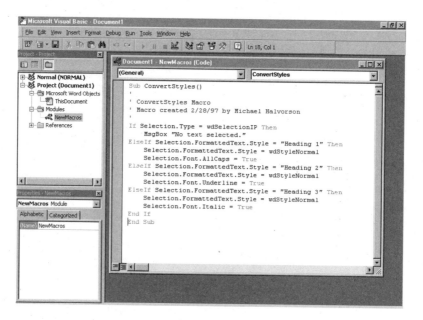

Run the macro

Now create some heads in your Word document and run the macro.

View Microsoft Word

1   Click the View Microsoft Word button on the Visual Basic Editor toolbar.

2   At the top of the document, type **First Head**, **Second Head**, and **Third Head** on three separate lines.

Place the heads on separate lines so you can test each level of formatting.

3   Select the first head and apply the Heading 1 style by using the Style drop-down list on Word's formatting toolbar.

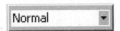

4   Format the second head with the Heading 2 style, and the third head with the Heading 3 style.

5   Now select First Head in your document and run the ConvertStyles macro.

Be sure to select one head only, and not multiple lines. When you run the macro, Word converts the selected head to all caps.

 NOTE   At this point, we'll assume you know how to start a macro. To review the five techniques you can use to run a macro in Word, see "Running a Macro" in Lesson 1.

6   Select Second Head and run the macro.

Word converts the second style to underlined type.

7   Select Third Head and run the macro.

Word converts the third style to italic type.

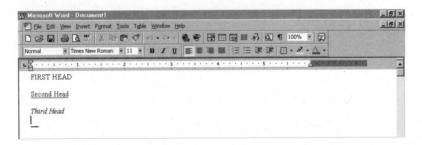

8   Now save your Word document to preserve the macro you just created. From the Word File menu, click Save As. Select the \WordVB\Less03 folder, type **MyLess03**, and then click Save.

Using Logical Operators in Conditional Expressions

Visual Basic lets you test more than one conditional expression in your If...Then and ElseIf clauses if you want to include more than one selection criterion in your decision structure. The extra conditions are linked together by using one or more of the following logical operators:

Logical operator	Meaning
And	If and only if both conditional expressions are True, then the result is True.
Or	If either conditional expression is True, then the result is True.
Not	If the conditional expression is False, then the result is True. If the conditional expression is True, then the result is False.
Xor	If one and only one of the conditional expressions is True, then the result is True. If both are True or both are False, then the result is False.

For example, the following decision structure uses the And logical operator to test a Word object:

```
If Application.UserName = "Michael Halvorson" And Price < 300 _
    Then
        MsgBox "Buy the product."
End If
```

You'll practice using this operator later in the lesson.

Writing Select Case Decision Structures

Select Case decision structures base branching decisions on one key variable.

Visual Basic also lets you control the execution of statements in your macros by using Select Case decision structures. A Select Case structure is similar to an If...Then...ElseIf structure, but it is more efficient when the branching depends on one key variable, or *test case*. In addition, Select Case structures make your macro code easier for others to read and easier to update later.

The syntax for a Select Case structure looks like this:

```
Select Case variable
Case value1
     program statements executed if value1 matches variable
Case value2
     program statements executed if value2 matches variable
Case value3
     program statements executed if value3 matches variable
  .
  .
  .
End Select
```

A Select Case structure begins with the Select Case keywords and ends with the End Select keywords. You replace the *variable* placeholder with the variable, property, or other expression that is to be the key value, or test case, for the structure. You replace *value1*, *value2*, and *value3* with numbers, strings, or other values related to the test case being considered. If one of the values matches the variable, the statements below its Case clause are executed and Visual Basic continues executing program code after the End Select statement.

You can include any number of Case clauses in a Select Case structure, and you can include more than one value in a Case clause. If you list multiple values after a case, separate them with commas.

The following example shows how a Select Case structure could be used to display an appropriate message about a person's age in a macro. If the Age variable matches one of the Case values, an appropriate message is displayed by using a message box.

The organization of a Select Case structure can make program logic clearer than an equivalent If...Then structure would.

```
Select Case Age
Case 16
     MsgBox "You can drive now!"
Case 18
     MsgBox "You can vote now!"
Case 21
     MsgBox "You can drink wine with your meals."
Case 65
     MsgBox "Time to retire and have fun!"
End Select
```

A Select Case structure also supports a Case Else clause that you can use to control how Visual Basic handles cases not captured by the preceding cases. Here's how it works with the Age example:

```
Select Case Age
Case 16
    MsgBox "You can drive now!"
Case 18
    MsgBox "You can vote now!"
Case 21
    MsgBox "You can drink wine with your meals."
Case 65
    MsgBox "Time to retire and have fun!"
Case Else
    MsgBox "You're a great age! Enjoy it!"
End Select
```

Using Comparison Operators with a Select Case Structure

A Select Case structure supports comparison operators just like an If...Then structure does.

Visual Basic lets you use comparison operators to include a range of test values in a Select Case structure. The Visual Basic comparison operators that can be used are =, < >, >, <, > =, and < =. To use the comparison operators, you need to include the Is keyword or the To keyword in the expression to identify the comparison you're making. The Is keyword instructs the compiler to compare the test variable to the expression listed after the Is keyword. The To keyword identifies a range of values. The following structure uses Is, To, and several comparison operators to test the Age variable and to display one of five messages:

```
Select Case Age
Case Is < 13
    MsgBox "Enjoy your youth!"
Case 13 To 19
    MsgBox "Enjoy your teens!"
Case 21
    MsgBox "You can drink wine with your meals."
Case Is > 100
    MsgBox "Looking good!"
Case Else
    MsgBox "That's a nice age to be."
End Select
```

If the value of the Age variable is less than 13, the message "Enjoy your youth!" is displayed. For the ages 13 through 19, the message "Enjoy your teens!" is displayed, and so on.

A Select Case decision structure is usually much clearer than an If...Then structure and is more efficient when you're making three or more branching decisions based on one variable or property. However, when you're making two or fewer comparisons, or when you're working with several different values, you'll probably want to use an If...Then decision structure.

In the following exercise, you'll use a Select Case structure to display the current document's paper type. You'll accomplish this by comparing the PageSetup object's PaperSize property to three different constants associated with paper.

 TIP The PaperSize macro is located in the Less03 document in the \WordVB\Less03 folder on your hard disk. You can either load and run the macro on your own, or type it in now from scratch.

Use Select Case to determine a document's paper size

Complete the following steps to create the PageSize macro:

1 From the Word Tools menu, click Macro, and then click Macros.

   Word opens the Macros dialog box. If the MyLess03.doc file is not listed as the active document in the Macros In list box, select it now.

2 Type **PageSize** in the Name text box, and then click Create.

   Word starts the Visual Basic Editor and opens a new macro procedure named PageSize in the Code window.

3 Type the following program statements:

```
Dim PaperType
PaperType = ActiveDocument.PageSetup.PaperSize
Select Case PaperType
Case wdPaperLetter
    MsgBox "Document type is Letter (8 1/2 x 11)."
Case wdPaperLegal
    MsgBox "Document type is Legal (8 1/2 x 14)."
Case wdPaperEnvelope10
    MsgBox "Document type is Envelope 10 (4 1/8 x 9 1/2)."
Case Else
    MsgBox "Type unknown. Check File/Page Setup/Paper Size."
End Select
```

The PageSize macro requires no user input. It simply stores the current paper size in a variant variable named PaperType, and then uses a Select Case structure to determine which type of paper is in use. The results are then displayed in a message box for the user.

The default paper size in word is Letter (8 1/2" x 11"), but this setting can be adjusted by using the Page Setup command on the File menu. If you're ever uncertain about the page size, simply run this macro.

NOTE   Occasionally, a document will use a paper type that is not accounted for in this macro. To handle this possibility, the Select Case structure uses an Else clause to display the message "Type unknown. Check File/Page Setup/Paper Size." However, you can add more functionality to your macro by adding more Case statements and paper size constants. To get a complete listing of the constants available, search for "PaperSize property" in the Visual Basic online Help.

Run the macro

Now run the macro to determine your document's paper size.

View Microsoft Word

1   Click the View Microsoft Word button on the Visual Basic Editor toolbar.

Word displays the MyLess03 document.

2   Run the PageSize macro.

Word displays a message box that describes the current document's paper type. Before you print, you can use this information to make sure you have the right type of paper in your printer.

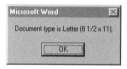

3   Experiment with the macro if you like by changing the paper type with the Page Setup command on the File menu. (The Paper Size tab controls the paper type.)

Save

4   When you're finished, click the Save button on Word's Standard toolbar to save the new macro to disk in the MyLess03 document.

Writing For...Next Loops

A For...Next loop lets you execute a specific group of program statements a set number of times in a macro. This can be useful if you are performing several related calculations, working with collections of Word objects, or processing several pieces of user input. A For...Next loop is really just a shorthand way of writing out a long list of program statements. Since each group of statements in the list would do essentially the same thing, Visual Basic lets you define one group of statements and request that it be executed as many times as you want.

The syntax for a For...Next loop looks like this:

In a For...Next loop, start *and* end *determine how long the loop runs.*

```
For variable = start To end
    statements to be repeated
Next variable
```

In this syntax statement, For, To, and Next are required keywords and = is a required operator. You replace the *variable* placeholder with the name of a numeric variable that keeps track of the current loop count, and you replace *start* and *end* with numeric values representing the starting and stopping points for the loop. The line or lines between the For and Next statements are the commands that are repeated each time the loop is executed.

For example, the following For...Next loop uses the TypeParagraph method to insert four carriage returns in a Word document:

```
For i = 1 To 4
    Selection.TypeParagraph
Next i
```

This loop is the functional equivalent of writing the Selection.TypeParagraph statement four times in a procedure. To the Visual Basic interpreter it looks the same as:

```
Selection.TypeParagraph
Selection.TypeParagraph
Selection.TypeParagraph
Selection.TypeParagraph
```

The variable used in the loop is i, a single letter that, by convention, stands for the first integer counter in a For...Next loop. Each time the loop is executed, the counter variable is incremented by one. (The first time through the loop, the variable contains a value of 1, the value of *start;* the last time through, it contains a value of 4, the value of *end.*) As you'll see in the following examples, you can use this counter variable to great advantage in your loops.

Using a Loop to Manage Tables

For...Next loops work best when you are processing information that conforms to a particular pattern. For example, For...Next loops are handy when you want to add, remove, or modify information in tables. Each Word document contains a Tables collection that holds each of the tables in a particular document. By using a combination of Table methods and properties, you can create tables, insert information, remove information, format the entries, and so forth.

In the next exercise, you'll create a macro named AutoTable that inserts a new table in the active document at the insertion point. The macro first prompts the user for the number of rows and columns in the table, then creates the table if it is at least two rows by two columns in size. The macro then uses a For...Next loop to add entries to each of the cells in the first column, and finally uses the AutoFormat command to format the entire table.

67

You can customize the AutoTable macro to create tables of almost any configuration.

 TIP The AutoTable macro is located in the Less03 document in the \WordVB\Less03 folder on your hard disk. You can either load and run the macro on your own, or type it in now from scratch.

Create a macro that automatically builds tables

The following steps show you how to build the AutoTable macro:

1 From the Word Tools menu, click Macro, and then click Macros.

2 Type **AutoTable** in the Name text box, and then click Create.

Word starts the Visual Basic Editor, and opens a new macro procedure named AutoTable in the Code window.

3 Type the following program statements:

```
Dim iRows As Integer, iColumns As Integer
Dim myTable

iRows = InputBox("Number of Rows?")
iColumns = InputBox("Number of Columns?")

If iRows > 1 And iColumns > 1 Then '2x2 table required
    Set myTable = ActiveDocument.Tables.Add(Selection.Range, _
        iRows, iColumns)
    For i = 2 To iRows
        myTable.Cell(i, 1).Range.InsertAfter "Item " & i - 1
    Next i
    myTable.AutoFormat Format:=wdTableFormatColorful2
Else
    MsgBox "Sorry, minimum table size 2 rows and 2 columns."
End If
```

This macro declares three important variables: iRows, an integer that contains the number of rows in the table; iColumns, an integer that contains the number of columns; and myTable, an object variable that represents the new table in the document. The main part of the macro is contained in an If...Then decision structure that uses the And logical operator to verify that a large enough table has been specified by the user. (This *bounds checking* prevents the macro from crashing if the user enters a number that is too small to define a usable table.)

Inside the If...Then decision structure, the For...Next loop uses a starting value of 2, so that text entry begins in the second row. (The first row is reserved for table headings.) The loop then uses the InsertAfter method to add text following the pattern Item 1, Item 2, Item 3, and so forth, until there are no more rows in the table.

The line continuation character preserves readability.

The line continuation character (_) used after the sixth line is simply a style we're using in this book to break lines that go beyond 68 characters in length (for readability) in a way that is acceptable to the Visual Basic interpreter. If you choose, you can type each of these long statements on one line if you remove the line continuation character. However, you may find the line continuation character useful if you want to see all your code at once. (The Code window can actually scroll to the right up to 1024 characters.)

IMPORTANT You cannot use a line continuation character to break a string that is in quotation marks.

Run the macro

Now run the macro to create a custom table in your document.

View Microsoft Word

1   Click the View Microsoft Word button on the Visual Basic Editor toolbar.

2   Move the insertion point to a place you'd like to create a table, and then run the AutoTable macro.

Word displays an input box prompting you for the number of rows in your table.

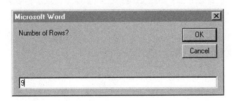

3   Type **9** and click OK.

Word displays a second input box prompting you for the number of columns.

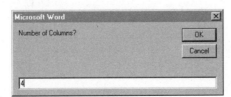

4   Type **4** and click OK.

Word creates a 9x4 table in the current document, fills the first column with text entries, and applies automatic formatting.

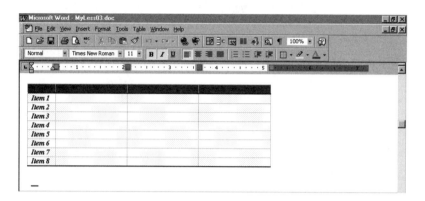

5   If you plan to use this macro often, return to the Visual Basic Editor and customize the macro code to insert appropriate table headings and column text using the InsertAfter method, and specify your own preferences for table formatting using the AutoFormat method.

 TIP   To see a list of the table formatting options that you can use with the AutoFormat method, search for "wdTableFormatColorful2" in the Visual Basic Object Browser.

Save

6   When you're finished, click the Save button on Word's Standard toolbar to save the new macro.

Using For...Each Loops

For...Next loops are very useful if you know exactly how many times a particular group of statements should run. But what if you simply want to process each object in a collection? Fortunately, the designers of Visual Basic included a special loop called For...Each that is specifically designed to march through each item in a collection, one by one. You'll find this especially useful when you're working with the Documents, Tables, Fields, Footnotes, Paragraphs, and Words collections.

The For...Each loop has the following syntax:

```
For Each element In collection
statements to be repeated
Next element
```

The following items are important:

- The *element* placeholder represents a variable name that you enter of type Variant. When the loop runs, *element* stands for each item in the collection one by one.

- The *collection* placeholder represents the name of a valid collection in Word, such as Documents or Paragraphs.

In the following exercise, you'll use a For...Each loop to check each open document in the Documents collection for a file named MyLetter.doc. If the file is found in the collection, the macro will make it the active document in Word. If the file is not found, the macro will load the file from the C:\WordVB\Less03 folder on your hard disk.

 TIP   The ShowLetter macro is located in the Less03 document in the \WordVB\Less03 folder on your hard disk. You can either load and run the macro on your own, or type it in now from scratch.

Use a For...Each loop to process a collection

Follow these steps to create the ShowLetter macro that makes MyLetter.doc the active document:

1   From the Word Tools menu, click Macro, and then click Macros.

2   Type **ShowLetter** in the Name text box, and then click Create.

Word starts the Visual Basic Editor, and opens a new macro procedure named ShowLetter in the Code window.

3   Type the following program statements:

```
Dim aDoc, docFound, docLocation
docLocation = "c:\WordVB\Less03\myletter.doc"

For Each aDoc In Documents
    If InStr(1, aDoc.Name, "myletter.doc", 1) Then
        aDoc.Activate
        Exit For
    Else
        docFound = False
    End If
Next aDoc

If docFound = False Then Documents.Open FileName:=docLocation
```

The macro begins by declaring three variables, all of type Variant. The aDoc variable will represent the current collection element in the For...Each loop, docFound will be assigned a Boolean value of False if the document is not found in the Documents collection, and docLocation will contain the path of the MyLetter.doc file on disk.

71

The For...Each loop cycles through each document in the Documents collection searching for the MyLetter file. If the file is detected by the InStr function (which detects one string in another), the file is made the active document. If the file is not found, the macro opens it by using the Open method of the Documents object.

Also note the Exit For statement, which we use to exit the For Next loop when the MyLetter file has been found and activated. Introduced here for the first time, Exit For is a special program statement you can use to exit a For Next loop when continuing will cause unwanted results. Periodically, you'll want to use Exit For in your own macros.

Run the macro

Now run the macro to display the MyLetter document in Word.

View Microsoft Word

New

1   Click the View Microsoft Word button on the Visual Basic Editor toolbar.

2   Click the New button twice to open two more Word documents.

   You should add a few documents to the Documents collection to test the macro properly.

3   From the Windows menu, click MyLess03 to make it the active window, and then run the ShowLetter macro.

   Word loads the MyLetter file from disk when the file is not found in the Documents collection. (This particular file is a short essay Michael wrote about the Italian Renaissance.)

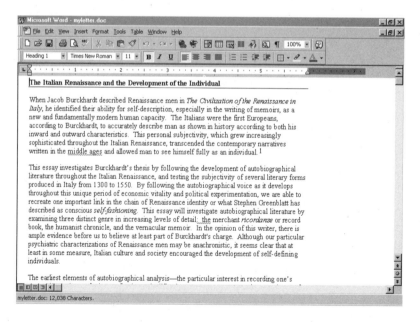

4 Make the MyLess03 document active again, and then run the ShowLetter macro.

This time Word finds the MyLetter document in the Documents collection and displays it with the Activate method.

Save

5 Close the MyLetter document and the two empty Word documents, and then click the Save button on Word's Standard toolbar to save the new macro to disk.

Using With Notation

As the macros in this lesson demonstrate, Word's object model comprises many interconnected objects, properties, and methods. As you've probably discovered, this busy hierarchy occasionally makes for some long object references in program code. Consider the following program statement, which uses the InsertAfter method to add the text *My Words* after the first paragraph in the active document:

```
ActiveDocument.Paragraphs(1).Range.InsertAfter Text:="My Words"
```

If you were to work extensively with the Range object in the first paragraph, you'd be in for a lot of typing. For example, consider the following three program statements that delete the first paragraph in the active document, create a new first paragraph containing the words *My Words*, and then insert a carriage return:

```
ActiveDocument.Paragraphs(1).Range.Delete
ActiveDocument.Paragraphs(1).Range.InsertAfter Text:="My Words"
ActiveDocument.Paragraphs(1).Range.InsertParagraphAfter
```

Although the typing chores in this particular routine are manageable enough, you'll quickly develop an "object hangover" if you use the same wordy object reference over and over again in a macro. Fortunately, Visual Basic provides some typing relief when repetition is the watchword: a convenient shorthand notation called the With statement.

With Statement Syntax

The With statement takes the following syntax:

```
With object
    .object references
End With
```

where the *object* placeholder represents a valid Word object, and *object references* are one or more methods or properties associated with the object (each preceeded by a period). For example, the following With structure deletes the first paragraph in the active document, creates a new paragraph containing *My Words*, and inserts a carriage return—the same work done by the program statements listed in the previous section.

```
With ActiveDocument.Paragraphs(1).Range
    .Delete
    .InsertAfter Text:="New text"
    .InsertParagraphAfter
End With
```

In sum, the With structure makes it easier to type program statements that use the same object notation. After identifying the primary object once, you simply use a period (.) to reference that object in subsequent statements.

TIP An added benefit of the With statement is that it makes your code faster to execute by the Visual Basic interpreter. Not only do you save time typing your code, but your macros run faster, too!

The following example uses the With statement and the Find method to replace all occurrences of the word *Mike* with *Michael* in the active document. The macro also uses the Replacement property, a handy setting that mimics the Replace dialog box in Word. You'll learn more about searching through documents in Lesson 7.

TIP The ReplaceText macro is located in the Less03 document in the \WordVB\Less03 folder on your hard disk. You can either load and run the macro on your own, or type it in now from scratch.

Use With notation to search and replace

Follow these steps to create the ReplaceText macro:

1   From the Word Tools menu, click Macro, and then click Macros.
    Word opens the Macros dialog box.

2   Type **ReplaceText** in the Name text box, and then click Create.
    Word opens the ReplaceText macro in the Code window.

3 Type the following program statements:

```
With Selection.Find
    .ClearFormatting
    .Text = "Mike"
    .Replacement.ClearFormatting
    .Replacement.Text = "Michael"
    .Execute Replace:=wdReplaceAll, Forward:=True, _
        Wrap:=wdFindContinue
End With
```

If you wish, change *Mike* to a search text that would be more useful for you, and replace *Michael* with a more suitable replacement text.

This particular With structure uses the Selection.Find object five times. In each of the first four calls, the macro sets a property that prepares Word for the search-and-replace operation. The ClearFormatting property tells Word to ignore formatting in its search—the equivalent to clicking the No Formatting button in the Find dialog box. The Text property then sets the Find text, the Replacement.ClearFormatting property ignores formatting in the replacement, and the Replacement.Text property identifies the Replacement text (*Michael*) that will be substituted for the Find text (*Mike*). Finally, the Execute method performs the search-and-replace operation throughout the entire document.

Run the macro

Let's see how the ReplaceText macro works.

View Microsoft Word

1 Click the View Microsoft Word button on the Visual Basic Editor toolbar. Word displays the MyLess03 document.

2 Type the following text at the bottom of your test document:

Mike, please add our Fall 1997 products to this list. And Mike, don't forget what Mike James told us about pricing last week.

3 Now run the ReplaceText macro to replace *Mike* with *Michael* throughout the document.

Word performs the search and makes three changes in the sample text you entered.

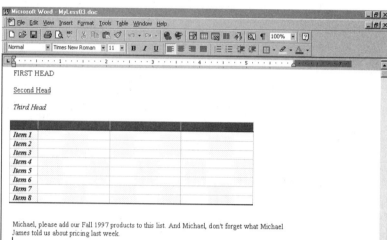

Save

4 Click the Save button on Word's Standard toolbar to save the macro.

Writing Do Loops

Do loops execute code until a specific condition is met.

Here's one last looping structure that you can use to manage repeating statements in your macros. As an alternative to a For...Next loop, you can create a structure called a Do loop, which executes a group of statements until a certain condition becomes True in the loop. Do loops are valuable because often you can't know in advance how many times a loop should repeat. For example, you might want to replace one word with another until a particular heading is encountered in your document. In such a situation, the work you need to do doesn't fit naturally into the bounds of a particular collection—you only need to repeat *until* your work is done.

A Do loop has several formats, depending on where and how the loop condition is evaluated. The most common syntax is:

```
Do While condition
    block of statements to be executed
Loop
```

For example, the following statements are a Do loop that will insert user-supplied text into a document, one word after the next, until the word *Done* is entered:

```
Do While InpName <> "Done"
     InpName = InputBox("Enter your text or type Done to quit.")
     If InpName <> "Done" Then Selection.TypeText Text:=InpName
Loop
```

The placement of the conditional test affects how a Do loop runs.

The conditional statement in this loop is *InpName <> "Done"*, which the Visual Basic interpreter translates as, "Loop as long as the InpName variable doesn't contain the word *Done*." This brings up an important fact about Do loops: if the condition at the top of the loop is not True when the Do statement is first evaluated, the Do loop is never executed.

In this example, if the InpName variable did contain the text string *Done* before the loop started (perhaps from an earlier assignment in the macro), Visual Basic would skip the loop altogether and continue with the line below the Loop keyword. Note that this type of loop requires an extra If...Then structure to prevent the exit value from being displayed when the user types it.

If you want the loop to always run at least once in a program, put the conditional test at the bottom of the loop. For example, the loop

```
Do
     InpName = InputBox("Enter your text or type Done to quit.")
     If InpName <> "Done" Then Selection.TypeText Text:=InpName
Loop While InpName <> "Done"
```

is essentially the same as the Do loop shown above, but the loop condition is tested after a name is received from the InputBox function. Putting the loop condition last has the advantage of updating the InpName variable before the conditional test in the loop, so a pre-existing Done value won't cause the loop to be skipped. Testing the loop condition at the bottom ensures that your loop will be executed at least once, but you'll often need to add a few extra statements to process the data.

The following exercise combines many of the elements you've encountered in this lesson, including the versatile Do loop.

Renumbering Graphics in a Chapter

If you use Word in a desktop publishing environment, you probably work with documents that contain placeholders for figures and graphics. One useful macro in this context is a utility that automatically numbers the graphics in a chapter, and carefully renumbers entries that are either missing numbers or are incorrectly numbered. For example, you want a formatting utility that can produce the following sequential output:

```
Graphic 1: The Visual Basic Editor
Graphic 2: Using Word Objects
Graphic 3: Do Loops
```

We used such a graphic numbering scheme in this book, and marked each callout with the Heading 3 style so that our compositor could identify the graphics later and move them in bulk into Adobe PageMaker, where we finalized our page layout.

The following exercise shows you how to search for each graphic in a chapter that is formatted with the Heading 3 style, and how to preface the artwork callout with the word *Graphic* and the current graphic number.

For this macro to work correctly, you should only format graphics with the Heading 3 style. If the graphic callout is already correct, the macro will skip the heading; however, the macro will also identify graphics that are numbered incorrectly and will renumber them as appropriate. For an author or editor, renumbering is the best part of the utility.

As you build the macro and study its contents, notice how the If, Do, and With structures work together to manage the search and replace operation.

 TIP The RenumberGraphics macro is located in the Less03 document in the \WordVB\Less03 folder on your hard disk. You can either load and run the macro on your own, or type it in now from scratch.

If you load the macro from disk, copy the macro to the Normal template before you test it on the Graphics.doc sample file. (Copy the macro with the Organizer command in the Macros dialog box.) If you type the macro directly into the Normal template as shown in the following exercise, you won't need to follow this step.

Create the RenumberGraphics macro

Follow these steps to build a macro that automatically renumbers graphics in a chapter based on Word's Heading 3 style. This time, you'll create the macro in the Normal template, so you can run it in all your documents.

1 From the Word Tools menu, click Macro, and then click Macros.
2 Type **RenumberGraphics** in the Name text box, select Normal.dot in the Macros In drop-down list, and then click Create.

Word opens the Normal template and places a procedure named RenumberGraphics in it.

3   Type the following program statements:

```
Dim GraphicNumber
GraphicNumber = 1
With ActiveDocument.Content.Find
    .ClearFormatting
    .Style = wdStyleHeading3
    Do While .Execute(FindText:="", Forward:=True, _
        Format:=True) = True
        With .Parent
            If .Words(1).Text = "Graphic " Then
                If .Words(2).Text <> GraphicNumber Then
                    .Words(2).Text = GraphicNumber
                End If
            Else
                .StartOf Unit:=wdParagraph, Extend:=wdMove
                .InsertAfter "Graphic " & GraphicNumber & ": "
            End If
            .Move Unit:=wdParagraph, Count:=1
        End With
        GraphicNumber = GraphicNumber + 1
    Loop
End With
```

In this macro, the GraphicNumber variable keeps track of the current graphic number. This variable is incremented by a Do loop each time a graphic is found in the document, and it is inserted into the text whenever a callout is needed. Note that two With structures are also used to simplify your references to the Find object and its parent object, Content. (The .Parent property is used to get an object reference one up in the current object hierarchy.)

The If...Then decision structure in the Do loop carefully checks the beginning of each paragraph that is formatted with the Heading 3 style, the Microsoft Press notation for graphic callouts. (If you like, you can use a different graphic style by modifying the wdStyleHeading3 constant.) If the first word in the paragraph is *Graphic*, then the next word in the paragraph is checked for the current graphic number. If the number is missing or incorrect, the correct number is added to the text using the Text property.

NOTE   This macro adds graphic callouts to each line formatted with the Heading 3 style, so be careful not to format any blank lines in your document with Heading 3, or they will also be labeled with a graphic number.

Practice renumbering graphics

Now run the macro in a test document that we have provided named
Graphics.doc.

*View Microsoft
Word*

Open

1 Click the View Microsoft Word button on the Visual Basic Editor toolbar.

2 Open the file Graphics.doc located in the \WordVB\Less03 folder.

This document contains five graphic callouts formatted with Heading 3
style. The first callout is correctly numbered and should be left alone by
the macro. The remaining callouts are either numbered incorrectly or
are missing a callout.

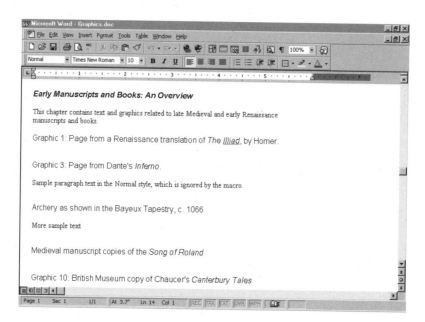

3 Run the RenumberGraphics macro, located in the Normal template.

Word uses a Do loop to scan each paragraph with Heading 3 formatting,
and correctly renumbers your graphics, as shown on the following page.

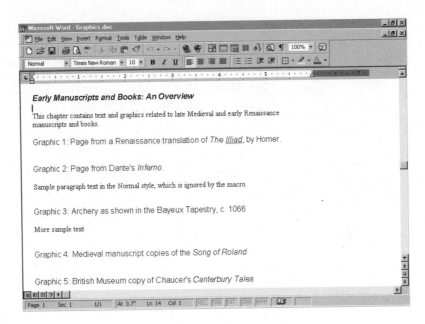

Not bad for just a few carefully organized program statements. If you do this sort of work often, customize the RenumberGraphics macro now so that it fits your needs, and put it to work!

4 When you're finished, close the Graphics sample document without saving your changes (you may want to test the macro again later), and then save the MyLess03 file to disk one last time.

You're finished recording macros in this chapter.

One Step Further: Avoiding an Endless Loop

Because of the relentless nature of Do loops, it is very important to design your test conditions so that each loop has a true exit point. If a loop test never evaluates to False, the loop will execute endlessly and your macro will no longer respond to input. Consider the following example:

```
Do
     Number = InputBox("Enter a number to square, -1 to quit.")
     Number = Number * Number
     MsgBox Number, , "Result"
Loop While Number >= 0
```

In this loop, the user enters number after number and the program squares each number and displays it in a message box. Unfortunately, when the user has had enough, he or she can't quit because the putative exit condition—*Number >= 0*—doesn't work. When the user enters –1, the program squares it and the Number variable is assigned the value 1. (The problem can be fixed by setting a different exit condition.)

 IMPORTANT If your macro gets trapped in an endless loop, press CTRL+BREAK to force the macro to exit.

Endless loops are a good thing to watch for when you're writing Do loops. Fortunately, they're pretty easy to spot if you test your macros thoroughly.

If you want to continue to the next lesson

➤ Keep Word running, and turn to Lesson 4.

If you want to quit Word for now

➤ From the File menu, click Exit. If you see a Save dialog box, click Yes.

Lesson Summary

To	Do this
Write a conditional expression	Use a comparison operator between two values.
Use a decision structure	Use an If...Then or Select Case statement and supporting expressions and keywords.
Make two comparisons in a conditional expression	Use a logical operator between comparisons (And, Or, Not, or Xor).

Execute a group of program statements a set number of times	Insert the statements between For and Next statements in a loop. For example:
	`For i = 1 To 10`
	`    MsgBox ("Press OK already!")`
	`Next i`

Process the elements in a collection	Use a For...Each loop. For example:
	`For Each aDoc in Documents`
	`    MsgBox aDoc.Name`
	`Next aDoc`

To	Do this

Streamline program code containing repeating objects	Use a With structure. For example:
	``
	With Selection.Find
	        .ClearFormatting
	        .Text = "U.S."
	        .Replacement.ClearFormatting
	        .Replacement.Text = "United States"
	        .Execute Replace:=wdReplaceAll, _
	              Forward:=True, _
	              Wrap:= wdFindContinue
	End With
	``

Execute a group of program statements until a specific condition is met	Insert the statements between Do and Loop statements. For example:
	``
	Do While Query <> "Yes"
	        Query = InputBox("Trotsky?")
	        If Query <> "Yes" Then MsgBox Query
	Loop
	``

Avoid an endless Do loop	Be sure the loop has a test condition that can evaluate to False.

For online information about	From the Visual Basic Help menu, click Contents And Index, click the Index tab, and then
Comparison operators	Search for "comparison operators"
Logical operators	Search for "logical operators"
If...Then decision structures	Search for "If"
Select Case decision structures	Search for "Select Case"
For...Next loops	Search for "For...Next"
For...Each loop	Search for "For Each"
Using the With statement	Search for "With"
Do loops	Search for "Do"

Preview of the Next Lesson

In Lesson 4, "Toolbars, Menus, and Dialog Boxes," you'll learn more about processing commands and managing input in your macros. You'll learn how to create custom toolbars, change Word's menus with program code, and use Word's dialog boxes programmatically.

Part 2

Polishing the User Interface

Toolbars, Menus, and Dialog Boxes

Estimated time
40 min.

In this lesson you will learn how to:

- Create custom toolbars and manage them with program code.
- Create custom menus and commands in Word and use them in your macros.
- Use Word's built-in dialog boxes to process information.

In Part II, you'll focus again on your macro's user interface—the toolbars, menus, windows, and dialog boxes a person sees when running your macros. In this lesson, you'll learn how to create custom toolbars and menus for your macros, and manage them with program code. You'll also learn how to use Word's built-in dialog boxes, such as Print and Font, to accomplish useful work in your macros without reinventing the wheel.

Creating Custom Toolbars

You don't need to use Visual Basic to create a custom toolbar in Word. In fact, creating and modifying toolbars is a general skill that you can use any time you want to customize Word's user interface. However, as your collection of macros grows, you may want to design a special toolbar that is set aside just for running macros. In addition, you may want to open a special-purpose toolbar while your macro is running to provide the user with useful options and commands. In this section, you'll learn how to build a custom toolbar with the Customize dialog box, and how to open and close a toolbar with Visual Basic program code.

TIP If you installed the sample files, the Macros toolbar is located in the Less04 document in the \WordVB\Less04 folder on your hard disk. You can either create the toolbar now from scratch, or open the Less04 document and display the toolbar using the Toolbars command on the View menu.

Create a new toolbar

The toolbar you create in this exercise will contain buttons that start the macros you constructed in Lesson 3. To create the toolbar in Word, follow these steps:

1 Open the Less04 document, located in the \WordVB\Less04 folder on your hard disk.

2 From the Word View menu, click Toolbars, and then click Customize.

The Customize dialog box appears.

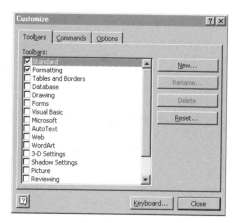

3 Click New to create a new toolbar.

4 Type **My Macros** in the Toolbar Name text box, and then verify that Less04 is the active document in the Make Toolbar Available To drop-down list.

TIP Click Normal in the Make Toolbar Available To drop-down list to place your toolbar in the Normal template and make it available to all of your Word documents.

5 Click OK to open the new toolbar.

Word displays the toolbar above the current document.

Now add some macro buttons to your new toolbar.

Add macro buttons to the toolbar

To add toolbar buttons that run macros, simply drag the macro names from the Commands tab in the Customize dialog box to the toolbar. Follow these steps:

1 Click the Commands tab in the Customize dialog box.

2 Click Macros in the Categories list.

A list of the available macros in the Normal template and in the active document appears in the Commands list.

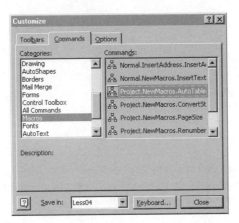

NOTE You can only copy macros to a toolbar if they are listed in the Normal template or the active document. If the Less04 document is not active in Word, open it now so that you may access its macros.

3 Drag a copy of the AutoTable macro from the Commands list to the My Macros toolbar.

As you drag the macro, it appears as an icon with an insertion pointer that will help you place the button. When you release the macro, it appears on the toolbar with its complete module name—Project.NewMacros.AutoTable. Now create a custom icon for the macro.

4 Click Modify Selection on the Commands tab, and then click Default Style.

Word changes the macro toolbar button to an icon.

5 Click Modify Selection again, and then click Change Button Image.

Word displays a selection of toolbar buttons you can use to give your macro a graphic representation.

6 Click the toolbar button containing the empty square.

Word changes the macro button to an empty square. Now you'll edit the button's bitmap image to create a table of rows and columns. (A visual representation of the AutoTable macro.)

7 Click Modify Selection, and then click Edit Button Image.

Word displays the Button Editor, a simple pixel editing program designed to customize toolbar buttons.

8   Create a 3-by-3 table inside the Picture window by clicking on the individual pixels of the toolbar button.

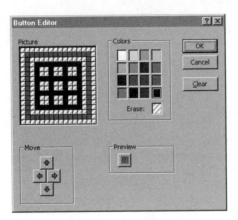

9   When you're finished, click OK to close the Button Editor.

Word displays the final toolbar button for the AutoTable macro.

10 Now repeat steps 3 through 6 five times to add five more macro buttons to the My Macros toolbar.

The remaining macros in the Less04 document are Convert Styles, Page Size, Renumber Graphics, Replace Text, and Show Letter, as shown in the following illustration. (You created these macros in the last lesson.) Use the toolbar buttons shown here, or create your own with the Button Editor.

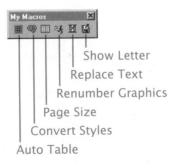

Save

11 When you're finished building the My Macros toolbar, click Close in the Customize dialog box, and then click the Save button.

The final My Macros toolbar appears on the screen, and you can dock or position it anywhere you like, just like a regular toolbar. In addition, you can hold the mouse pointer over one of the toolbar's buttons to see a ToolTip identifying the name of the macro. Click the AutoTable button on the My Macros toolbar now and try it out!

 TIP You can copy a custom toolbar from one document to another document or template by pressing ALT+F8, clicking the Organizer button, clicking the Toolbars tab, and then dragging the toolbar from one location to the next. For more information about the Organizer feature, see "One Step Further" in Lesson 2.

Opening a Toolbar with Program Code

Periodically, you may want to open one or more toolbars while a macro is running to give a user access to additional macros or Word commands. For example, you might want to create a special formatting macro that opens all of Word's text formatting and drawing toolbars, plus your own custom toolbar that contains formatting-related macros.

The CommandBars object controls toolbars and menus.

The secret to opening, closing, and customizing toolbars within a macro is using the CommandBars object, which lets you adjust the current settings of Word's toolbars and menus bars by using a short list of special properties and methods. The following exercise shows how you can open the My Macros toolbar from within a macro.

Use the CommandBars object to open a toolbar

1 From the Word Tools menu, click Macro, and then click Macros.

   Word opens the Macros dialog box.

2 Type **OpenMacros** in the Name text box, and then verify that Less04 is selected in the Macros In drop-down list.

3 Click Create.

   Word starts the Visual Basic Editor, and opens a new macro procedure named OpenMacros in the Code window.

4 Type the following program statements:

```
Dim Reply As Integer
Reply = MsgBox("Display My Macros toolbar?", vbOKCancel)
If Reply = 1 Then  'if OK button clicked
    With CommandBars("My Macros")
        .Visible = True
        .Position = msoBarFloating
    End With
End If
```

This macro uses a MsgBox function to ask if the user would like to open the My Macros toolbar. The answer is stored in an Integer variable named Reply. If the user clicks the OK button in the message box, the Reply variable will hold a value of 1, and the macro will use the CommandBars object to display the My Macros toolbar in a floating position. If the user clicks the Cancel button, the If...Then decision structure will skip the program statements that open the toolbar.

 TIP You can reference any valid Word toolbar by placing its name in double quotation marks and parentheses after the CommandBars object, as shown in the With statement above. For a list of the valid toolbar names, click Toolbars from the Word View menu. To close a toolbar from within a macro, simply set its Visible property to False.

Run the macro

Now run the macro to open the My Macros toolbar in your document.

View Microsoft Word

1 Click the View Microsoft Word button on the Visual Basic Editor toolbar.

2 Press ALT+F8 to open the Macros dialog box, and then double-click the OpenMacros macro.

Word displays a message box asking if you want to open the My Macros toolbar.

3 Click OK to open the toolbar.

Word opens the toolbar and places it in a floating position over your document. You can now run macros by clicking buttons on the My Macros toolbar, or you can close the toolbar by clicking the Close button on the toolbar's title bar.

![Save icon] **4** When you're finished experimenting with toolbars, click the Save button on Word's Standard toolbar to save the new macro.

Save

Creating Custom Menus

Creating new menus in Word is very similar to creating new toolbars. You open a new menu by clicking New in the Commands tab of the Customize dialog box, and you add commands to the menu by dragging them from the Commands tab to the menu bar.

You can create a custom menu to hold new combinations of Word commands, or you can add one or more macros to your custom menus. Fundamentally, menus are analogous to toolbars; the commands are just represented differently in menus: toolbars use buttons, menus use words. In the following exercise, you'll create a new menu named Macros on the menu bar that contains the six macros you've been using in this lesson.

Create a custom menu

Follow these steps to create a new menu:

1 From the Word Tools menu, click Customize.

The Customize dialog box appears.

2 Click the Commands tab.

3 Scroll to the bottom of the Categories list, and click the New Menu item.

Word places the New Menu item in the Commands list box.

4 Drag the New Menu item to the menu bar in the location you would like to place it.

If you're creating a special-purpose macros menu, we recommend you place it to the left of the Help menu. As you drag the menu, Word changes the mouse pointer to an insertion pointer to help you position the menu.

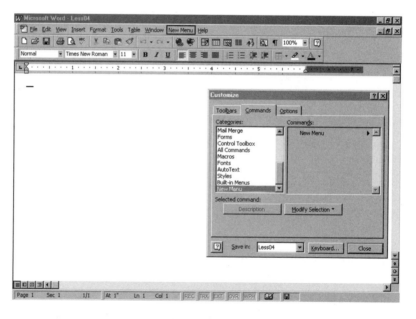

5 Click the new menu with the right mouse button (that is, "right-click" the menu), and then change the Name field in the pop-up window to **Macros** and press ENTER.

Always rename a new menu after you create it.

Now add some macro commands to your new menu.

Add macro commands to the Macros menu

To add macros to your new menu, simply drag the macro names from the Commands tab in the Customize dialog box to the menu. Follow these steps:

1 Click Macros in the Categories list.

A list of the available macros in the Normal template and in the active document appears in the Commands list.

 NOTE You can only copy macros to a menu or toolbar if they are listed in the Normal template or the active document. If the Lesso04 document is not active in Word, open it now so that you may access its macros.

2 Drag a copy of the AutoTable macro from the Commands list to the Macros menu.

An insertion pointer appears to help you position the macro on the empty Macros menu. When you release the mouse button, the macro appears on the menu with its complete module name—Project.NewMacros.AutoTable.

3 Click the Modify Selection button on the Commands tab, and then change the Name field to **&AutoTable** and press ENTER.

The ampersand (&) in front of the command name will underline the letter *A* and make it an *access key*, a keyboard shortcut for running the command when the menu is open.

 TIP By convention, the first letter of a command name is used as its access key, unless the letter is already being used as an access key elsewhere on a menu.

4 Now repeat steps 2 and 3 five times to add the ConvertStyles, Page Size, Renumber Graphics, Replace Text, and Show Letter macros to the Macros menu.

These are the remaining macros you created in Lesson 3. (You don't need to add the other Lesson 4 macros, unless you want to.)

5 When you're finished customizing the Macros menu, click Close in the Customize dialog box.

The final Macros menu appears on the menu bar.

6 Click the Macros menu now to display it on the screen.

Your new menu opens and displays your collection of macros. Click the Page Size macro now to try out your new menu!

7 When you're finished customizing the menu, click the Save button to save the new menu in your document.

Save

 NOTE In Lessons 7 through 11, we'll use the custom menu feature to automatically add the book's menus to your menu bar, so you can run the macros without using the Macros dialog box.

Disabling a Menu with Program Code

As you did with toolbars, you can modify certain elements of a menu by using program code in a macro. For example, you might find it useful to disable one or more of Word's menus while your macro is running to prevent the user from issuing potentially dangerous commands. Again, the trick to modifying a menu is using the CommandBars object, which lets you adjust one or more property settings, or call a menu-related method.

The following exercise shows you how to disable or enable Word's Window menu from within a macro. Although this simple routine is just for learning purposes, you can easily incorporate it into a more sophisticated macro that temporarily disables one or more menus while you perform useful work.

Use the Enabled property to disable a menu

1   From the Word Tools menu, click Macro, and then click Macros.

   Word opens the Macros dialog box.

2   Type **DimWindowMenu** in the Name text box, and then verify that Less04 is selected in the Macros In drop-down list.

3   Click Create.

   Word starts the Visual Basic Editor, and opens a new macro procedure named DimWindowMenu in the Code window.

4   Type the following program statements:

```
Dim Reply As Integer
Reply = MsgBox("Disable Window menu?", vbYesNo)
If Reply = vbYes Then     'if Yes clicked, disable menu
    CommandBars("Window").Enabled = False
ElseIf Reply = vbNo Then 'if No clicked, restore menu
    CommandBars("Window").Enabled = True
End If
```

   This macro uses a MsgBox function to ask if the user wants to disable the Window menu. (The vbYesNo constant displays a message box with Yes and No buttons.) If the user clicks Yes, the Enabled property of the CommandBars object is set to False, and the Window menu is disabled. If the user clicks No, the Enabled property is set to True, and the Window menu is enabled. (Enabling the Window menu with program code allows you to use the same macro to disable and enable the Window menu.)

TIP   In this macro, we used the vbYes and vbNo constants in the If...Then decision structure to make the program code easier to read. You could have also used 6 (for vbYes) and 7 (for vbNo), the integer equivalents identified in the Visual Basic for Applications type library.

Run the macro

Now return to Word and run the macro.

*View Microsoft
Word*

1   Click the View Microsoft Word button on the Visual Basic Editor toolbar.

2   Press ALT+F8 and double-click the DimWindowMenu macro.

The macro asks you if you want to disable the Window menu.

3   Click Yes to disable the menu.

The macro disables the Window menu and stops. Until you restore the Window menu with this macro, you will not be able to open it.

4   Run the macro again, and this time click No when you are asked to disable the menu.

The macro enables the Window menu, and it is available for use. Now save your Word document to preserve the macro you just created.

Save

5   Click the Save button on the toolbar.

Using Built-in Dialog Boxes

In Lesson 5, you'll learn how to build your own dialog boxes with toolbox controls. But before you create your own masterpiece, take a moment now to learn what you can do with Word's built-in dialog boxes, the handy information-gathering tools that Word uses to collect input and set options, including Print, Page Setup, and Font.

The Dialogs Collection

*The Show
method opens a
Word dialog
box.*

Each of Word's dialog boxes is included in a special collection called Dialogs. To display a dialog box, you simply type the word Dialogs, followed by the constant that represents the dialog box you want to open, and the Show method. For example, the following program statement displays the Print dialog box in a macro:

```
Dialogs(wdDialogFilePrint).Show
```

Once the dialog box is open, you can use it just like a regular dialog box. Confirm or cancel the options presented, to suit your needs.

The complete list of dialog box constants is available in the Object Browser (search for "wdWordDialog"), and you can also explore your options in the Code window by typing the Dialogs collection name followed by an open parenthesis. However, you'll also find comfort in the naming convention used to define most of the constants, which usually allows you to guess the correct name without using the Object Browser or the Auto List feature. Each constant begins with *wdDialog* and then contains the menu name, the command name, and any necessary submenus or buttons that are required to open the dialog box, without any intervening spaces.

Displaying Dialog Box Tabs

To display a particular tab in a dialog box, use a special tab constant with the DefaultTab property. For example, the following With structure sets the default tab in the Page Setup dialog box to Page Size and then opens the dialog box using the Show method:

```
With Dialogs(wdDialogFilePageSetup)
    .DefaultTab = wdDialogFilePageSetupTabPaperSize
    .Show
End With
```

Tab constants are usually a mouthful, as the tab constant *wdDialogFilePageSetupTabPaperSize* demonstrates. However, they follow the same practical naming conventions that the dialog box constants do; they begin with the text *wdDialog*, contain the name of the menu and command needed to open the dialog box, and end with the text *Tab* and the tab name. If a dialog box has many tabs, displaying the relevant one for the user will save considerable confusion.

 TIP You can see the complete list of tab constants by searching for "wdWordDialogTab" in the Object Browser. The tab constants for each dialog box are also displayed by the Auto List feature in the Code window.

Using Page Setup in a Macro

Let's put the program code we just developed into a macro to see how it works. In Lesson 3, you created a simple macro named PageSize that used a MsgBox function and a Select Case decision structure to display the page size of the current document. (The macro used Word constants to detect the Letter, Legal, and Envelope 10 paper sizes.) Modify the PageSize macro now so that it allows the user to change the current paper size if desired.

Open a built-in dialog box

Complete the following steps to build a revised PageSize macro named ChangePageSize:

1 From the Word Tools menu, click Macro, and then click Macros.

2 Type **ChangePageSize** in the Name text box, and then verify that Less04 is selected in the Macros In drop-down list.

3 Click Create.

Word starts the Visual Basic Editor and opens a new macro procedure named ChangePageSize in the Code window.

4 Type the following program statements:

```
PaperType = ActiveDocument.PageSetup.PaperSize
Select Case PaperType
Case wdPaperLetter
    Prompt = "Document type is Letter (8 1/2 x 11). OK?"
Case wdPaperLegal
    Prompt = "Document type is Legal (8 1/2 x 14). OK?"
Case wdPaperEnvelope10
    Prompt = "Document type is Envelope (4 1/8 x 9 1/2). OK?"
Case Else
    Prompt = "Type unknown. OK?"
End Select
Reply = MsgBox(Prompt, vbYesNo)
If Reply = vbNo Then   'if No clicked, open Page Setup
    With Dialogs(wdDialogFilePageSetup)
    .DefaultTab = wdDialogFilePageSetupTabPaperSize
    .Show
    End With
End If
```

The Select Case decision structure in this macro is a little different than the one in the PageSize macro. Rather than calling the MsgBox function inside the Select Case structure, we wait until the end to save a little typing (the MsgBox function is only listed once). The MsgBox function asks the user if the current page size is correct. If the user clicks No, the With structure developed above sets the default tab in the Page Setup dialog box to Paper Size, and then displays the dialog box. The user can then change the current page setting or click Cancel to end the macro.

Run the macro

Now run the macro to see how the Page Setup dialog box looks.

*View Microsoft
Word*

1   Click the View Microsoft Word button on the Visual Basic Editor toolbar.

Word displays the MyLess04 document.

2   Run the ChangePageSize macro.

The macro displays a message box that describes the current document's paper type, and asks if it is OK.

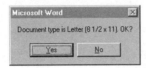

3   Click No to change the paper size.

The macro opens the Page Setup dialog box with the Paper Size tab displayed.

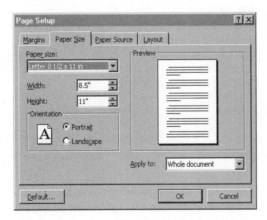

4   Use the Paper Size drop-down list to change the paper size to Legal, and then click OK.

Word changes the current document's paper size to Legal.

5   Run the macro again, and use the Page Size tab to change the page size back to Letter.

Save

6   When you're finished experimenting with the macro, click the Save button to save the new macro to disk in the MyLess04 document.

One Step Further: Setting Dialog Box Options

If a dialog box has optional settings, you can also adjust them by changing one or more dialog box properties with program code. This capability lets you design a dialog box to contain just the default settings that you want; it's a little like arranging the plates, bowls, and silver on the table for an honored guest. It will both save the user time and let you subtly recommend the options the user should select.

Try using the Font and Points properties now to adjust two default settings in the Font dialog box.

 NOTE Unfortunately, the Auto List feature in the Visual Basic Code window does not display dialog box settings in a properties list box, so you'll need to know the exact options you want to customize in advance. (The Word documentation calls these dialog box settings "arguments," not "properties.") For the complete list of the dialog box settings available, search for "built-in Word dialog boxes, argument list" in the Microsoft Word Visual Basic online Help.

Configure the Font dialog box

1 Press ALT+F8, type **FormatText**, and then click Create.

Word opens a new macro named FormatText in the Code window.

2 Type the following program statements:

```
With Dialogs(wdDialogFormatFont)
    .Font = "Times New Roman"
    .Points = 24
    .Show
End With
```

This macro uses a With structure to set the default font to Times New Roman and the default point size to 24, and then opens the Font dialog box using the Show method. As you enter the macro, note that Font and Points are not listed as properties in the Auto List list box. Don't worry; these are legitimate arguments supported by the Font dialog box. Word will recognize them.

Now run the macro to format some text with your new settings.

View Microsoft Word

3 Click the View Microsoft Word button, and then type **Mozart's Hoffmeister String Quartet** in your Word document.

4 Select the text, and then run the FormatText macro.

The macro opens the Font dialog box with your new default settings. Font has been set to Times New Roman, and Size has been set to 24 points.

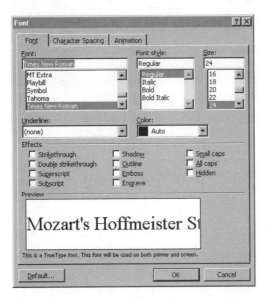

5 Click OK to accept the default formatting settings.

Word formats the selected text in 24-point Times New Roman. By using default settings, you suggested a particular formatting option and saved the user a little formatting time—a nice touch.

6 Click the Save button to save the new macro to disk.

You're finished recording macros in this lesson.

Save

If you want to continue to the next lesson

➤ Keep Word running, and turn to Lesson 5.

If you want to quit Word for now

➤ From the File menu, click Exit. If you see a Save dialog box, click Yes.

Lesson Summary

To	Do this
Create a new toolbar	From the Word View menu, click Toolbars, click Customize, click the Toolbars tab, and then click New.
Display a toolbar in a macro	In a With statement, set the Visible property of the toolbar to True, and specify a location with the Position property. For example: ```\nWith CommandBars("My Macros")\n .Visible = True\n .Position = msoBarFloating\nEnd With\n```
Create a new menu	From the Word Tools menu, click Customize, click the Commands tab, click New Menu in the Categories list, and then drag the new menu to the menu bar.
To disable a menu	Set the Enabled property of the menu to False. For example: ```\nCommandBars("Window").Enabled = False\n```
Open a built-in dialog box	Specify the Dialogs collection with the dialog box constant and the Show method. For example: ```\nDialogs(wdDialogFilePrint).Show\n```
Display a specific tab in a dialog box	Use the DefaultTab property with the Dialogs object. For example: ```\nWith Dialogs(wdDialogFilePageSetup)\n .DefaultTab = _\n wdDialogFilePageSetupTabPaperSize\n .Show\nEnd With\n```
Set a dialog box option	Specify a dialog box argument with the Dialogs object. For example: ```\nWith Dialogs(wdDialogFormatFont)\n .Font = "Times New Roman"\n .Points = 24\n .Show\nEnd With\n```

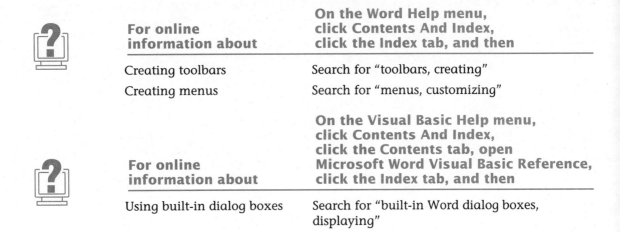

For online information about	On the Word Help menu, click Contents And Index, click the Index tab, and then
Creating toolbars	Search for "toolbars, creating"
Creating menus	Search for "menus, customizing"

For online information about	On the Visual Basic Help menu, click Contents And Index, click the Contents tab, open Microsoft Word Visual Basic Reference, click the Index tab, and then
Using built-in dialog boxes	Search for "built-in Word dialog boxes, displaying"

Preview of the Next Lesson

In Lesson 5, "Working with UserForms," you'll learn how to create new dialog boxes called UserForms to process user input. You'll learn how to create objects on a UserForm with toolbox controls, how to customize objects with property settings, and how to program objects with Visual Basic code.

Working with UserForms

Estimated time
50 min.

In this lesson you will learn how to:

- Create a simple UserForm with the Label, Image, and CommandButton controls.
- Use the TextBox control to display paragraphs in a Word document.
- Use the OptionButton, CheckBox, ListBox, and ComboBox controls to build a graphical ordering system.
- Manage multiple UserForms in a macro.

In Lesson 4, you learned how to use Word's built-in dialog boxes to run commands and process input in your macros. In this lesson, you'll learn how to create your own custom dialog boxes called UserForms. You'll learn how to open UserForms in your macro, how to create objects with toolbox controls, how to configure objects with property settings, and how to customize objects with event procedures. The toolbox controls you'll learn how to use include Label, CommandButton, TextBox, Image, OptionButton, CheckBox, ListBox, and ComboBox. When you're finished, you'll have all the tools you need to build the ultimate user interface for any macro.

Getting Started with UserForms: The MusicTrivia Macro

The best way to get started with UserForms is to create a simple macro that opens a custom dialog box and uses it to display information. In this section, you'll create a MusicTrivia macro that asks the user a simple question about a popular rock and roll instrument. Along the way, you'll learn the three fundamental steps to creating a Visual Basic UserForm: designing the user interface, setting properties, and writing event procedures.

Designing the User Interface

A UserForm is simply a custom dialog box that you create in the Visual Basic Editor by using programmable interface objects called toolbox controls. To open a UserForm in the Visual Basic Editor, you click UserForm from the Insert menu. Each UserForm appears in a separate Project window in the Visual Basic Editor, and is also listed in the Forms folder in the Project Explorer. The first UserForm is named UserForm1; subsequent UserForms are named UserForm2, UserForm3, and so on.

Whenever a UserForm is active in the Visual Basic Editor, a palette of toolbox controls also appears in a window, which allows you to add programmable interface objects to your UserForm. If you've used a drawing program such as Paint, you have many of the skills you need to use toolbox controls. To build the interface objects, you click a control in the toolbox, and then you "draw" the interface object by dragging with the mouse. This is usually a simple matter of clicking to position one corner of the object and then dragging to create a rectangle that is exactly the size that you want. After you create the object—a text label, for example—you can resize it by using the selection handles, or you can relocate it by dragging. You can also resize or move the UserForm itself to create a dialog box in exactly the size and location you want.

You create interface objects on your UserForm with toolbox controls.

In the following exercise, you'll create the UserForm for the MusicTrivia macro by using toolbox controls.

Create the user interface

1   Start Word and open the Less05 document in the C:\WordVB\Less05 folder.

The Less05 document contains all the completed macros in this lesson. You can simply run the MusicTrivia macro in the Less05 document now, but we also recommend that you follow these instructions to build a copy of the macro step by step. It takes a little practice to create a UserForm with toolbox controls.

2   From the Word Tools menu, click Macro, and then click Macros.

Word opens the Macros dialog box, the place where you create and run Visual Basic macros.

3   Type **MyMusicTrivia** in the Name text box, and then click the Macros In drop-down list and select the Less05 document.

4   Click Create.

Word starts the Visual Basic Editor and opens a new macro procedure named MyMusicTrivia in the Code window.

5   Type the following program statements to load and open the UserForm:

```
Load UserForm1
UserForm1.Show
```

Every macro that opens a UserForm needs these two program statements to bring the UserForm into memory and display it. In this simple macro, these are the only two lines you'll type in the macro. The remaining program statements will be entered into event procedures associated with the objects on the UserForm. (You will learn more about event procedures in the next lesson.)

6   From the Insert menu, click UserForm.

The Visual Basic Editor opens a new UserForm in a window, and displays the toolbox controls. The UserForm is named UserForm1.

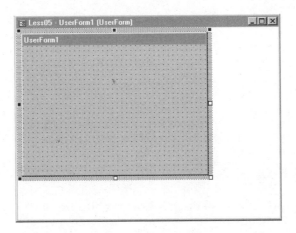

*Label
control*

7 Click the Label control in the toolbox, and then place the mouse pointer over the UserForm.

The Label control is selected, and the mouse pointer changes to crosshairs when it rests on the form. The crosshairs are designed to help you draw the rectangular shape of a label. When you hold down the left mouse button and drag, the label object takes shape and snaps to the grid formed by the intersection of dots on the form. Try creating a label that will hold the text of your MusicTrivia question now.

> **TIP** To learn the name of a control in the toolbox, hold the mouse over the control until its ToolTip appears.

8 Move the mouse pointer to the middle of the UserForm (near the left edge), hold down the left mouse button, and then drag down and to the right. Stop dragging and release the mouse button when your label object looks like the one in the following illustration:

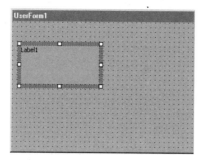

The purpose of a label object is to display formatted text on a UserForm. The first label object on a form is named Label1; subsequent labels are named Label2, Label3, and so on. You'll add text to the label object later in this exercise when you practice setting object properties.

*Label
control*

9 Click the Label control in the toolbox again, and then create a second, smaller label object below the first one.

Each label object on a UserForm maintains its own set of properties and methods. By creating two separate label objects, you'll be able to manipulate them individually with program code.

*Image
control*

10 Click the Image control in the toolbox, and create a large, square image object on the right side of the form.

The purpose of an image object is to display clip art, photographs, bitmaps, and other electronic artwork on a UserForm. (Specifically, an image object can display .ico, .wmf, .bmp, .cur, .jpg, and .gif files.) You'll use this image object to display a photograph of the musical instrument that demonstrates the answer to the musical trivia question.

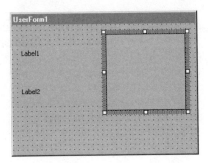

CommandButton control

11 Click the CommandButton control in the toolbox, and create a command button object at the bottom of your UserForm, on the left side.

The purpose of a command button object is to create dialog box buttons on a UserForm. Typical command buttons include OK and Cancel, but you can also create your own button types.

12 Click the CommandButton control again, and then create a second command button object at the bottom of your UserForm, on the right side.

You're finished creating objects on your UserForm. If the final dialog box doesn't look like the following illustration, use the mouse to fine tune the size and location of your objects.

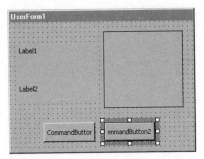

Setting Properties

After you create objects on your UserForm with toolbox controls, your next step is to customize the objects with property settings. As you learned in Lesson 1, a property setting is a quality or characteristic of an object that can change as your macro runs. You can change the property settings for objects on a UserForm by using the Properties window at *design time* (when your macro is being built), or by using program code at *run time* (while your macro is executing).

In the following exercise, you'll customize each object on the MusicTrivia UserForm with one or more property settings.

 TIP To make the purpose of your objects easier to identify in event procedures, you can change the names of the objects on your UserForm to something more intuitive by using the Name property in the Properties window. In short macros such as this one, devising a well-thought-out naming convention is not that important, but when you write larger macros, you may want to consider it. For more information about naming conventions, search for "naming conventions" in the Visual Basic online Help.

Use the Properties window

1 Click the first label object on the UserForm.

Before you can set a property for an object, you must select the object on the UserForm. When you select the first label object, its name (Label1) appears at the top of the Properties window in the Object drop-down list.

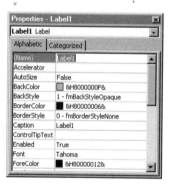

 TIP To see more of the Properties window, double-click its title bar to display it in its fully expanded position. To return the Properties window to a docked position, double-click the title bar again.

2 In the Properties window, double-click the text (Label1) to the right of the Caption property to select it, and press DELETE.

The default text setting for the Caption property is deleted. Now enter a new caption.

3   Type **What rock and roll instrument is often played with sharp, slap-ping thumb movements?** and press ENTER.

The contents of the Label1 object on the form change to match your trivia question. Since the label object's WordWrap property is set to True by default, the text wraps inside the label object.

4   Click the Label2 object on the UserForm, and follow the same steps to change its Caption property to **The Bass Guitar**.

5   With the Label2 object still selected, click the Visible property, and change its setting to **False**.

You'll keep the answer hidden until the first command button is pressed.

6   Click the Image1 object on the form.

Now you'll adjust the PictureSizeMode, Picture, and Visible properties of the image object to display a photograph of a bass guitar when the user clicks a command button.

7   Click the PictureSizeMode property, and select 1 – fmPictureSizeModeStretch in the drop-down list.

This property setting resizes artwork in an image box so that it fits exactly.

8   Click the Picture property, and then click the button containing three dots in the setting field.

A dialog box appears prompting you to select a piece of artwork for the image box.

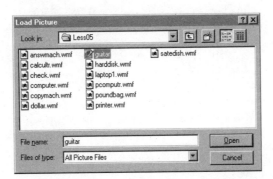

9   Select the C:\WordVB\Less05 folder, and then double-click guitar.bmp.

The photograph of a hip Seattle bass player appears in the image box. (Look closely—he's currently demonstrating the slap-bass technique.)

10 Click the Visible property, and set it to **False**.

You'll keep the photograph hidden until the user clicks the first command button.

11 Now select the first command button object on the form and change its Caption property to **Answer**.

12 Change the Caption property of the second command button to **Quit**.

13 Finally, click the UserForm itself (not the title bar or an object), and set the Caption property of the UserForm to **Music Trivia**.

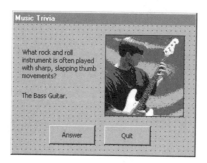

You're finished setting properties for the macro.

Writing Event Procedures

The final step in creating a UserForm is writing the program code for the interface objects on the UserForm. Fortunately, most of the objects on a UserForm already "know" how to work when the macro runs, so you just need to add the final touches with a few carefully designed event procedures. An event procedure is a special routine that runs when an object on your form is manipulated at run time. (Technically, event procedures run when a specific *event* is triggered in the macro, such as a click, a double-click, or a drag-and-drop operation.) UserForm event procedures use the same Visual Basic macro language you're familiar with, so you'll have little trouble figuring out what to do. As with Word macros, the trick to learning the ropes is understanding what the most important properties and methods do, and then executing them in the proper sequence with program code.

In this simple macro, you just need to write "click" event procedures for the two command button objects: CommandButton1 and CommandButton2. The rest of the UserForm runs automatically.

Write event procedures with the Code window

1 Double-click the CommandButton1 object (the button with the Answer caption).

The Visual Basic Editor opens the click event procedure for the CommandButton1 object in the Code window.

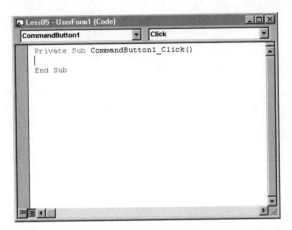

2   Type the following code between the Private Sub and End Sub statements:

```
Image1.Visible = True
Label2.Visible = True
```

These program statements make the Image1 and Label2 objects visible on the UserForm when the user clicks the Answer button.

3   Click the Object drop-down list in the Code window, and select the CommandButton2 object.

4   Type the following statement between Private Sub and End Sub:

```
Unload UserForm1
```

This line unloads the MusicTrivia UserForm and closes the macro when the user clicks the Quit button.

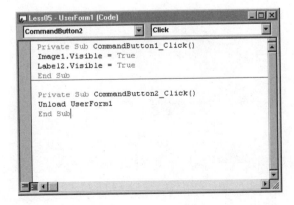

TIP Use the Unload statement whenever you want to close a UserForm and return to the Word macro that opened it.

Save

5 Now click the Save button to save your UserForm and macro to disk.

Run the MusicTrivia macro

Congratulations, you've built your first UserForm. Now return to Word and run the MyMusicTrivia macro.

View Microsoft Word

1 Click the View Microsoft Word button on the Visual Basic Editor toolbar.

2 Press ALT+F8 and double-click MyMusicTrivia.

The macro runs and displays your UserForm on the screen. Pretend you don't know the answer to our little puzzler.

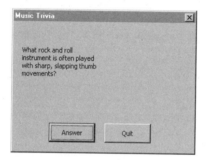

3 Click the Answer button.

The answer and photograph appear on the form, just as you specified in the CommandButton1 event procedure.

4 Click the Quit button to close the macro.

The UserForm unloads and the macro stops.

NOTE If your program didn't display the expected results, check the program statements in your event procedures, and the property settings you made. If you forgot to set the Image1 and Label2 Visible properties to False, Visual Basic won't hide them when your macro starts.

Now let's move on to some other toolbox controls.

Displaying Paragraphs with the TextBox Control

The Label control is useful if you want to display a short sentence on a UserForm, but if you want to exhibit or solicit large amounts of text, you'll want to use the TextBox control. A text box is a rectangular storage container for words, sentences, and paragraphs—the basic stuff of Word documents. You can receive text via a TextBox control, and provide your macro with raw material for text processing, comparing, or printing. Or you can display text with the TextBox control; the source can be either material from an existing Word document, or information from the operating system or the macro itself. Best of all, the TextBox control is designed with ease of use in mind. You can display it with or without scroll bars, and you can select, copy, and paste information to and from a text box just like a Word document.

 TIP To create a text box object that can handle multiple lines, set the text box object's Multiline property to True, and set the ScrollBars property to 2-fmScrollBarsVertical or 3-fmScrollBarsBoth. You can also set the WordWrap property to True if you don't want to use horizontal scroll bars.

The ParaScan Macro

The following exercise demonstrates how you can use the TextBox control to display each paragraph in a Word document, one by one. The macro contains Next, Format, and Delete buttons, too, so you can quickly scan a document and make formatting adjustments or delete unwanted material. As you practice using the utility, you'll learn more about using program code to manipulate the contents of a Word document.

Run the ParaScan macro

1 Press ALT+F8 to open the Macros dialog box, and then double-click the ParaScan macro.

Word runs the macro and displays the ParaScan UserForm.

2 Start the macro by clicking Next on the UserForm.

The macro selects the first paragraph in the Less05 document and copies it to the text box object on the UserForm. The four buttons at the bottom of the UserForm describe your options: you can scan the next paragraph by clicking Next, you can format the current paragraph by clicking Format, you can delete the current paragraph by clicking Delete, or you can quit the macro by clicking Quit.

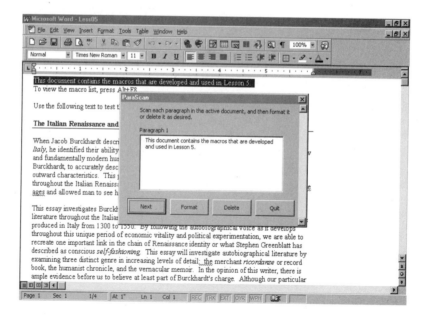

3 Click Next seven times to select the eighth paragraph in the document.

This paragraph is too long to fit entirely in the text box, but if you click the text box, a vertical scroll bar will appear to let you view the hidden text.

4 Now click Format to change the font formatting in the paragraph.

The macro opens the Font dialog box so that you can quickly make the formatting changes you want to.

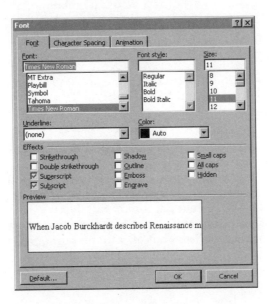

5 Change the font to 9 point, change the color to Blue, and then click OK.

The macro formats the selected paragraph as you requested.

6 Click Next again, and then click Delete.

The macro highlights a new paragraph and then deletes it when you click Delete.

7 Click Next a few more times to see how the ParaScan macro works, and then click Quit to close the macro.

TIP We wrote the ParaScan macro primarily for demonstration purposes, but if you'd like to use it to manage your own documents, copy it to the Normal template now with the Organizer tool so that you can use it with all your documents. (Until you do, it is only available in the Less05 document.)

How Does ParaScan Work?

ParaScan is a two-part macro. The first part is a simple two-line procedure named ParaScan that uses the Load statement and the Show method to open and display the UserForm2 dialog box on the screen. The real work of the macro happens in the second part, a custom UserForm with an event procedure for each command button object in the user interface: Next, Format, Delete, and Quit.

Public variables hold their values in all event procedures.

Something new you'll see in this macro is a global or *public* variable named Num, which keeps track of the current paragraph in the document. A public variable is declared at the top of a module with the Public keyword, in a special section called Declarations. When you declare a public variable in a macro, the variable holds its value in all event procedures in the macro. By contrast, variables declared within an event procedure are *local* to the event procedure, meaning that only the event procedure that defines the variable has access to it, and that the variable loses its value once the event procedure is finished.

Loading text in a text box object   When the user clicks Next, the CommandButton1_Click event procedure is executed. This event procedure increments the Num variable, which tracks the current paragraph number in the document (1, 2, 3, and so on). Using the paragraph number, the routine then selects the current paragraph and copies it to the Text property of the TextBox1 object. The current paragraph number is also displayed in the Label1 caption, and if the paragraph is the last one in the document, the Next button is disabled. (Clicking the Next button with no paragraphs left would cause a run-time error.)

```
Private Sub CommandButton1_Click()
Num = Num + 1
ActiveDocument.Paragraphs(Num).Range.Select
TextBox1.Text = ActiveDocument.Paragraphs(Num).Range
Label1.Caption = "Paragraph " & Num
If Num = ActiveDocument.Paragraphs.Count Then
    CommandButton1.Enabled = False
End If
End Sub
```

Opening the Font dialog box   The second command button object (Format) simply opens Word's built-in Font dialog box, so that the user can format the selected paragraph. As you learned in Lesson 4, a built-in dialog box is displayed when you use one of Word's dialog box constants with the Dialogs collection and the Show method.

```
Private Sub CommandButton2_Click()
Dialogs(wdDialogFormatFont).Show
End Sub
```

Deleting a paragraph   The third command button (Delete) deletes the paragraph that is currently selected in the Word document and is visible in the TextBox1 object. Deleting the text is the easy part—a simple matter of using the Delete method with the active range, as the first line of the event procedure demonstrates.

```
Private Sub CommandButton3_Click()
ActiveDocument.Paragraphs(Num).Range.Delete
If Num >= 2 Then Num = Num - 1
ActiveDocument.Paragraphs(Num).Range.Select
TextBox1.Text = ActiveDocument.Paragraphs(Num).Range
Label1.Caption = "Paragraph " & Num
If Num = ActiveDocument.Paragraphs.Count Then
    CommandButton1.Enabled = False
End If
End Sub
```

The rest of the event procedure clarifies what happens next. If there are two or more paragraphs in the document, the new selected paragraph simply becomes the paragraph directly above. However, if there is only one paragraph in the document, the paragraph count remains the same—in Microsoft Word there can never be "zero" paragraphs. If the new active paragraph is the last paragraph in the document, the Next button is disabled so that the user cannot specify a paragraph outside of the valid range. (Such an action would produce a run-time error.)

Unloading the UserForm   Finally, the last command button in the UserForm (Quit) terminates the macro by unloading the UserForm. This is always the best way to close a UserForm.

```
Private Sub CommandButton4_Click()
Unload UserForm2
End Sub
```

Controls for Gathering Input

Visual Basic provides several methods for gathering input in a macro. As you just learned, text boxes can accept typed input, built-in dialog boxes offer a variety of standard input formats, and menus and toolbars provide visual representations of frequently used commands. In this exercise, you'll learn how to use four additional toolbox controls that will help you collect input in a macro. You'll learn about the OptionButton control, the CheckBox control, the ListBox control, and the ComboBox control. You'll explore each of these tools as you run a macro called InvoiceMaker, a custom utility that prepares an invoice for computer equipment in your document using a variety of graphical input tools. As you run the macro, you'll get some hands-on experience with several tried-and-true techniques for gathering information in an application for Windows.

121

The InvoiceMaker Macro

The InvoiceMaker macro simulates an electronic ordering environment in which you see what you're ordering as you make your selection. If you work in a business that does a lot of order entry, you may want to expand this macro into a full-featured graphical order entry program someday. (Graphical tools like this are popular on the World Wide Web.) As you experiment with InvoiceMaker, spend some time observing how the option button, check box, list box, and combo box elements work in the macro. They were created in a few short steps by using toolbox controls and a UserForm.

Run the InvoiceMaker macro

1   Press ALT+F8 to open the Macros dialog box, and then double-click the InvoiceMaker macro.

Word runs the macro and displays the InvoiceMaker UserForm.

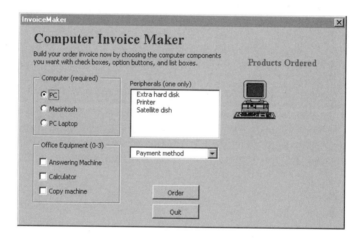

The InvoiceMaker UserForm contains option button, check box, list box, combo box, image box, command button, and label objects. These work together to create a simple order entry program that demonstrates how the Visual Basic input objects work. When the InvoiceMaker macro is run, it loads Windows metafiles from the \WordVB\Less05 folder on drive C and displays them in the six image boxes on the form.

NOTE If you installed the practice files in a location other than the default C:\WordVB folder, the statements in the macro that load the artwork from disk will contain an incorrect pathname. (Each statement begins with c:\wordvb\less05, as you'll soon see.) If this is the case, you can make the macro work by renaming the practice files folder to \WordVB, or by changing the pathnames in the Code window using either the editing keys or the Replace command on the Edit menu.

Option buttons allow the user to select one item from a list.

2 Click the PC Laptop option button in the Computer box.

The image of a laptop computer appears in the Products Ordered area on the right side of the UserForm. In the Computer box, *option buttons* are used to gather input from the user. Option buttons force the user to choose one (and only one) item from a list of possibilities. The user can click the various option buttons repeatedly. After each click, the current choice is graphically depicted in the order area to the right.

NOTE The artwork in this macro is displayed by a collection of six image objects. The artwork we use are all Windows metafiles (.wmf files), which are electronic images designed for resizing that take up very little disk space. When the PictureSizeMode property of an image object is set to 1-fmPictureSizeModeStretch, a Windows metafile looks quite sharp. You'll find the complete collection of Windows metafiles in the C:\WordVB\Less05 folder.

Check boxes let the user select any number of items.

3 Select the Answering Machine, Calculator, and Copy Machine check boxes in the Office Equipment box.

Check boxes are used in a program when more than one option at a time can be selected from a list. Clear the Calculator check box, and notice that the picture of the calculator disappears from the order area. Since each user interface element is live and responds to click events as they occur, order choices are reflected immediately.

List boxes let the user select one item from a variable-length list of choices.

4 Click Satellite Dish in the Peripherals list box.

A picture of a satellite dish is added to the order area. A *list box* is used to get a single response from a list of choices. List boxes can contain many items to choose from (scroll bars appear if the list is longer than the list box), and unlike option buttons, a default selection is not required. In a Visual Basic macro, items can be added to, removed from, or sorted in a list box while the macro is running.

Combo boxes take up less space than list boxes.

5 Now select U.S. Dollars (sorry, no credit) from the payment list in the Payment Method combo box.

A *combo box,* or drop-down list box, is similar to a regular list box, but it takes up less space. Visual Basic automatically handles the opening, closing, and scrolling of the list box. All you do as a programmer is write code to add items to the list box before the macro starts and to process the user's selection. You'll see examples of each task in the InvoiceMaker code.

After making your order selections, your screen should look something like this:

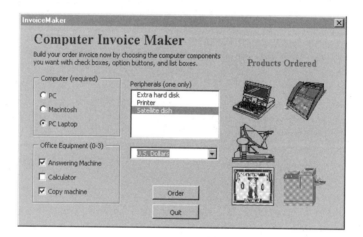

6 Now click the Order button to create an invoice in Word with the selections you have made.

The macro opens a new document in Word and creates a simple invoice for your order. (We didn't include pricing, tax, or shipping figures in this example because it is just for demonstration purposes.) Notice the header, current date, and closing "thank you" message that the macro created, in addition to the content of your order.

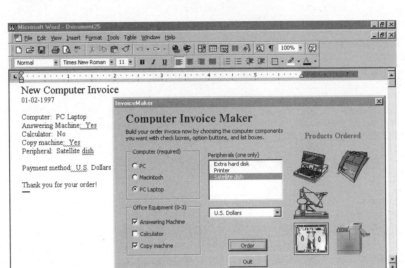

7   Practice making a few more changes to the order list in the macro. Try different computers, peripherals, and payment methods, and then click the Order button to build a second invoice.

Each time you click the Order button, the macro creates an invoice in a new Word document.

8   When you're finished experimenting with the macro, click Quit.

The program closes when you click Quit, and the Visual Basic Editor appears.

Looking at the InvoiceMaker Program Code

You've had some practice using a few of the new input controls; now take a look at the program code to see how they work. Since most of the controls offer multiple selections, a common theme in the event procedures that control them is an If...Then or Select Case decision structure. The key item in these structures is either the Value property, which changes when a check box is selected, or the ListIndex property, which changes when an item in a list is selected.

Examine the CheckBox code and ListBox code

1 Be sure the macro has stopped running, and then double-click the Answering Machine check box in the Office Equipment frame to display the CheckBox1_Click event procedure in the Code window.

2 Resize the Code window, and you'll see the following program code:

```
Private Sub CheckBox1_Click()
If CheckBox1.Value = True Then
    Image2.Picture = LoadPicture("c:\wordvb\less05\answmach.wmf")
    Image2.Visible = True
Else
    Image2.Visible = False
End If
End Sub
```

The CheckBox1_Click event procedure contains the program code that is run when a user selects the Answering Machine check box in the macro. The important keyword here is CheckBox1.Value, which should be read as "the Value property of the first check box object." CheckBox1 is the name of the first check box created on a form; subsequent check boxes are named CheckBox2, CheckBox3, and so on. The Value property is a quantity that changes when a user selects the check box on the form. When an X or a check mark appears in the check box, the Value property is set to 1; when the check box is blank, the Value property is set to 0.

The Value property can be set by using the Properties window when you are designing your check box (so that the check box can contain a default setting), or the property can be changed by the user when the program is running (when a check box is selected). In the code above, the Value property is evaluated by an If...Then...Else decision structure. If the property evaluates to 1, the program loads the picture of an answering machine into the second image box on the form and makes the picture visible. Otherwise, when the Value property is 0, the answering machine picture is hidden from view.

3 Close the Code window, and double-click the Peripherals list box on the form.

When the user clicks an item in a list box, Visual Basic returns the name of the item to the macro in the ListBox1.Text property.

The ListBox1_Click event procedure appears in the Code window. The following statements appear:

```
Private Sub ListBox1_Click()
Select Case ListBox1.ListIndex
Case 0
    Image3.Picture = LoadPicture("c:\wordvb\less05\harddisk.wmf")
Case 1
    Image3.Picture = LoadPicture("c:\wordvb\less05\printer.wmf")
```

```
Case 2
    Image3.Picture = LoadPicture("c:\wordvb\less05\satedish.wmf")
End Select
Image3.Visible = True
End Sub
```

Here you see the code that executes when the user clicks an item in the Peripherals list box in the macro. In this case, the important keyword is ListBox1.ListIndex, which means, "the ListIndex property of the first list box object." After the user makes a choice in the list box, the ListIndex property returns a number that corresponds to the location of the item in the list box. (The first item is numbered 0, the second item is numbered 1, and so on.)

The actual text of the choice (the name of the list box item) is also returned in the ListBox1.Text property, and Visual Basic programmers often use this feature as a method for receiving input in their macros. In the code above, ListBox1.ListIndex is evaluated by the Select Case decision structure, and a different Windows metafile is loaded depending on the value of the ListIndex property. If the value is 0, a picture of a hard disk is loaded; if the value is 1, a picture of a printer is loaded; if the value is 2, a picture of a satellite dish (our dream peripheral) is loaded.

Statements in the UserForm_Initialize event procedure run when the program starts.

4 Close the Code window, and double-click the form (not any of the objects) to display the code associated with the form itself.

The UserForm_Initialize event procedure appears in the Code window. This is the routine that executes each time the InvoiceMaker UserForm is loaded or *initialized*. Programmers put program statements in this special location when they want something executed every time a macro loads. Often, as in the InvoiceMaker macro, the statements define an aspect of the user interface that couldn't be created by using toolbox controls or the Properties window.

```
Private Sub UserForm_Initialize()
Image1.Picture = LoadPicture("c:\wordvb\less05\pcomputr.wmf")
ListBox1.AddItem "Extra hard disk"
ListBox1.AddItem "Printer"
ListBox1.AddItem "Satellite dish"
ComboBox1.AddItem "U.S. Dollars"
ComboBox1.AddItem "Check"
ComboBox1.AddItem "English Pounds"
End Sub
```

The first line loads the personal computer Windows metafile into the first image box. This is the default setting reflected in the Computer option button box. The next three lines add items to the Peripherals list box (ListBox1) in the macro. The words in quotes will appear in the list box when the list box is opened on the UserForm. Below the list box program

127

statements, the items in the Payment Method combo box (Combo1) are specified. The important keyword in both these groups is AddItem, a special method that adds text to the list box and combo box objects.

Examine the code that creates the invoice

Finally, let's take a look at the Word-related commands that build the invoice in a new document.

1 Click the CommandButton1 object in the Code window's Object drop-down list.

   The CommandButton1_Click event procedure appears in the Code window. The program code in this routine is quite long—about 65 lines—because at least one program statement is needed for each line in the invoice. In addition, several decision structures are required to determine the exact contents of the input objects on the UserForm and enter them appropriately.

2 Locate the three local variables that are declared at the top of the event procedure:

```
Dim Box$, Extras$, Money$ 'declare variables for selections
Documents.Add              'open a new document for invoice
```

   These variables will hold the contents of the input objects, and make your macro easier to read and modify later. Below the Dim statement, we use the Documents object with the Add method to open a new document in Word. The new document will contain the computer equipment invoice; when the macro is finished, the user can save it, print it, or discard it.

3 Examine the seven Selection statements that come next in the event procedure:

```
Selection.Font.Size = 16   'display invoice header and date
Selection.TypeText Text:="New Computer Invoice"
Selection.TypeParagraph
Selection.Font.Size = 11
Selection.TypeText Date$
Selection.TypeParagraph
Selection.TypeParagraph
```

   This code uses the Selection object to display a header for the invoice containing the current date. To make the header stand out, 16-point type is used. The Date$ function is also employed to record the current date in the invoice. The date comes from your computer's system clock, and can be modified using the Windows Control Panel.

4 Now, examine the remaining decision structures in the event procedure that process the selections you made on the UserForm.

Each decision structure evaluates a different object created by the input controls, and enters the appropriate selection in the invoice. The first decision structure is a typical example: it contains three If...Then decision structures that test the Value properties of the three option button objects on the form (these option buttons contain the computer options available). Each If statement builds a text string with the Box$ variable that identifies the computer selected by name. After the computer type is printed, the TypeParagraph method enters a carriage return at the end of the line.

```
                                'display new computer type
If OptionButton1.Value = True Then Box$ = "IBM PC Compatible"
If OptionButton2.Value = True Then Box$ = "Apple Macintosh"
If OptionButton3.Value = True Then Box$ = "PC Laptop"
Selection.TypeText Text:="Computer:   " & Box$
Selection.TypeParagraph
```

5 Take a few minutes to examine any other parts of the macro that interest you, and then move on to the next exercise.

One Step Further: Managing Multiple UserForms in a Macro

The macros in this lesson have used just one UserForm to display and receive information, but you can use as many UserForms as you want to prompt and entertain your users. (The only limitations are those of your system resources.) You can create additional forms by using the UserForm command on the Insert menu. They are displayed in a macro by using the Load statement and the Show method, and they are closed by using the Unload statement. And since each UserForm maintains its own collection of objects, properties, and event procedures, you can create general purpose UserForms for export to other projects, or special purpose UserForms for a particular situation.

In this exercise, you'll create a second UserForm for the InvoiceMaker macro that displays a useful screen of information about contacting the computer manufacturer. The UserForm will open when the user clicks the Questions? button, and it will close when the user click the Close button.

 TIP To create a copy of the active UserForm in your macro that will be saved as a stand-alone file (not part of a Word document), click Export File from the Visual Basic File menu, and then specify the UserForm you want to copy. To add an existing UserForm to a macro you are working on, click Import File from the File menu and specify a UserForm that has previously been exported.

Add a second form to InvoiceMaker

1   In the Project Explorer, click the UserForm3 icon in the Less05 document, and then click the View Object button.

    Visual Basic displays the InvoiceMaker UserForm in the development environment.

CommandButton control

2   Click the CommandButton control in the toolbox, and then create a third command button object on the InvoiceMaker UserForm, just above the Order button.

3   In the Properties window, set the Caption property of the new command button object to **Questions?**.

4   Double-click the Questions? button, and then type the following code in the CommandButton3_Click event procedure:

```
Load UserForm4
UserForm4.Show
```

    These statements will display your new UserForm when the user clicks the Questions? button.

5   Close the Code window, and then click UserForm from the Insert menu.

    Visual Basic opens a new UserForm named UserForm4 in the development environment.

Label control

6   Click the Label control in the toolbox, and then create a large Label object in the middle of the UserForm.

7   With the Properties window, set the Caption property of the label object to **Please call us 24-hours a day at 1-800-555-5555 if you have questions about your order. We ship product within 24-hours of receiving your invoice.**

CommandButton control

8   Click the CommandButton control in the toolbox, and then create a command button object at the bottom of the new UserForm.

9   Set the Caption property of the command button to **Close**.

10 Click the UserForm itself (not the title bar or one of the objects), and then set the UserForm's Caption property to **Contacting Us**.

    Now add the program code that closes the new UserForm when the user clicks the Close button.

11 Double-click the Close button, and then type the following program statement in the command button's event procedure:

```
Unload UserForm4
```

Save

12 Close the Code window, and click the Save button to save your changes to disk.

Now run the macro and test the second UserForm.

13 Return to Word, and then press ALT+F8 and run the InvoiceMaker macro.

14 Make a few order selections on the first UserForm, and then click the Questions? button.

The InvoiceMaker macro displays your second form, which provides useful contact and shipping information.

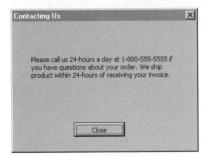

15 Click·the Close button to close the second form, and then click the Quit button to close the InvoiceMaker macro.

Congratulations! You've learned several useful skills in this lesson that will help you write your own professional-looking Word applications in the near future.

If you want to continue to the next lesson

➤ Keep Word running, and turn to Lesson 6. If you are asked whether you want to save the changes to the current macro, click Yes.

If you want to quit Word for now

➤ From the Visual Basic File menu, click Close And Return To Word. Then quit Word by clicking Exit from the File menu. If you see a Save dialog box, click Yes.

Lesson Summary

To	Do this	Button
Create a label object	Click the Label control in the toolbox, and draw the label.	A
Create a text box object	Click the TextBox control in the toolbox, and draw the box.	abl
Create a command button object	Click the CommandButton control in the toolbox, and draw the button.	▭
Create an image box object	Click the ImageBox control in the toolbox, and draw the box.	🖾
Change a property at run time	Change the value of the property by using program code. For example: `TextBox1.Text = "Hello!"`	

Load a picture at run time	Call the LoadPicture function, and assign the result to the Picture property of an image object. The syntax for this statement would be
	
	`Object.Picture = _`
	`    LoadPicture(SelectedFile)`
	
	where *Object* is the name of the object and *SelectedFile* is a variable that holds the filename of a graphic. For example:
	
	`SelectedFile = "c:\truck.bmp"`
	`Image1.Picture = _`
	`    LoadPicture(SelectedFile)`	

Create an option button	Use the OptionButton control. To create multiple option buttons, place more than one option button object inside a box you create by using the Frame control.	⊙
Create a check box	Click the CheckBox control, and draw a check box.	☑
Create a list box	Click the ListBox control, and draw a list box.	🗒
Create a drop-down list box	Click the ComboBox control, and draw a drop-down list box.	🗒

To	Do this	Button
Add items to a list box	Include statements with the AddItem method in the UserForm_Initialize procedure of your macro. For example:	

```
ListBox1.AddItem "Printer"
```

For online information about	**On the Visual Basic Help menu, click Contents And Index, click the Index tab, and then**
Visual Basic controls	Search for the control name you want to learn about
Managing UserForms in a macro	Search for "UserForm object"

Preview of the Next Lesson

In the next lesson, "Event Handling," you'll learn how to run macros each time a particular "event" occurs in Word, such as the opening or closing of a document. You also learn how to use special routines called event handlers in your procedures, so your macros don't stop working when something unexpected happens.

Event Handling

In this lesson you will learn how to:

Estimated time
35 min.

- Create a macro that automatically runs commands each time you open a new document in Word.
- Use the Close event to update a log file each time a particular document closes.
- Create an error handler to trap run-time errors in a macro.

In Lesson 5, you learned how to manage the click events associated with input objects on UserForms. In this lesson, you'll take a broader look at event handling in Word. You'll learn how to write "auto" macros that manage global events in the word processor, such as opening a new document or quitting Word. You'll also learn how to use the New, Open, and Close events in individual documents and templates to run special commands. Finally, you'll learn how to create general purpose error handlers that prevent your macros from crashing if an unexpected error occurs.

Creating Auto Macros

Periodically, you'll want to perform a specific action when you open or close an existing document, or create a new one. For example, each time you close a document you may want to save your changes, create a backup file, and restore the toolbars that you closed in your editing session. Word allows for this by setting aside five automatic macros (or "auto" macros) for the periodic events that happen in the word processor, as shown in the following table. If you create a macro and give it one of these names, Word will automatically run the macro when the event occurs.

This macro	Runs when
AutoExec	You start Word or load a global template.
AutoNew	You create a new document.
AutoOpen	You open an existing document.
AutoClose	You close a document.
AutoExit	You quit Word or unload a global template.

Although you can place an auto macro in any Word document, many auto macros are created in the Normal template, so that they are globally available throughout the word processor. In the following example, you'll create an AutoNew macro in the Normal template that automatically displays the current page size when you open a new document and gives you the opportunity to change it. The code for this macro comes from the ChangePageSize macro you developed in Lesson 4.

 TIP To prevent an auto macro from running while you are working in Word, simply hold down the SHIFT key before the macro event takes place. For example, hold down the SHIFT key (and keep it down) just before you quit Word to disable the AutoExit macro. You can also disable an auto macro with program code by using the WordBasic.DisableAutoMacros statement.

Use AutoNew to set page size

If you want, you can use an AutoNew macro to set formatting options in your document, such as font size and spacing, or to insert boilerplate text, but these adjustments are usually best made by changing styles in Word's default template. Rather, you should use AutoNew to run commands that can't be conveniently added to a template, such as program statements that load UserForms for input, or that adjust the default settings in your document. Follow these steps to create an AutoNew macro that asks you to specify the page size for each document that you create.

1 Start Word and open the Less06 document in the C:\WordVB\Less06 folder.

2 From the Word Tools menu, click Macro, and then click Macros.

    Word opens the Macros dialog box.

3   Type **AutoNew** in the Name text box, and then click the Macros In drop-down list and select Normal.dot.

By creating the AutoNew macro in the Normal template, you're asking Word to run it each time a user opens a new document.

4   Click Create.

Word starts the Visual Basic Editor and opens the AutoNew macro in the Code window.

5   Type the following program statements, or copy the ChangePageSize source code and paste it into the AutoNew procedure.

```
Dim PaperType, Prompt, Reply
PaperType = ActiveDocument.PageSetup.PaperSize
Select Case PaperType
Case wdPaperLetter
    Prompt = "Document type is Letter (8 1/2 x 11). OK?"
Case wdPaperLegal
    Prompt = "Document type is Legal (8 1/2 x 14). OK?"
Case wdPaperEnvelope10
    Prompt = "Document type is Envelope (4 1/8 x 9 1/2). OK?"
Case Else
    Prompt = "Type unknown. OK?"
End Select

Reply = MsgBox(Prompt, vbYesNo)
If Reply = vbNo Then   'if No clicked, open Page Setup
    With Dialogs(wdDialogFilePageSetup)
    .DefaultTab = wdDialogFilePageSetupTabPaperSize
    .Show
    End With
End If
```

As you learned earlier, this macro uses the PaperSize property to determine the current page size and the Page Setup dialog box to adjust the page size, if necessary. More important, however, are the name and location of the AutoNew procedure. By placing AutoNew in Normal.dot, you'll make the macro available to all documents.

Run the macro

Now run the macro.

View Microsoft Word

New

1 Click the View Microsoft Word button on the Visual Basic Editor toolbar.

2 Click the New button on the Word toolbar.

Word opens a new document and runs the AutoNew macro. The default page size is displayed in a message box, and you are asked to verify the setting.

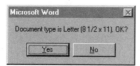

3 Click No, and then specify the Envelope 10 size in the Page Setup dialog box.

4 Click OK to close the dialog box.

Word adjusts the current page size to Envelope 10.

5 Close the new Word document and discard your changes.

You won't be using the new document. Unless you always plan to use the macro, rename or delete the AutoNew macro in the Normal template.

6 Return to the Visual Basic Editor, scroll to the top of the AutoNew procedure, and change AutoNew to ChangePageSize.

By modifying the procedure name, you change the macro name and thus the automatic effect of the macro.

Save

7 Click the Save button on the toolbar to save your changes.

You've demonstrated the power of the AutoNew macro. If you find this feature useful, consider using it in the future to display instructions, notices to employees, custom UserForms, toolbars, menus, and other essential items. You can also use the AutoExec, AutoOpen, AutoClose, and AutoExit macros to exploit other global Word events.

Use the Close event to update a log file

In the last exercise, you placed an auto macro in the Normal template to run a specific sequence of program statements each time a new document was created. You have two additional options when creating auto macros: you can save the macro in a favorite document template, so that it is available to all the documents based on that template, or you can place the macro in a single document by using the Document object's Open, Close, and New events. In the following steps, you'll create an auto macro in the Less06 document that uses the Close event to create a log file on disk that records the time and date whenever you close the Less06 document.

TIP   The Close event code is located in the Less06 document in the \WordVB\Less06 folder on your hard disk. (You'll find it in the ThisDocument class, under the Document object.) You can either load and run the macro on your own, or type it in now from scratch.

1   Open the Visual Basic Editor, and display the Less06 project in the Project Explorer.

2   Open the Microsoft Word Objects folder in the Less06 project, and double-click ThisDocument.

The class module ThisDocument is selected in the Project Explorer and is opened in the Code window. By default, each Word document includes a ThisDocument class module, which you can use to define special document properties and document-related events.

3   In the Code window's Object drop-down list, select the Document object.

Within the ThisDocument class module, the Document object controls the New, Open, and Close events.

4   In the Procedure drop-down list, click the Close event.

The Close event in the Less06 project is activated each time the Less06 document is closed. You'll customize this event procedure now by

139

adding program code that updates a log file each time the Less06 document closes.

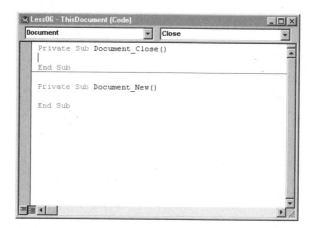

```
Less06 - ThisDocument (Code)                      _ □ ×
Document                 ▼   Close                      ▼
    Private Sub Document_Close()

    End Sub

    Private Sub Document_New()

    End Sub
```

TIP A log file is a simple text file that contains basic information about how a document has been worked on. Typical log files include the user name, access times, and any error messages that occurred during the editing session. By looking at the log file periodically in a word processor or text editor, you or your supervisor can see who updated the master file and when it happened.

5 Type the following program code in the Close event procedure:

```
Open "c:\wordvb\less06\less06.log" For Append As #1
Print #1, "Closed by "; Application.UserName, Date$, Time$
Close #1
```

The Open, Print, and Close statements are used to manage text files.

This routine uses three new Visual Basic statements that manage text files: Open, Print, and Close. The Open statement opens a text file on disk for sequential (that is, line by line) file output. The file is Less06.log, a simple, unformatted text file. Because the file is opened in Append mode, each new log entry is appended to the end of the file, preserving the previous records. In the second line, the Print statement sends a log entry to the file by identifying the open file by number and using four text arguments that create the record. Finally, the Close statement closes the text file after the log entry has been posted.

Run the macro

Now run the macro and see how it works.

View Microsoft Word

Save

1   Click the View Microsoft Word button on the Visual Basic Editor toolbar.

2   Verify that the Less06 document is active, and then click the Save button on the Word toolbar to save the macro to disk.

3   From the File menu, click Close to close the Less06 document and trigger the Close event.

Word runs the Close event macro and updates the log file located in the C:\WordVB\Less06 folder.

4   Open the Less06 document again and close it immediately to add a second entry to the log file.

Running the macro twice will verify that the Append feature is working correctly. Now open the log file and see what it looks like.

5   From the File menu, click Open, select All Files in the Files Of Type drop-down list, and then open the Less06.log file in the C:\WordVB\Less06 folder.

The log file shows the exact time you closed the Less06.doc file. Bingo, it works!

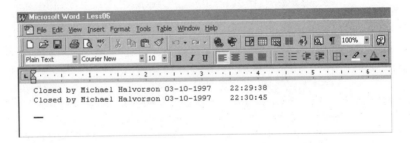

6   Close the Less06.log file and open the Less06.doc file again.

You're ready to move on to error handlers.

TIP   If you like the idea of creating a full-featured logging system to track your editorial work, create an Open event procedure that records the time and date you opened the Less06 file for editing. You can also use the Open, Print, and Close statements in an AutoOpen or AutoClose macro to record each editing operation you make for all your documents—nothing will get by you then!

Handling Run-Time Errors

Have you experienced a run-time error in a Word macro yet? A *run-time error,* or *program crash,* is an unexpected event that happens while your macro is running and that Visual Basic can't recover from. It's not that Visual Basic isn't tough enough to handle the glitch; it's just that the interpreter hasn't been told what to do with it.

An error handler helps your program recover from run-time errors.

Fortunately, you don't have to live with occasional errors that cause your macros to halt unexpectedly. Word lets you write special routines, called *error handlers,* to respond to run-time errors. An error handler tells the macro how to continue when one of its statements doesn't work. Error handlers are placed in the same procedures that the potentially unstable statements are in, and they handle, or *trap,* a problem by using a special error handling object named Err. The Err object has a Number property that identifies the error and lets your macro respond to it. For example, if a routine that inserts a table into your document causes an error, your error handler might display a custom error message and then disable the feature until the user fixes the problem.

When to Use Error Handlers

Most run-time errors are caused by external events.

You can use error handlers in any situation in which an unexpected action might result in a run-time error. Typically, error handlers are used to process external events that influence a macro—for example, events caused by a failed network drive, an open floppy drive door, or a printer that is offline. The following table lists potential problems that can be addressed by error handlers.

Problem Class	Description
Network problems	Network drives or resources that unexpectedly fail, or "go down"
Floppy disk problems	Unformatted or incorrectly formatted disks, open drive doors, or bad disk sectors
Offline printers	Printers that are offline, out of paper, or otherwise unavailable
Selection problems	Selected text in a format that the macro cannot recognize
Range problems	A value that is outside the valid range, such as an invalid table entry or paragraph number
Clipboard problems	Problems with data transfer or the Clipboard
Logic errors	Syntax or logic errors undetected by the interpreter and previous tests, such as an incorrectly spelled filename

Setting the Trap: The On Error Statement

The On Error statement identifies the error handler.

The program statement used to detect a run-time error is On Error. You place On Error in a macro procedure, right before you use the statement you're worried about. The On Error statement sets, or *enables,* an event trap by telling Word where to branch if it encounters an error. The syntax for the On Error statement is:

```
On Error GoTo label
```

where *label* is the name of your error handler.

Error handlers are typed near the bottom of a macro procedure, following the On Error statement. Each error handler has its own label, which is followed by a colon for identification purposes—ErrorHandler: or TableError:, for example. An error handler usually has two parts. The first part typically uses the Err.Number property in a decision structure (such as If...Then or Select Case) and then displays a message or sets a property based on the error. The second part is a Resume statement that sends control back to the program so that the program can continue.

Resume

In the Resume statement, you can use the Resume keyword alone, use the Resume Next keywords, or use the Resume keyword with a label you'd like to branch to, depending on where you want the macro to continue.

Resume, Resume Next, and Resume label return control to the macro.

The Resume keyword returns control to the statement that caused the error (in hopes that the error condition will be fixed or won't happen again). Using the Resume keyword is a good strategy if you're asking the user to fix the problem, for example by selecting a different paragraph or putting paper in the printer.

The Resume Next keywords return control to the statement *following* the one that caused the error. Using the Resume Next keywords is the strategy to take if you want to skip the command and continue working.

You can also follow the Resume keyword with a label you'd like to branch to. This gives you the flexibility of moving to any place in the event procedure you want to go. A typical location to branch to is the last line of the procedure.

An Invalid Table-Entry Error Handler

The following example shows how you can create an error handler to recover from out-of-range errors associated with tables. You'll add the error handler to a macro that attempts to create a table with input from the user. (The macro crashes if the user enters zero, a negative number, or a number greater than 63.) You can use the same technique to add error-handling support to any Word macro—just change the error numbers and messages.

NOTE The following macro uses an error number (from the Err.Number property) to diagnose a run-time error. To see a complete listing of error numbers, search for "error codes" in the Visual Basic online Help.

Detect the run-time error

The first step in detecting a run-time error is understanding the problem. Complete the following steps to find the run-time error in the RuntimeError macro:

1   Open the Less06.doc document in Word, press ALT+F8, and run the RuntimeError macro.

   The macro prompts you for the number of rows in your table.

2   Type **5** and click OK.

   The macro prompts you for the number of columns in your table.

3   Type **0** and click OK.

   The macro attempts to create a five-row by zero-column table in the document, and generates a run-time error that stops the macro when it fails.

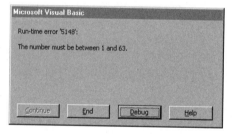

This is the run-time error we want to trap and redirect, so that our macro doesn't crash.

 TIP If you ever get stuck in an endless loop and can't get out when you are testing an error handler, press CTRL+BREAK to stop the macro.

Create a table-entry error handler

1   Click End in the Error dialog box, and then press ALT+F8 to open the Macros dialog box.

2   Select the RuntimeError macro, and then click Edit.

Word displays the RuntimeError macro in the Visual Basic Editor.

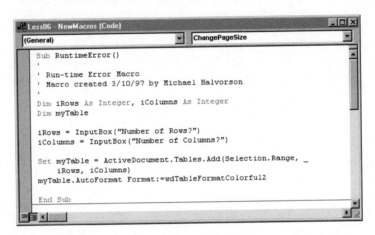

3   Type the following statements near the top of the procedure, below the Dim statements:

```
On Error GoTo TableError
TryAgain:
```

The first statement enables the error handler in the procedure and tells Word where to branch if a run-time error occurs. The second statement tells Word where to go if it needs to repeat the command. Now you'll add the TableError error handler to the bottom of the procedure.

4   Move one line below the AutoFormat statement (the last statement before End Sub), and type the following program code:

```
StopTrying:
Exit Sub  'exit procedure

TableError:
If Err.Number = 5148 Then 'if table out of range
    MsgBox "Row range 1-32,767. Column range 1-63.", , _
        "Invalid Table Range"
    Resume TryAgain
Else
    MsgBox "Table cannot be created", , "Unknown Error"
    Resume StopTrying
End If
```

145

The conditional expression in the error handler's If...Then statement tests the Err.Number property to see if it contains the number 5148, the error code that is returned when a table entry is out of range. If a table error has occurred, the macro gives the user the opportunity to fix the problem by entering a new set of row and column numbers and then continuing with creating the table.

If the error was not related to the table, the macro assumes that there was some other problem with the table that created an error. In that case the error handler branches to the StopTrying label at the top of the error handler, and exits via Exit Sub. In either case, the error handler prints a message for the user and stops the macro from being prematurely terminated. You could add more ElseIf statements and error numbers to the error handler to give the user more specific and useful information about the problem.

You can use an Exit Sub statement to skip over an error handler in a procedure.

If the program encounters no table problems or if the user fixes an initial problem, the macro continues until the Exit Sub statement ends the event procedure. Exit Sub is a general purpose statement that you can use to end any Visual Basic procedure before the End Sub statement is executed. In this case, Exit Sub prevents the error handler from running after the program successfully creates the table. If possible, you should always have a single exit point (one Exit Sub statement) in your procedure.

Test the error handler

1 Return to Word and run the RuntimeError macro again.

2 Enter **5** for the number of rows, and click OK.

3 Enter **0** for the number of columns, and click OK.

Word generates a run-time error, but the error handler traps the error and displays the following message.

4 Click OK to close the error handler.

Now type a new set of table dimensions.

5 Type **5** for the number of rows, and click OK.

6 Type **4** for the number of columns, and click OK.

Lickety split, Word creates a five-by-four table in your document and formats it with auto formatting.

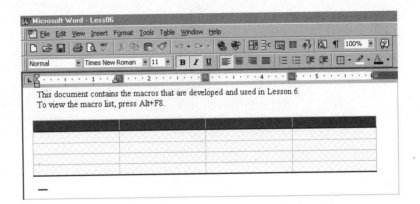

 TIP If you want to demonstrate the "Unknown Error" section of your error handler, click the Cancel button in Step 5 when you are prompted for a row number. Canceling the dialog box will produce run-time error 13 (Type Mismatch), and your macro will display the "Unknown Error" message you created—a bulletproof macro!

One Step Further: More Techniques for Error Handlers

The Err.Description property contains an explanation of a run-time error.

The Err object contains a few other properties that you might want to use to display additional information in your error handlers. The Err.Description property contains the error message returned to Word when a run-time error occurs. You can use this message as an additional source of information for the user, whether or not you plan to handle the error with program code. For example, the following error handler uses the Description property to display an error message if an error occurs when you are loading artwork from a floppy disk into an Image object on a UserForm.

```
On Error GoTo DiskError
Image1.Picture = LoadPicture("a:\prntout2.wmf")
Exit Sub                    'exit procedure

DiskError:
MsgBox Err.Description, , 'Loading Error'
Resume                      'try LoadPicture function again
```

147

You can use this technique to trap floppy disk problems such as unformatted disks, missing files, or an open drive door. The error handler uses the Resume statement to try the loading operation again when the user fixes the problem and clicks OK in the message box. When the file eventually loads, the Exit Sub statement ends the procedure.

Specifying a Retry Period

Another strategy you can use in an error handler is to try an operation a few times and then jump over the problem if it isn't resolved. For example, the following error handler uses a counter variable named Retries to track the number of times an error message has been displayed, and then the program skips the loading statement if it fails twice:

```
Retries = 0                      'initialize counter variable
On Error GoTo DiskError
Image1.Picture = LoadPicture("a:\prntout2.wmf")
Exit Sub                         'exit the procedure

DiskError:
MsgBox Err.Description, , "Loading Error"
Retries = Retries + 1            'increment counter on error
If Retries = 2 Then
    Resume Next
Else
    Resume
End If
```

This is a useful technique if the error you're handling is a problem that can occasionally be fixed by the user. The important thing to remember here is that Resume retries the statement that caused the error, and Resume Next skips the statement and moves on to the next line in the procedure. When you use Resume Next, be sure that the next statement really is the one you want to execute, and when you continue, make sure that you don't accidentally run the error handler again. A good way to skip over the error handler is to use the Exit Sub statement; you can also use Resume Next with a label that directs Word to continue executing below the error handler.

If you want to continue to the next lesson

➤ Keep Word running, and turn to Lesson 7. If you see a Save dialog box, click Yes.

If you want to quit Word for now

➤ From the Visual Basic File menu, click Close And Return To Word. Then quit Word by clicking Exit from the File menu. If you see a Save dialog box, click Yes.

Lesson Summary

To	Do this
Create a global macro to manage Word events	Create an AutoExec, AutoNew, AutoOpen, AutoClose, or AutoExit macro in the Normal template.
Control file-related events at the document level	Write a macro for the Document object's New, Open, or Close events in the ThisDocument class module.
Detect run-time errors in your macros	Enable error handling by using the statement On Error GoTo *label.*
Process run-time errors	Create an error-handling routine beneath a label identifying the error handler.
Continue after an error	Use Resume, Resume Next, or Resume *label.*
Exit a procedure before an End Sub statement	Use the Exit Sub statement.

For online information about	On the Visual Basic Help menu, click Contents And Index, click the Contents tab, open Microsoft Word Visual Basic Reference, click the Index tab, and then
AutoExec, AutoOpen, AutoNew, AutoClose, and AutoExit	Search for "auto macros"
Open, New, and Close events	Search for "events," and then double-click Using Events With The Document Object

For online information about	On the Visual Basic Help menu, click Contents And Index, click the Index tab, and then
The Err object	Search for "Err"
Visual Basic error codes	Search for "trappable errors"

Preview of the Next Lesson

In the next lesson, "Understanding Word Objects," you'll focus again on Word's expansive collection of objects, and you'll explore advanced topics that leverage the Visual Basic fundamentals you've learned in Parts 1 and 2. You'll learn how to use the Document object, the Range object, and the Words collection to create powerful analysis and navigation tools, and you'll learn how to use the Object Browser to learn more about Word's object model. In Part 3, we pick up the pace a bit, so buckle up and have some fun!

Power Programming with Objects

Exploring Microsoft Word Objects

Estimated time
40 min.

In this lesson you will learn how to:

- Conceptualize Word objects in Visual Basic.
- Use the Object Browser.
- Work with Word objects, including Document, Range, Selection, Character, Word, and Paragraph objects.

So far in this book, you've explored Word's Visual Basic programming environment, and how to use its tools—the Code window, modules, the Properties and Project Explorer windows—to create macros and custom functions that change the structure and appearance of elements in a Word document. You've also learned about programming structures, variables, and user-interface enhancements such as menus, toolbars, simple dialog boxes, and UserForms. You've also had a taste of the ways you can work with the elements of a Word document—its objects, the objects' properties, and the methods that these objects support.

In this lesson, we'll take a deeper look at the huge range of objects that you can find in Word documents, and we'll begin to learn how to manipulate the structure of a Word document through its objects. First, though, we'll discuss Word's object model and working with objects using object variables.

There are a bewildering number of objects in a Word document and in the Visual Basic programming language. Rather than grappling with the entire spectrum of objects available in Word, it's best to start with the objects presented in this lesson and then learn about only those additional objects you need to get a particular job done. Often, there's more than one way to get the same job done.

In this section you'll concentrate on a few objects you can access in a Word document, but we'll defer discussion of the formats you can change for these objects—that is, changing their properties—to Chapter 9, "Changing Word Object Formats."

Learning More About Word's Object Model

There are several ways to learn about the types of Visual Basic objects available in Word:

- You can access Help directly.
- You can record macros and study the resulting Visual Basic code. If you select the name of an object used in the code and press F1, the Visual Basic Editor presents a Help screen that tells more about the object you've selected.
- You can use the Object Browser, described a little later in this lesson.

Use Visual Basic Help to explore Word's object model

The best place to get an overview of the vast array of objects available to you is to start with the list in Visual Basic Help. For more information on Word's object model, do the following:

1 In the Visual Basic Editor, click Microsoft Visual Basic Help.

The Assistant window appears, where you can type a topic to search for.

2 In the Assistant window, type **object model**, and click the Search button.

The Assistant presents a list of Help topics on working with objects.

3 In the list presented, click Microsoft Word Objects.

The following window appears:

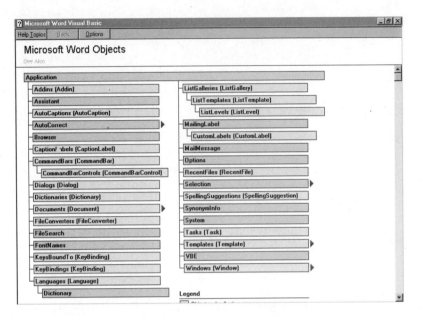

This Help screen displays a box for each class of object found in the Word application. Click a box to jump to a Help screen offering more information about the corresponding object.

You'll be investigating many of Word's less-often-used objects in later chapters, but for now let's take a tour of the primary objects you'll encounter in the Word environment.

An object model, such as that corresponding to a Word document, is rather like a set of carved Russian dolls, each one containing another inside—something like this:

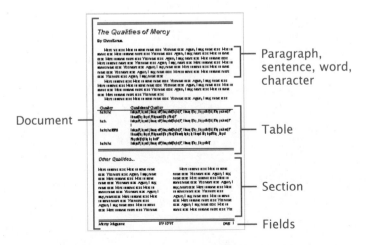

NOTE Sometimes these hierarchical, nested objects in a Word document are called *formatting domains*. Each formatting domain corresponds to a series of Word objects that belong to the domain. For example, when you select text in a Word document and apply a new font to the selection, you are working with the character formatting domain, and as far as Visual Basic is concerned, you are changing the Font property of the Selection object.

Choosing a Starting Point

The method for presenting macro code in the next few lessons will be a little different than it was in the previous parts of the book. To explore Word's diverse object model, you'll be loading and running several short macros that show you how to organize your objects in program code. You can either enter them from scratch as you have been doing, or you can simply load the routines supplied with this book.

If you want to follow along with the prepared lesson

1   Start Microsoft Word and open Less07.doc in the practice files folder.

When you open this document, Word adds the Lesson07Macros menu to the menu bar, which lists the macros created in Lesson 7. You can run any of the macros by simply pulling down the Lesson07Macros menu and clicking the name of the macro you want.

2   From the Tools menu, click Macro, and then click Visual Basic Editor.

3   In the Project Explorer window, locate the Lesson07Proj07 project and click the + symbol next to the Modules folder to display the modules in the project.

4   The Lesson module in the Lesson07Proj07 project contains larger macros that we use to illustrate functional applications of Visual Basic in Word. The Examples module contains short sample macros used to illustrate minor points, but which may not be useful macros by themselves.

As you work through this lesson, you can use any of several ways to run your macros, as described in the section, "One Step Further," in Lesson 1, "Creating Your First Macro." To make it easy, however, you can use the custom menu called Lesson7Macros, which lists the practice and example macros for this lesson.

NOTE There's another module in the Less07 project called Background, which contains "housekeeping" macros created for the practice file. There is also a short macro inside the ThisDocument object that notifies you that the Lesson07Macros menu has been added. You can study or ignore these macros, but don't change them.

If you want to enter the lesson's macros from scratch

1 Start Microsoft Word, create a new document, and save it as **Less07.doc**.

2 From the Tools menu, click Macro, and then click Visual Basic Editor.

3 In the Project Explorer window, select the Project heading for the Less07 document; in the Properties window, change the name of the project to **Proj07**.

4 In the Project Explorer window, select the Less07 project and click Module from the Insert menu. With the new module selected, change the name of the module to **Lesson**. This is the module in which you'll be entering code.

5 If you want to enter the example code also, create another module and name it **Examples**.

As you enter the macros presented in this lesson, you can associate each macro with a menu command, as we've done with the Lesson07Macros menu, or you can use some other way to run your macros, such as using a toolbar button, a key sequence, or the Macros dialog box.

Introducing the Application Object

The highest level of object available to you within the Word environment is the Word application itself. Like other objects, the Word Application object has its own properties, methods, and events.

The DisplayBarState Property

The DisplayBarState property, for example, controls whether the status bar at the bottom of the Word window is visible. The following example shows one way to use the DisplayBarState property:

You can run this macro by clicking Examples and then ToggleStatusBar from the Lesson07Macros menu.

```
Sub ToggleStatusBar()
    barState = Application.DisplayStatusBar
    Application.DisplayStatusBar = Not barState
End Sub
```

If you are typing your code in by hand, insert this code at the end of the Macros module that you created earlier in the lesson. All macros discussed in this lesson can be created in this same manner.

This short macro gets the current state of the status bar from the DisplayStatusBar property of the Application object, and stores it in the barState variable; if the status bar is visible, barState is True. The next line of the macro uses the Not operator to reverse the value stored in the barState variable and set the DisplayStatusBar property. Therefore, the macro "toggles" the state of the status bar in a way that's analogous to flipping a switch from on to off, or from off to on.

The ListCommands Method

To take another example, the following one-line macro uses the ListCommands method of the Application object to create a new document containing a table listing all the commands in Word and the key sequences that activate them:

You can run this macro by clicking Examples and then ListCommands from the Lesson07Macros menu.

```
Sub ListCommands()
    Application.ListCommands ListAllCommands:=True
End Sub
```

When you run the ListCommands macro, you'll see a table similar to this:

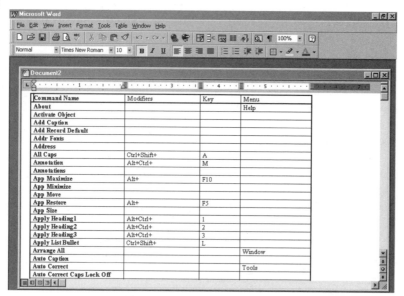

The ListFontNames Macro

The Application object also contains all other objects in the Word environment, including many objects that don't exclusively pertain to Word documents themselves. For example, the FontNames collection of the Application object contains the names of all the fonts installed on your system. You can use a For Each structure in the following macro to display each of these font names.

158

You can run this macro by clicking Examples and then ListFontNames from the Lesson07Macros menu.

```
Sub ListFontNames()
    Documents.Add
    For Each thisFont in FontNames
        With Selection
            .InsertAfter thisFont & vbCr
            .MoveUp Unit:=wdParagraph, Count:=1
            .MoveDown Unit:=wdParagraph, Count:=1, Extend:=wdExtend
            .Font.Name = thisFont
            .MoveDown Unit:=wdParagraph, Count:=1
        End With
    Next
End Sub
```

When you run the ListFontNames macro, it creates a document similar to this:

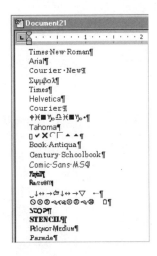

The macro first creates a new document, which then becomes the active document. It then generates a list of installed fonts by using a For Each loop to insert the name of each item in the FontNames collection into the new document, with each item separated by a carriage return (the constant vbCr). Then each font name is selected and formatted with the font itself.

Even though you don't see it in the macro, the FontNames object belongs to the Application—but you usually don't have to explicitly cite the Application object. Therefore, the statements

```
For Each thisFont in FontNames
```

and

```
For Each thisFont in Application.FontNames
```

are equivalent. (This is true of many, if not most, of the objects cited in macros you'll encounter.)

Introducing the Document Object

An instance of a Document object is an entire Word document, including all the objects found in it: its text, paragraphs, tables, sections, and the formats (that is, properties) each object offers. Many of these objects (like the Document object itself) are hierarchical—that is, they act as containers for other objects.

Investigate the Document object

Because it displays in one place all the objects available to you in Visual Basic, the Object Browser offers an excellent way to learn about objects. Let's play with the Object Browser by taking a closer look at the Document class:

1 In the Visual Basic Editor, click Object Browser from the View menu.

   The Object Browser window should appear.

2 From the Project/Library drop-down list, click Word. (If you had selected the <All Libraries> item, you would have seen a list of the object classes made available by every object library that's open, but you want to narrow the focus to those made available by Word alone.)

3 In the Classes list, click Document.

4 In the Members of 'Document' list, click the Name property. At this point, the Object Browser window should look like this:

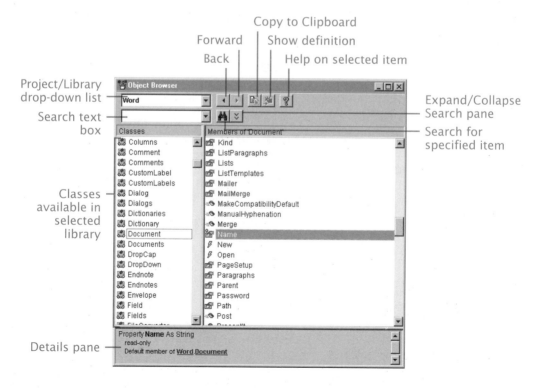

The properties, methods, and functions that belong to any instance of a Document object appear in the Members of 'Document' list. To the left of each item, a tiny icon is displayed that describes its purpose. Some examples of Document members (and one from the Constants class) are shown here:

Icon	Class Member / Description	Example
Property	Document.Content	`thisRange =` `Documents("MySpringBreak").Content`
	Finds the document object named MySpringBreak in the Documents collection, and returns a range consisting of the main body of the document.	
Method or Function	Document.Activate	`Documents("MySummerVacation"). _` `Activate`
	Finds the document object named MySummerVacation and activates it.	
	Document.Undo	`undone3 = _` `Documents("MySabbatical").Undo(3)`
	Finds the document object named MySabbatical, undoes the last three actions, and stores True in the undone3 variable if these actions were successfully undone.	
Default	Document.Name (The blue dot means the member is the default property or method for the object, if it is not specified.)	`thisDocument = ActiveDocument`
	Puts the Name property of the active document into the thisDocument variable.	

Event	Document.Open	`Sub Document.Open()`
		`your code`
		`End Sub`

	Stored in the ThisDocument module, runs the routine called Document_Open when the document is opened.	
Constant	Constants.vbCr	`Selection.InsertAfter vbCr`
	Inserts a new paragraph after the currently selected text.	

To see how these statements might work in practice, run the DocumentActivate macro in the Less07.doc practice file.

You can display items in the Members list in order of their type by right-clicking the list and then clicking Group Members.

161

TIP You can copy or drag text from the Details pane to the Visual Basic routine you're developing. If text in the Details pane is underlined, you can click the underlined word to jump to an item in Help that describes the underlined word.

Objects are recorded in *object libraries.* You can see a list of the object libraries available to the Object Browser by right-clicking anywhere in the Object Browser window to display the shortcut menu for the Object Browser, and then clicking References. When you do this, Visual Basic displays the References window shown here.

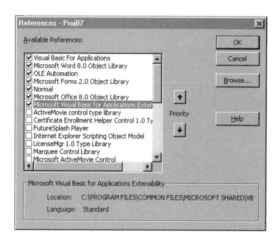

 TIP You can also get information about any of the items listed in the Object Browser by selecting the object and pressing F1.

Introducing the Range Object

Learning to work with the Range object may be the most important task you'll face as a beginning Visual Basic programmer. What is a range? That can vary depending upon the application you are using. In Word, *a range* is an uninterrupted series of characters in a document. A range usually has a beginning character position and an end character position, but it can also consist solely of a location in a document with no characters at all.

Ranges are similar to selections, but although you can define and use as many ranges in a document as you need, there can be only one selection in each pane of a window in a document. Ranges are also similar to bookmarks (a bookmark is a series of characters in a document that are associated with a name). However, a bookmark belongs to and remains with the document in which it is defined, while a variable in which a range is stored remains only as long as the macro is running, or in the case of a public variable, as long as the document remains open.

 NOTE For more on using bookmarks to keep track of text in a document, see "Working with Bookmarks" in Lesson 8, "Navigating in a Word Document."

Let's consider a few examples. Assume the beginning of a document starts with this text:

```
Dammit, Jim, I'm a doctor, not a VB programmer!
||||||||||||||||||||||||||||||||||||||||||||||||
0123456789012345678901234567890123456789012345
```

The Range method

You use the Range method on an instance of a Document object to return a Range object. For example, using the above text, the macro

```
Sub TestRange1()
  thisRange = ActiveDocument.Range(Start:=0, End:=11)
  MsgBox thisRange
End Sub
```

uses the Range method to return a Range object consisting of everything from the first character in the active document to the eleventh character, store the range in a variable, and display a message box containing that text:

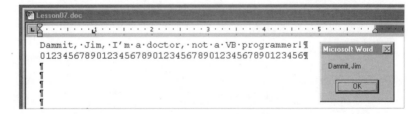

Similarly, you can set any of the formats of a given range by changing its associated property. For example, running the macro

```
Sub TestRange2()
  thisRange = ActiveDocument.Range(Start:=0, End:=12)
  thisRange.Italic = True
End Sub
```

causes the text *Dammit, Jim,* to be formatted in italic.

Introducing Sentence and Word Objects

A "word" in Visual Basic is any string of characters delimited by a space or punctuation mark (except an apostrophe). The words in a document, range, or selection are represented by the Words collection. Each item, or "word," in the Words collection is itself a Range object that corresponds to the characters in the document that make up the word.

Similarly, a sentence is defined a little differently in Visual Basic than in standard English, as you'll see in a moment.

Let's create a few routines to see clearly what items are considered words and sentences.

A Custom Word Count Routine

Word's Word Count feature is very handy, but if you only want a word count for a document, you still have to wait for a full repagination so that Word can determine the number of pages in the document before you can see the statistics in the Word Count dialog box. You can develop a slightly different version of this feature that quickly gives you only the information you need.

Create the MyCounter macro

1   In the Proj07 module, enter the following code (or follow along from the code supplied in the practice file):

```
Sub MyCounter()
  'Test for the type of selection.
  If Selection.Type = wdSelectionIP Then
    Set thisRange = ActiveDocument.Content
  Else
    Set thisRange = Selection.Range
  End If

  'Count the objects.
  nChars = CStr(thisRange.Characters.Count)
  nWords = CStr(thisRange.Words.Count)
  nSents = CStr(thisRange.Sentences.Count)

  'Display the statistics.
  endLine = Chr(13)
  msgTitle = "MyCounter Macro"
  msg1 = "Characters: " + nChars + endLine
  msg2 = "Words: " + nWords + endLine
  msg3 = "Sentences: " + nSents + endLine
  msgTot = msg1 + msg2 + msg3
  answer = MsgBox(msgTot, vbInformation, msgTitle)
End Sub
```

2   Switch back to Word and assign the MyCounter macro to a toolbar button, menu, or key sequence (or you can use the MyCounter command on the Lesson07Macros menu).

The first part of this macro simulates the behavior of Word's Word Count feature. If you select text before choosing Word Count from the Tools menu, Word displays statistics for the selected text; otherwise, Word displays statistics for the entire document.

To implement this, you have the macro check the selection's Type property; if the wdSelectionIP constant is returned, the selection is an insertion point. It's important to include this step, because using the Count property in the next section of the macro will cause an error (and stop the macro) unless there is something in the selection to count.

Next, of course, you count the characters, words, and sentences in the range stored in the thisRange variable.

Finally, the macro displays a message box that returns the requested information. Each item of data is displayed on a new line ending with the ASCII character 13, which corresponds to a carriage return.

 TIP   Rather than use MsgBox, which has a limited ability to display information in a well-formatted way, you could create a custom UserForm and create a gridlike structure similar to that found in Word's Word Count dialog box. For more information on creating UserForms, see Lesson 5, "Working with UserForms."

Run the MyCounter macro

Some items you may not consider words are taken to be words by Visual Basic in Word. To illustrate, let's consider an example:

1   Click Show/Hide ¶ in the standard toolbar so that you can see each white space character (that is, spaces, tab characters, and paragraph marks).

2   Enter the following text (the opening paragraph of *Moby Dick* by Herman Melville) in the Less07 practice file (the ¶ symbol means there's a paragraph mark at the end of each line of text). This text should be in an unaltered copy of the Less07 practice file.

```
Call me Ishmael. Some years ago--never mind how long ¶
precisely--having little or no money in my purse, ¶
and nothing particular to interest me on shore, ¶
I thought I would sail about a little and see the ¶
watery part of the world. ¶
```

3   Select all five lines of text and click MyCounter from the Lesson07Macros menu.

When you do this, the macro displays this dialog box:

If you count the words, characters, and sentences yourself using the human definition of these terms, you'll conclude that there are fewer of each in the text than the macro represents. If you click Word Count from the Tools menu, Word reports the following statistics (among others):

Item	What Word Count reports	What MyCounter macro reports
Words	42	54
Characters with spaces	223	230
Sentences	Not reported	6

 NOTE In the next lesson, you'll develop a macro that records this word count information in a table, to help you track your writing output, for example. You could run this routine at regular intervals to assess the number of characters added every hour.

A Routine for Counting Words and Sentences

To get a clearer idea of what elements are considered word and sentence objects in Visual Basic, let's add code to the MyCounter macro that sequentially selects each word object in the Lesson07 document.

Create the WordSelectorForward macro

1   Switch to the Visual Basic Editor and open the Lesson module in the Proj07 project.

2   Find the MyCounter macro, and insert the following code at the top of the module (that is, before the MyCounter macro):

```
Public thisRange as Variant
Public nWords, thisWordIndex As Integer
Public nSents, thisSentIndex As Integer
```

3   After the MyCounter macro, enter the following procedures:

```
Sub WordSelectorForward()
'Selects the next indexed item in thisRange.
'Key sequence: Ctrl+Period
  thisWordIndex = thisWordIndex + 1
  If thisWordIndex => nWords + 1 Then thisWordIndex = 1
  thisRange.Words(thisWordIndex).Select
End Sub
```

4   Switch to Word, and click Customize from the Tools menu.

5   In the Customize dialog box, click Keyboard.

The Customize Keyboard dialog box appears, as shown here:

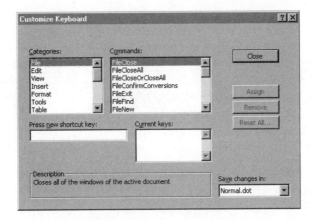

6   In the Customize Keyboard dialog box, click Less07 from the Save Changes In list. From the Categories list, click Macros. From the Macros list, click WordSelectorForward. Finally, click in the Press New Shortcut Key text box and press CTRL+PERIOD.

This macro simply iterates though each item in the Words collection, by incrementing the thisWordIndex variable and then selecting the associated range of the "word" inside the selected text.

167

You may wonder why you're creating only one routine, rather than additional WordSelectorBack, SentSelectorForward, and SentSelectorBack macros. Stay tuned; we're waiting to perfect our first macro.

Run the WordSelectorForward macro

Before testing the WordSelectorForward macro, you have to run the MyCounter macro, in order to initialize the values of the public thisRange, nWords, and nSents variables. If you don't run MyCounter first, these variables won't have meaningful values, and Visual Basic will display an error dialog box stating that the object requested by the macro doesn't exist.

Run the WordSelectorForward macro once by choosing the macro from the Lesson07Macros menu or pressing CTRL+PERIOD. You'll see that as far as Visual Basic is concerned, a Word object consists of the word itself and the space character after it, if any:

Press CTRL+PERIOD two more times. When you do this, you'll see the following text selected:

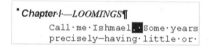

Clearly, a period and the space after it are also considered instances of a Word object. If you keep pressing CTRL+PERIOD, you'll see that each item in the Words collection of the thisRange Range object becomes selected. When you get to the last item in the collection, thisWordIndex is set back to 1, which corresponds to the first item in the collection.

Now try this experiment:

1   Keep pressing CTRL+PERIOD until the text *Ishmael* is selected again.

2   Press the DELETE key to delete the text.

3   Keep pressing CTRL+PERIOD until the selection moves to the end of the paragraph. When you press CTRL+PERIOD again, Word switches to the Visual Basic Editor and displays an error message stating that the requested object doesn't exist.

What happened? When you deleted *Ishmael,* the number of items in the collection decreased by one, but the WordSelectorForward routine still used the previous number of words in the collection that was stored in nWords. The moral of this story is that you can determine the number and continuity of each item in a collection at a single point in time, but the user's actions can change that collection, making the data concerning it incorrect.

How can you fix the WordSelector macro so that it's more robust? You can edit it so that it tests for the number of objects in the collection every time the macro is run.

Edit the WordSelectorForward macro

You can make this macro work every time, even if an element in thisRange is deleted, by creating a new version of the macro as follows:

1   Switch to the Visual Basic Editor, open the Lesson module, and find the WordSelectorForward macro.

2   Make the following changes in the macro (text in boldface is new):

```
Sub WordSelectorForward()
'Selects the next indexed word in thisRange.
'Key sequence: Ctrl+>
    thisWordIndex = thisWordIndex + 1
    wordCount = thisRange.Words.Count
    If thisWordIndex = wordCount + 1 Then thisWordIndex = 1
    thisRange.Words(thisWordIndex).Select
End Sub
```

3   Add the equivalent versions of the WordSelectorBack, SentSelectorForward, and SentSelectorBack macros, as shown here:

```
Sub WordSelectorBack()
'Selects the previous indexed word in thisRange.
'Key sequence: Ctrl+Comma
    thisWordIndex = thisWordIndex - 1
    wordCount = thisRange.Words.Count
    If thisWordIndex <= 0 Then thisWordIndex = wordCount
    thisRange.Words(thisWordIndex).Select
End Sub

Sub SentSelectorForward()
'Selects the next indexed sentence in thisRange.
'Key sequence: Ctrl+Shift+Period
    thisSentIndex = thisSentIndex + 1
    sentCount = thisRange.Sentences.Count
    If thisSentIndex => sentCount + 1 Then thisSentIndex = 1
    thisRange.Sentences(thisSentIndex).Select
End Sub
```

```
Sub SentSelectorBack()
'Selects the previous indexed sentence in thisRange.
'Key sequence: Ctrl+Shift+Period
    thisSentIndex = thisSentIndex - 1
    sentCount = thisRange.Sentences.Count
    If thisSentIndex <= 0 Then thisSentIndex = sentCount
    thisRange.Sentences(thisSentIndex).Select
End Sub
```

4 As described earlier in this lesson, assign the key sequences indicated within the code's comments to each macro.

Some of these shortcut keys conflict with and override those assigned to Word's commands. (You'll probably find that, for example, assigning CTRL+PERIOD conflicts with the Grow Font command.) As long as you store the key assignment in the Less07 practice file, however, the key assignment will revert to Grow Font when you close the practice file.

All of these macros are virtually identical and work with either the Words or the Sentences collection objects. When you run either of the sentence macros, you'll see that sentences aren't allowed to extend beyond the end of a paragraph, even if it looks like English usage would suggest otherwise.

 NOTE As you'll see in the next chapter, you can extend this type of macro to other objects found in a Word document, providing another way to navigate in your documents.

If you want to continue to the next lesson

➤ Keep Word and Word's Visual Basic Editor running, and turn to Lesson 8.

If you want to quit Word for now

➤ Switch to Word, and click Exit from the File menu. If you see a Save dialog box, click Yes.

Lesson Summary

To	Do this
View the objects in the Word Object Library	In the Visual Basic Editor, click Object Browser.
View the members of a specific class	In the Object Browser, click the name of the library you want to view from the Project/Library drop-down list.
Make a library available for use	In the Visual Basic Editor, click References from the Tools menu, and select the library you want to use.
Find any character in a document	Use the Start and End arguments of the Range method. For example: `ActiveDocument.Range(Start:=0, End:=6)`
Count the numbers of characters, words, or sentences in a range	Use the Count property of the Characters, Words, or Sentences collection objects. For example: `nWords = CStr(thisRange.Words.Count)`
Select any item in a Characters, Words, or Sentences collection	Index the appropriate collection and use the Select method on the item. For example: `thisRange.Words(thisWordIndex).Select`

For online information about	From the Visual Basic Help menu, click Contents And Index, click the Contents tab, open Microsoft Word Visual Basic Reference, click the Index tab, and then
The Document object	Search for "Document object"
Selections	Search for "working with the Selection object"
Ranges	Search for "working with Range objects"

For online information about	From the Visual Basic Help menu, click Contents And Index, click the Index tab, and then
Using the Object Browser	Search for "Object Browser"

171

For online information about	Select the name of the object and then
Any object in the Visual Basic Editor	Press F1

Preview of the Next Lesson

In the next lesson, "Navigating in Word," you'll learn how to find your way around a Word document using the objects you've explored in this chapter; you'll also learn about some new objects, such as bookmarks, fields, tables, windows, stories, and hyperlinks.

Navigating in Word

Estimated time
40 min.

In this lesson you will learn how to:

- Navigate in a Word document.
- Create routines that let you navigate with bookmarks.
- Move around in tables by creating a macro that logs document statistics.
- Use events to control macro execution.

In the last lesson, you explored Word's object model and how to use Word objects such as ranges, selections, characters, and words to manipulate the text in a Word document. In this lesson, we'll expand on this theme, but we'll focus on the ways you can navigate among the vast array of objects found in a Word document. Along the way, you'll develop a set of macros that help the user jump to any location in the active document using the bookmarks that have been defined in the document, and you'll create a macro that lets you generate a table containing statistics on your progress in creating a document.

Start the lesson

1 Start Microsoft Word and open Less08.doc in the practice files folder.

When you open this document, Word adds the Lesson08Macros menu to the menu bar, which lists the macros created in Lesson 8. As you work through the examples in this lesson, you can run your macros by clicking their names on the Lesson08Macros menu, which is added when you open the Lesson08 practice file on disk.

2 From the Tools menu, click Macro, and then click Visual Basic Editor.

3 Find and open the Macros module in the Proj08 project.

 NOTE There's another module in the Less08 project called Background, which contains "housekeeping" macros created for the practice file. There is also a short macro inside the ThisDocument object that notifies you that the Lesson08Macros menu has been added. You can study or ignore these macros, but don't change them.

Navigating Using the Browser Buttons

Tucked away down in the lower-right corner of the document window in Word are some useful tools for finding objects in a Word document: the Browser buttons. The Browser buttons (called Navigator Buttons in Word's online Help) consist of the Previous Object, Select Browse Object, and Next Object buttons. You may be familiar with the two double-arrowed buttons as Previous Page and Next Page buttons. Here you will explore their functionality further.

Previous object
Select browse object
Next object

Browsing objects

Let's create a macro to record the action of choosing an object from the palette of browse objects.

1 Activate the Less08 document and then start the Macro Recorder by clicking Macro from the Tools menu and then clicking Record New Macro. In the Record Macro dialog box, make sure the new macro will be recorded in the Less08.doc file, and click OK.

2 Click the Select Browse Object button.

A palette of objects appears.

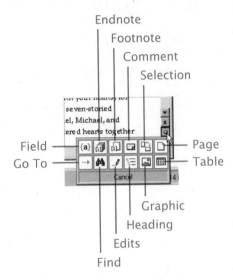

3 Choose a class of object to browse by clicking it.

4 Click the Next or Previous button.

Each object in the document of the class you've chosen is selected in turn.

5 Turn off the Macro recorder by clicking the Stop button on the Stop Recording toolbar.

If you switch to the Visual Basic Editor, open the New Macros module in the Proj08 project, and view the macro you just created, you'll see code similar to the following:

```
Sub SetBrowser()
    Application.Browser.Target = wdBrowseEdit
    Application.Browser.Next
End Sub
```

The Target property of the Browser object takes any of a dozen constants that set the Browser to find a class of object in the active document, such as comments, endnotes, fields, footnotes, graphics, headings, pages, sections, and tables. (In this case, the Edits option was selected so the constant is wdBrowseEdit.) Once you've specified the object to find, you can use the Next and Previous methods to jump to each item in the document; this corresponds to clicking the Next and Previous Browser buttons.

The Browser, however, presents just one of many ways to structure a user interface for navigating in a Word document using its objects.

Create a navigation toolbar

Let's create a new Navigation toolbar that holds various types of navigation controls. In order to make this toolbar available to every open document, we'll store the new toolbar in the Normal.dot template.

1   In Word, right-click any toolbar.

    The Toolbar shortcut menu appears, which lists all the toolbars you can currently display.

2   From the Toolbars shortcut menu, click Customize.

    The Customize dialog box appears.

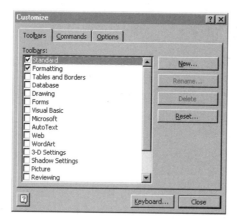

3   Click the Toolbars tab and click New. Type **Navigation** in the Toolbar Name text box, and in the Make Toolbar Available To list, click Normal.dot. Finally, click OK.

    Word displays a Navigation toolbar stub to which you can add toolbar buttons. Let's add some.

4   Click the Commands tab, and in the Categories list, click Edit.

5   In the Commands list, click Find, and drag it onto the empty Navigation toolbar.

    The toolbar displays a Find button.

6   Following the same procedure you did in step 5, add the Find Next and Go To commands to the toolbar.

7 In the Categories list, click View, and drag Document Map from the Commands list onto the Navigation toolbar.

8 In the Categories list, click Insert, and drag Bookmark from the Command list onto the Navigation toolbar.

9 Click Close to close the Customize dialog box.

When you're done, the new Navigation toolbar should look like this:

We added several tools because they're useful, even though they don't require writing macros to implement. For example, we added a button for opening the Document Map pane because it's a cool utility for quick navigation: when you click the button, a pane opens up on the left side of the document window showing the headings that exist in the document—something like the following figure. If you click a heading, Word jumps to the associated location in the document. Take some time to experiment with your new navigation toolbar.

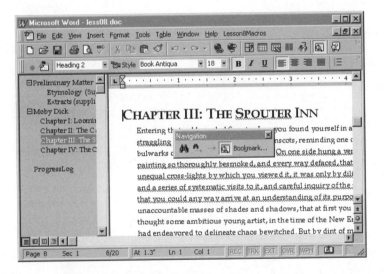

Now let's add a few controls to this toolbar that do require macro programming. First we will add a set of controls that help you manage bookmarks.

Navigating Using Bookmarks

The Browser buttons and the Document Map features of Word are useful for jumping back and forth among Word objects. So are bookmarks. A *bookmark* is a range of text (or simply a position between two characters) to which you've assigned a name. You can see the list of existing bookmarks by clicking Bookmark from the Insert menu; when you do this, Word displays this dialog box:

Bookmarks are useful, but they don't have an easy-to-use interface. Let's write a set of procedures for making it simpler to navigate using bookmarks. When we're done, we'll have added a combo box to the Navigation toolbar that will list the bookmarks defined in the active document. Clicking an item in the list will select the range associated with the bookmark. And clicking in a document window to bring it to the front will update the list so that the list always reflects the bookmarks in the active document.

This is one of the more complex projects in this book; from a programmer's viewpoint, it is composed of many parts. In order to implement the behavior we've just described, we'll create the following:

- A routine called AddBookmarkCombo that adds a combo box to the Navigation toolbar listing the bookmarks in the active document.

- A routine called BookmarkChoice that records the action of choosing a bookmark from the list.

- A routine called App_DocumentChange that updates the bookmark list whenever the user clicks a document window to bring it to the front. In order to do this, we will create a new type of module called an *event class* module containing a procedure that runs when a document is activated.

So that the list of bookmarks will get updated whenever a document is activated, we'll create this system of macros in the Normal.dot template.

If you don't want to enter the code from scratch

Most of the exercises in this book assume you'll be entering code into modules in the practice files. Because this system of macros works best when run in a global context, its code should be installed in the Normal template. If you aren't entering the exercise code from scratch, you can move the modules containing the Bookmark routines from the Less08 document to the Normal template as follows:

1   Switch to the Visual Basic Editor and find the module named NavBook in the Less08 practice file.

2   With the pointer over the NavBook module, hold down the left mouse button, drag the NavBook module over the Normal project, and then release the mouse button. This creates a copy of the NavBook module in the Normal template.

3   In the same way, transfer a copy of the MyEventClassModule module to the Normal template.

Create the AddBookmarkCombo procedure

If you want to add your own code, the first step is to create a procedure that adds a Bookmark combo box, containing a list of the bookmarks in the active document, to the Navigation toolbar.

1   Switch to the Visual Basic Editor and create a module named **NavBook** in the Normal template.

2   In the NavBook module, enter the following code:

```
Sub AddBookmarkCombo()
    'Find the Navigation toolbar and display it.
    Set navBar = CommandBars("Navigation")
    navBar.Visible = True
      'Add the combo box.
    Set booklistControl = navBar.Controls.Add( _
      Type:=msoControlComboBox)

      'Set the control's name and associated procedure.
    With booklistControl
      .Tag = "BookmarkListTag"
      .OnAction = "NavBook.BookmarkChoice"

      'Add a list of the current bookmarks.
      For Each thisBookmark In ActiveDocument.Bookmarks
        .AddItem thisBookmark
      Next thisBookmark
    End With
End Sub
```

This procedure stores the CommandBar object named "Navigation" in the myBar variable, makes sure it's visible, and then adds a combo box to it. The associated object for this is CommandBarComboBox, which doesn't have a Name property. Instead, we set the Tag property to BookmarkListTag in order to give the new combo box a unique identifier should you later add another combo box to the Navigation toolbar. The BookmarkList tag will be used in the App_DocumentChange procedure we'll create later in this lesson to find the combo box so that we can update its contents.

The OnAction property of the combo box specifies a procedure to run when the user selects an item from the list. We specify the module and procedure name so that Word will be able to find the procedure even if a routine in a different module or procedure is also named BookmarkChoice.

Finally, the macro gets each instance of a bookmark from the Bookmarks collection object and adds its name to the list in the combo box.

Run the AddBookmarkCombo procedure

To create the Bookmark combo box, do the following:

1 Switch back to Word, and activate the Less08.doc practice file.

2 Click Normal.NavBook.AddBookmarkCombo from the Lesson08Macros menu.

   This runs the copy of the routine in the Normal template, rather than the copy of the routine in the Less08 practice file.

   When you do this, the macro adds the combo box to the Navigation toolbar and adds the bookmarks defined in Less08.doc, as shown here:

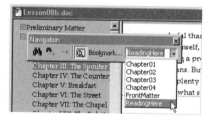

TIP You could create another combo box on the Navigation menu that redefines an existing bookmark, rather than taking you to it. For example, if you were working on a document and needed to work on three locations in the document at one time, you could create three bookmarks called PointA, PointB, and PointC, and another combo box called SetBookmarkList. Choosing one of these bookmarks from the SetBookmarkList combo box would redefine the chosen bookmark as the current selection, and you could later jump to the new bookmark location by choosing it from the BookmarkList combo box.

Create the BookmarkChoice routine

Now that we've created the BookmarkList list box, let's implement the routine that gets called when the user selects a bookmark from the list.

➤ While still in the NavBook module in the Normal template, enter the following procedure just after the AddBookmarkCombo routine:

```
Sub BookmarkChoice()
   'Find the Navigation toolbar.
   Set navBar = CommandBars("Navigation")

   'Find the BookmarkList box on the toolbar.
   Set booklistControl = navBar.FindControl _
     (Type:=msoControlComboBox, _
     Tag:="BookmarkListTag")

   'Get the number of the item chosen,
   'and go to the associated bookmark.
   With booklistControl
      chosenItem = .List(.ListIndex)
      ActiveDocument.Bookmarks(chosenItem).Select
   End With
End Sub
```

As in the AddBookmarkCombo routine, this procedure begins by identifying the Navigation toolbar and assigning it to the object variable navBar. It then uses the FindControl method to return a CommandBarComboBox object having its Tag property set to BookmarkListTag. The CommandBarComboBox object has an associated List collection object containing the names of the bookmarks we've entered in the list, and the ListIndex property stores the number of the last item chosen. To expand this expression would result in a statement like this:

```
chosenItem = booklistControl.List(booklistControl.ListIndex).Name
```

Create an application-level event handler

Next, we'll create a routine that updates the Bookmark combo box whenever the user activates a document. This involves a little extra footwork, because we have to create a new type of module, called a Class module, in which we define a handler that is called when the activation event occurs.

 NOTE For more information on creating event handlers, see Lesson 6, "Event Handling."

A class module is a special type of module that holds the definition of a class (in this case, an event class), including the definition of its properties and methods.

1   Switch to the Visual Basic Editor and locate the Normal project in the Project window.

2   Right-click anywhere in the Normal project; in the shortcut menu that appears, click Class Module from the Insert submenu.

The Visual Basic Editor inserts a new class module in the project.

3   In the Properties window, change the name of the new class module from *Class1* (or whatever name appears) to **MyEventClassModule**.

4   Double-click the MyEventClassModule to open a code window for it, and enter the following statements:

```
Public WithEvents App As Word.Application

Private Sub App_DocumentChange()
'Event handler for switching between documents.
  'Find the Bookmarks combo box on the Navigation toolbar,
  'using its Tag property.
  Set navBar = CommandBars("Navigation")
  Set booklistControl = navBar.FindControl _
    (Type:=msoControlComboBox, _
    Tag:="BookmarkListTag")

  'If the combo box doesn't exist--that is, if
  'FindControl returned Nothing, exit procedure.
  If booklistControl Is Nothing Then Exit Sub

  'Delete contents of combo box by repeatedly
  'removing the first item on the list.
  With booklistControl
    For booklistControlIndex = 1 To booklistControl.ListCount
      booklistControl.RemoveItem 1
    Next
  End With
```

```
'Get Bookmarks collection from the active document, and
'add the name of each bookmark into a line of the combo box.
With booklistControl
    For Each thisBookmark In ActiveDocument.Bookmarks
      .AddItem thisBookmark
    Next thisBookmark
  End With
End Sub
```

The first statement in this code declares the App object variable as containing a reference to the Word application itself. The App object variable responds to events initiated in the Word application. The App_DocumentChange routine traps the DocumentChange event, which occurs whenever a document is created, opened, or activated.

First, this routine finds the combo box on the Navigation toolbar; if the FindControl method of the CommandBar object fails (that is, if there is no such control) FindControl returns the Nothing value to the booklistControl variable. The routine tests for this value and aborts the routine if the combo box doesn't exist.

If the combo box exists, the routine executes a For...Next loop for the number of items appearing in the list (its ListCount property) and repeatedly deletes the first item on the list, until every item on the list has been removed.

Next, the routine adds an item to the list for every bookmark in the active document, using the Bookmarks collection object.

Register the event handler

The last step is to connect the declared class object in the class module MyEventModule with the Application object and to write a short procedure that registers the event handler.

1   In the Visual Basic Editor, switch back to the NavBook module, and at the top of the module, enter the following code:

```
Dim X As New MyEventClassModule
Sub Register_Event_Handler()
  Set X.App = Word.Application
End Sub
```

2   Switch back to Word and register the handler by clicking Register_Event_Handler from the Lesson08Macros menu.

You can think of the registration process as the "glue" that links the DocumentChange event handler from the MyEventClassModule with the Word application itself, so that the event of activating a document window is passed to the correct routine.

As a debugging step, you could also call the Register_Event_Handler routine from the AddComboBox procedure, just in case you're working with the handler and introduce a bug into it; reregistering the routine whenever you create the combo box lets Word "know" that there's a new version of the routine.

If you were going to prepare this set of bookmark navigation macros for a system intended to be run by other users, you would probably want to call the Register_Event_Handler routine from an Auto_Open macro in the ThisDocument object that belongs to the same project that contains the code (in this case, the Normal.dot template) so that the registration process would be invisible to the user.

 NOTE For more information on auto-open event handlers, see Lesson 6, "Event Handling."

Now let's verify that the App_DocumentChange and BookmarkChoice routines are working correctly.

Test the bookmark navigation system

1 Open at least two documents that contain bookmarks. You can use the TextBk1 and TextBk2 files that accompany the Less08 practice file, if you want, or you can add bookmarks to any set of open documents and then use those documents.

2 Activate a document and pull down the Bookmark combo box. Whenever you activate a document, the App_DocumentChange procedure updates the Bookmarks combo box listing the bookmarks in the document.

3 Select an item from the list in the Bookmarks combo box. When you do this, the BookmarkChoice routine causes the associated bookmark to become selected.

You can adapt this technique for navigating among any of several classes of objects found in a Word document, such as tables, fields, and headings. For example, you can create a TableList tool for the Navigation toolbar that lists the tables in the active document by the names you've given them, assuming that the caption for each has been formatted in a specified style.

 TIP The bookmarks you create in a document are saved with the document and remain in it after you've closed it. This contrasts with variables you use in a Visual Basic macro to temporarily store ranges; when the macro ends and the document containing these ranges is closed, this information is lost. To store this information between editing sessions, transfer the range information to a bookmark before the document is closed.

Navigating Using Object Collections

Using object collections in a Word macro frees you from the need to do exhaustive testing for the characteristics of the material in the document to find out what you're working with. For example, let's say you want to find all the tables in a document and add a one-point border around each cell. Using the following code, you can create a macro that will place the insertion point at the beginning of the document, advance the selection character by character, and test whether the insertion point is inside a cell:

```
Sub MakeCellBorders()
    'Place insertion point at beginning of document.
    ActiveDocument.Range(0,0).Select
    'Find the number of characters in the document.
    numChars = ActiveDocument.Characters.Count
    'Step through each character.
    For nChar = 1 to numChars
      'Select the character.
      ActiveDocument.Characters(nChar).Select
      'If it's in a table, put borders around the cell.
      If Selection.Information(wdWithInTable) Then
        Selection.Cells(1).Borders.Enable = True
      End If
    Next
End Sub
```

The first thing this macro does is place the insertion point before the first character in the document, using the Range method. The number of characters in the document is then stored in the numChars variable, which is used in the For...Next loop that follows. This loop iterates once for every character, selecting it, and testing the character to see if it occurs in a table. If so, the Border property of the first cell in the selection (that is, the cell containing the selection) is set to True.

Obviously, this macro is pretty inefficient programming, not the least reason being that the macro takes forever because it has to process each character in the document. This process further slows down the macro because it requires a call to the display interface, adding unnecessary steps to each iteration of the For...Next loop. Also, the routine adds borders to the cell containing the character even if the cell already has borders. Interestingly, the selection moves more slowly the deeper into the document the macro proceeds, probably because the Select method of the Characters collection object counts from the beginning of the document each time it's used.

> **TIP** Every once in a while you'll write code (such as that in the
> MakeCellBorders procedure) that virtually freezes Word while it
> chugs along. When you decide you've had enough, press
> CTRL+BREAK to stop the macro.

You can speed this macro up a bit by having the process start at the beginning
of the current selection, as shown in this edited version of the MakeCellBorders
macro (statements in bold type mark the changed code):

```
Sub MakeCellBorders2()
  'Find the starting character position.
  startChar = Selection.Range.Start
  'Find the number of characters in the document.
  numChars = ActiveDocument.Characters.Count
  'Step through each character.
  For nChar = startChar to numChars
    'Select the character.
    ActiveDocument.Characters(nChar).Select
    'If it's in a table, put borders around the cell.
    If Selection.Information(wdWithInTable) Then
      Selection.Cells(1).Borders.Enable = True
    End If
  Next
End Sub
```

To test this macro, place the insertion point just before the table, and then click
MakeCellBorders2 from the Lesson08Macros menu. When you run the macro,
you'll see the selection move across the table, character by character. When the
selection moves beyond the last character in a cell, it selects the end-of-cell
marker. When the selection moves beyond the last cell in the first row, the
macro stops and displays an error dialog box that states that the "requested
member of the collection does not exist," because an end-of-row marker is in
fact inside a table, but isn't inside a cell.

A much better way to get to each cell in the active document is to use the
Tables collection of the Document object to change the format of each table,
regardless of its position:

```
Sub UnMakeCellBorders()
  'Test if there are any tables in the active document.
  If ActiveDocument.Tables.Count >= 1 then
    'Turn off borders for each table.
    For each thisTable in ActiveDocument.Tables()
      thisTable.Borders.Enable = False
    Next thisTable
  End if
End Sub
```

This routine takes a much more direct route. If there is at least one table in the active document, it sets the Borders property to False for each table in the Tables collection object of the document. Notice that no object in the active document is actually selected, but that the border format of each table changes nonetheless.

Let's consider another application that works with the cells and rows in a table using the Tables collection. Let's say you want to record your progress in a writing assignment by periodically recording the current number of pages, words, and characters in the document in a table at the end of the document. To do this, you need to do the following:

- Create a new table to hold the data, and define a bookmark we'll call NextRow that marks the first empty row in the table, so that when you open the document again, the macro will be able to start up where it left off.

- Write a macro called DateTimeStamp that enters a timecode recording the date and time the statistics were collected.

- Write a macro called LogProgress that stores the location of the current selection, jumps to the first empty row of the table, enters the data there, and jumps back to where you where working.

Create the progress log table

First, create the table in which the LogProgress macro will record statistics:

1   Go to the end of the Less08 document, and enter a level 1 heading called **Progress Table**.

2   With the insertion point at the beginning of the next line, click Insert Table, and insert a table that has five columns and two rows.

3   In the first row of the table, enter the headings **Timecode**, **Words**, **Characters**, **Paragraphs**, and **Comments**.

Progress Table

Timecode	Words	Characters	Paragraphs	Comments

4   Click in the first cell of the second row, click Bookmarks from the Insert menu, and create a bookmark named **NextRow**.

Create and test the DateTimeStamp macro

Next, create a macro that inserts the current date and time in a predetermined format:

1 Switch to the Visual Basic Editor, and add to the Less08 document a new module called **NavTable**.

2 In the NavTable module, enter the following procedure:

```
Sub DateTimeStamp()
   'Insert a field containing the date and time.
   Selection.Fields.Add _
      Range:=Selection.Range, _
      Type:=wdFieldEmpty, _
      Text:="DATE [\@ ""YYMMDD.HHmm""]", _
      PreserveFormatting:=True

   'Select the field.
   Selection.MoveLeft _
      Unit:=wdWord, _\
      Count:=1, _
      Extend:=wdExtend
   'Convert it into straight text.
   Selection.Fields.Unlink
   'Move insertion point to just after timecode.
   Selection.MoveRight _
      Unit:=wdWord, _
      Count:=1
End Sub
```

3 Switch to Word, activate the Less08 document if necessary, and click DateTimeStamp from the Lesson8Macros menu.

When you run the macro, Word inserts the timecode in a format similar to the ANSI date format, which is economical and which also lets you easily sort entries in a table or in other lists. The Visual Basic code that inserts this field was recorded using the custom field code *YYMMDD.HHmm*, which inserts two digits each for the year, month, day, hour, and minute. Next, the macro selects the newly created field, converts it into straight text using the Unlink method applied to the Fields collection object, and then advances the insertion point to the end of the timecode text.

NOTE We could have implemented a "purer" Visual Basic approach by using the Now function to return the current date and time, and the Year, Month, Day, Hour, and Minute functions to extract each unit of the date and time. The macro could finally assemble them again into a text string and insert the result into the cell. The gain would be a minor improvement in execution time at the expense of more programming effort.

Create and test the LogProgress macro

Now create the routine that manages the insertion of the timecode and the current document statistics in the next available row in the table:

1 At the end of the NavTable module, enter the following code:

```
Sub LogProgress()
    'Store location of current selection.
    ActiveDocument.Bookmarks.Add _
        Range:=Selection.Range, _
        Name:="LastEdit"

    'Go to NextRow bookmark.
    Selection.GoTo What:=wdGoToBookmark, Name:="NextRow"

    'Enter the timecode.
    DateTimeStamp

    'Enter the word count.
    Selection.MoveRight Unit:=wdCell
    numWords = ActiveDocument.Words.Count
    Selection.TypeText Text:=CStr(numWords)

    'Enter the character count.
    Selection.MoveRight Unit:=wdCell
    numChars = ActiveDocument.Characters.Count
    Selection.TypeText Text:=CStr(numChars)

    'Enter the paragraph count.
    Selection.MoveRight Unit:=wdCell
    numParas = ActiveDocument.Paragraphs.Count
    Selection.TypeText Text:=CStr(numParas)

    'Create a new row (equivalent to pressing
    'the Tab key in the last cell of the table).
    Selection.MoveRight Unit:=wdCell
    Selection.MoveRight Unit:=wdCell
```

```
'Redefine the NextRow bookmark.
ActiveDocument.Bookmarks.Add _
   Range:=Selection.Range, _
   Name:="NextRow"

'Reselect what was selected when LogProgress ran.
ActiveDocument.Bookmarks("LastEdit").Select

'Start an OnTime event that calls this macro.
Application.OnTime _
   When:=Now + TimeValue("00:15:00"), _
   Name:="LogProgress"
End Sub
```

2   Switch back to Word, select any text in the Less08 document, and click LogProgress from the Lesson8Macros menu.

The first time you run this macro, it stores the location of the current selection as a bookmark called LastEdit in the active document. We could have stored the Selection.Range information in a variable, but it is better to have the document itself "remember" the location of the last edit, so that the user can easily return to the location the next time the document is opened and the macro is run.

The LogProgress macro then jumps to the location of the NextRow bookmark we defined earlier in this lesson, and calls the DateTimeStamp procedure to enter the timecode in the first cell of the table. Next, the number of words, characters, and paragraphs are entered in the next three cells; the macro leaves the last cell open for comments you can enter later.

You could add an item in this comments column that lists the name of the heading before the current selection when the LogProgress macro runs. You could do this by temporarily setting the selection to the predefined bookmark, /HeadingLevel, finding the name of the first Heading object within it, and inserting that name in the fifth column of the table.

Next, two copies of the statement

```
Selection.MoveRight Unit:=wdCell
```

move the selection two cells to the right. This has the effect of pressing the TAB key twice—first to get to the comments column, and again inside the comments column, which is the lower-right cell in the table; when you do this manually in Word, another row is added to the bottom of the table.

Next, the macro redefines the NextRow bookmark and jumps back to the location of the LastEdit bookmark so the user can continue working on the document.

The last step of the LogProgress macro uses a little trick to cause the recording process to repeat at regular intervals. The OnTime method of the Application object takes two parameters, a specified time and the name of a procedure to run when that time occurs. The When argument, *Now + TimeValue("00:15:00")*, sends a message to the Word application to wait for 15 minutes, and the Name argument specifies that the LogProgress procedure run again at that time. In effect, the LogProgress macro calls itself every 15 minutes.

 TIP In order to make this system of macros more complete, you would probably want to use an Auto_Open procedure to call LogProgress and start logging statistics, and an Auto_Close procedure to record final statistics at the moment the user closes the document. You could also record these actions in the comment column of the Progress Log table.

If you want to continue to the next lesson

➤ Keep Word and Word's Visual Basic Editor running, and turn to Lesson 9.

If you want to quit Word for now

➤ From Word's File menu, click Exit. If you see a Save dialog box, click Yes.

Lesson Summary

To	Do this
Navigate using the Browser buttons	Set the target of the Application's Browser object. For example: `Application.Browser.Target = wdBrowseTable` `Application.Browser.Next`
Move a copy of a module into another project	Hold the left mouse button down with the pointer over the module you want to copy, and drag the module to the project in which you want to create the copy.
Create a new class module	In the Project Explorer, right-click in the project to which you want to add the class module, and then click Class Module from the Insert submenu.
Stop a macro during execution	Press CTRL+BREAK.

For online information about	From the Visual Basic Help menu, click Contents And Index, click the Index tab, and then
Calling procedures globally	Search for "calling procedures with the same name"

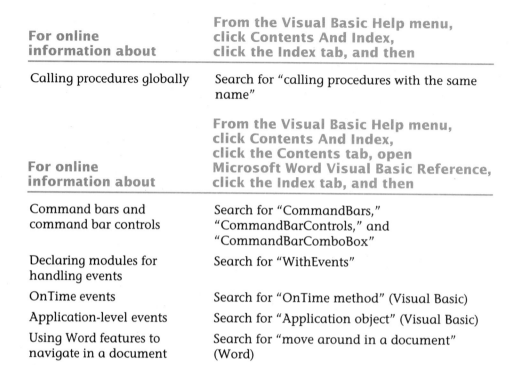

For online information about	From the Visual Basic Help menu, click Contents And Index, click the Contents tab, open Microsoft Word Visual Basic Reference, click the Index tab, and then
Command bars and command bar controls	Search for "CommandBars," "CommandBarControls," and "CommandBarComboBox"
Declaring modules for handling events	Search for "WithEvents"
OnTime events	Search for "OnTime method" (Visual Basic)
Application-level events	Search for "Application object" (Visual Basic)
Using Word features to navigate in a document	Search for "move around in a document" (Word)
The DocumentChange event	Search for "DocumentChange" (Word)

Preview of the Next Lesson

In the next lesson, "Changing Word Object Formats," you'll experiment with changing the properties of objects in a Word document by using the document's style sheet, as well as by creating a document from scratch.

Changing Word Object Formats

Estimated time
50 min.

In this lesson you will learn how to:

■ Experiment with setting formats of Word objects through their properties.

■ Create a set of procedures for working with style sheets.

■ Automatically generate a Word document that lists your Visual Basic code in an easy-to-read format.

In this lesson, you'll explore some ways to get and change the properties of objects found in a Word document, such as characters, paragraphs, headings, tables, and headers. We'll focus mainly on character and paragraph styles, but most of the principles covered in this lesson are applicable to the formats of any object in a Word document.

Start the lesson

1   Start Microsoft Word and open Less09.doc in the practice files folder.

When you open this document, Word adds the Lesson09Macros menu to the menu bar, which lists the macros created in Lesson 9.

2   From the Tools menu, click Macro, and then click Visual Basic Editor.

3   Find and open the Macros module in the Proj09 project.

As you work through the examples in this lesson, you can run your macros by clicking on any of the commands on the Lesson09Macros menu, which lists the practice and example macros for this lesson, and is added when you open the Less09.doc practice file on disk.

NOTE There's another module in the Less09 project called Background that contains housekeeping macros we've created for the lesson. You can study or ignore these macros, but don't change them.

Managing Format Properties

From a Visual Basic programmer's perspective, when you use Word to change a format (to make some text you've selected italic, for example), you are setting properties of the characters in the range of characters you've selected.

When you specify a range in a document or selection, and the content of the range consists of more than one type of object, setting a property of an object applies to every other object of the same type in the range. For example, you can set a range to refer to the entire body of the active document and change the style of every paragraph in the document by using this code:

```
Sub SetAllContentNormal()
    ActiveDocument.Content.Style = wdStyleNormal
End Sub
```

Each built-in style has a reserved name that you can set through a corresponding Visual Basic constant in a macro: wdStyleNormal for the Normal style, wdStyleHeading1 for the Heading 1 style, and so on. You can find a table listing the reserved constant names for these styles in the Less09.doc practice file.

To set the style of every paragraph in the current selection to the Normal style, you could use this code:

```
Sub SetRangeNormal()
    Selection.Range.Style = wdStyleNormal
End Sub
```

To set the style of every paragraph in the document to the Normal style, you could also use the following routine:

```
Sub SetAllParasNormal()
    For Each thisPara In ActiveDocument.Paragraphs
        thisPara.Style = wdStyleNormal
    Next thisPara
End Sub
```

If you run the SetAllContentNormal or SetRangeNormal macros, you can reverse the effect by choosing Undo from the Edit menu. Interestingly, you can't undo the SetAllParasNormal macro, though, because the For Each...Next loop iterates once for every paragraph in the document, and only the last formatting effect can be undone.

Getting Format Properties

You can get information about the formats that have been applied to a range of text in a Word document as well. For example, you can determine the name of the style and the description of the formats belonging to the style of the first paragraph in the selection by using the following routine:

```
Sub GetStyleDescription()
  thisStyle = Selection.Style
  styleDesc = Selection.Style.Description
  MsgBox _
    prompt:=thisStyle + vbCr + styleDesc, _
    Title:="GetStyleDescription"
End Sub
```

Click the second heading in the Less09 practice file and run this macro. You'll see this message box:

If the selection consists of more than one paragraph, the information returned is that of the first paragraph in the range. The Style property of the Selection object returns a Style object, and the default property of the Style object is its NameLocal property, which is the name given the style in the active document. (You can verify this by clicking Object Browser from the View menu, clicking Style in the Classes list, and finding the NameLocal property in the Members Of 'Style' list.)

The Description property of the Style object consists of the same text you see in Word's Style dialog box, shown here:

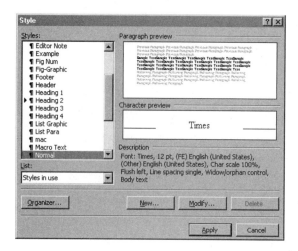

Another way to get to the Description property would be to replace the statement

```
styleDesc = Selection.Style.Description
```

with the statement

```
styleDesc = ActiveDocument.Styles(thisStyle).Description
```

Here, we're using the style name to identify the Style object we want, not through the Selection object but through the Styles collection, which belongs to the Document object.

Working with Style Sheets

In order to learn more about using Visual Basic to manage styles and style sheets, let's develop a set of macros that you can use for experimentation. This set of macros reads each item in the Styles collection and places six properties of each Style object into an array; each row of this array contains the following information:

Property name	Meaning
NameLocal	The name of the style in the specified document
Type	Whether the style is a paragraph or character style
BaseStyle	The name of the style that the style is based on

Property name	Meaning
BuiltIn	Whether the style is built-in (True) or user-defined (False)
InUse	Whether the style has been defined or redefined in the document (True), or is built-in but unused (False)
Description	The formats belonging to the style

Listing the Styles in a Document

Create the StyleMapper procedure

1 In the Visual Basic Editor, right-click in the Project Explorer window, click Insert, and then click Module.

The Visual Basic Editor inserts a new module.

2 In the Properties window, change the name of the module from *Module1* to **StyleProcs**.

3 In the StyleProcs module, enter the following code:

```
Public styleArray(256, 5) As String
Public docName As Variant
Public nRows As Integer

Sub StyleMapper()
   'Get document object.
   Set docName = ActiveDocument

   GetStyleArray
   CreateStyleTableDoc
   FormatStyleTableDoc
End Sub
```

The first three lines in the StyleProcs module declare global variables that the procedures in the module will use: an array of string values that will hold the table of style properties, the Document object whose style sheet we want to extract (in this case, the Less09.doc practice file), and the maximum number of rows in the table. Using global variables is a little more convenient than passing these values back and forth as arguments to procedures.

The StyleMapper procedure is simply an executive routine that stores a reference to the active document in the docName variable; then it calls three routines that read the properties mentioned above into the array, create a new document holding a table containing the values in the array styleArray (declared at the beginning of this code), and then format the resulting table.

Create the GetStyleArray procedure

➤ In the StyleProcs module and after the StyleMapper procedure, enter the following code:

```
Sub GetStyleArray()
  'Set up array to hold style table.
  nRows = 1
  styleArray(0, 0) = "Type"
  styleArray(0, 1) = "Style Based On"
  styleArray(0, 2) = "Style Name"
  styleArray(0, 3) = "Built-In?"
  styleArray(0, 4) = "In Use?"
  styleArray(0, 5) = "Description"
  For Each thisStyle In docName.Styles
    If thisStyle.Type = 1 Then
      styleArray(nRows, 0) = "Para"
    Else
      styleArray(nRows, 0) = "Char"
    End If
    styleArray(nRows, 1) = thisStyle.BaseStyle
    styleArray(nRows, 2) = thisStyle.NameLocal

    If thisStyle.BuiltIn = True Then
      styleArray(nRows, 3) = "Yes"
    Else
      styleArray(nRows, 3) = "No"
    End If

    If thisStyle.InUse Then
      styleArray(nRows, 4) = "Yes"
    Else
      styleArray(nRows, 4) = "No"
    End If
    styleArray(nRows, 5) = thisStyle.Description
    nRows = nRows + 1
  Next thisStyle
End Sub
```

The first row in the array holds the table headings in the order shown in the listing, because we'll eventually sort the table not by style name, but first by style type (character or paragraph), second by base style, and third by style name. This presentation makes the relationships between the styles in the style sheet easier to follow.

The For...Next block in the routine steps through each style in the Styles collection that belongs to the active document and extracts their associated properties. In the case of the Type, BuiltIn, and InUse properties, we use an If...Then...Else structure to translate the Type, True, and False values into values that will be easier to read in the finished table. At the end of each iteration, the nRows variable is incremented so that when the For...Next loop is done, nRows contains the row number of the last row in the table.

Create the CreateStyleTableDoc procedure

Now let's create a routine that creates a new document and enters the style sheet data.

➤ In the StyleProcs module and after the StyleMapper procedure, enter the following code:

```
Sub CreateStyleTableDoc()
   'Create new document--recorded statements.
   Documents.Add
   If ActiveWindow.View.SplitSpecial = wdPaneNone Then
      ActiveWindow.ActivePane.View.Type = wdNormalView
   Else
      ActiveWindow.View.Type = wdNormalView
   End If

   For k = 0 To nRows - 1
      rowText = styleArray(k, 0) + vbTab
      rowText = rowText + styleArray(k, 1) + vbTab
      rowText = rowText + styleArray(k, 2) + vbTab
      rowText = rowText + styleArray(k, 3) + vbTab
      rowText = rowText + styleArray(k, 4) + vbTab
      rowText = rowText + styleArray(k, 5) + vbCr
      Selection.TypeText Text:=rowText
   Next k
End Sub
```

This procedure performs the equivalent of clicking New from the File menu and setting the document to Normal View. Next, it takes the styleArray variable and reads its values into the document, separating each value from the next by a tab character, and ending each line with a carriage return.

Create the FormatStyleTableDoc procedure

Next, create a routine for converting the tab-delimited style sheet information into a table.

➤ In the StyleProcs module and after the CreateStyleTableDoc procedure, enter the following code:

```
Sub FormatStyleTableDoc()
  'Select All
  Selection.WholeStory
  'Convert tab-delimited text to a table.
  Selection.ConvertToTable _
    Separator:=wdSeparateByTabs, _
    NumColumns:=6, _
    Format:=wdTableFormatNone, _
    ApplyBorders:=True, _
    ApplyShading:=True, _
    ApplyFont:=True, _
    ApplyColor:=True, _
    ApplyHeadingRows:=True, _
    ApplyLastRow:=False, _
    ApplyFirstColumn:=True, _
    ApplyLastColumn:=False, _
    AutoFit:=False
    'NumRows:=15,

  'Select the table.
  ActiveDocument.Tables(1).Select
  'Sort the table by char or para style,
  'then by BaseStyle,
  'then by LocalName.
  Selection.Sort _
    ExcludeHeader:=True, _
    FieldNumber:="Column 1", _
    SortFieldType:=wdSortFieldAlphanumeric, _
    SortOrder:=wdSortOrderAscending, _
    FieldNumber2:="Column 2", _
    SortFieldType2:=wdSortFieldAlphanumeric, _
    SortOrder2:=wdSortOrderAscending, _
    FieldNumber3:="Column 3", _
    SortFieldType3:=wdSortFieldAlphanumeric, _
    SortOrder3:=wdSortOrderAscending, _
    Separator:=wdSortSeparateByTabs, _
    SortColumn:=False, _
    CaseSensitive:=False, _
    LanguageID:=wdLanguageNone

    'Set the column widths.
  Selection.Cells.AutoFit
```

```
        'Format first row as table heading, in case table
      'runs to more than one page.
      Selection.Rows(1).HeadingFormat = True
      Selection.Rows(1).Shading.Texture = wdTexture10Percent

        'Insert paragraph before table, in Heading 1 style.
      ActiveDocument.Tables(1).Rows(1).Select
      Selection.SplitTable

      Selection.InsertBefore docName + " Stylesheet"
      Selection.Style = "heading 1"
    End Sub
```

This procedure consists mostly of code that we recorded. It starts with the action of clicking Select All from the Edit menu and then clicking Text To Table from the Table menu. We've left the recorded code as-is so you can see all the options available, but notice that we moved the NumRows argument to the end of the list and commented it out; doing this is like leaving the Number Of Rows box in the Convert Text To Table box unconstrained, and lets the macro enter an indeterminate number of entries to be converted.

Once the table has been created, we select it through the Tables collection and sort the table by Type, Base Style, and Style Name (again using recorded code). The next statements in the procedure adjust the column widths to accommodate the text in each column and format the first row in the table in a heading format so that if the table runs to more than one page, the headings will be repeated at the top of each new page. The last block of code performs the equivalent of clicking Split Table from the Tables menu, inserting an empty paragraph above the first row of the table so that we can later enter a heading that lists the name of the document containing the listed style sheet.

Running the StyleMapper macro

➤ Switch to Word and click StyleMapper from the Lesson09Macros menu. When you do this, the macro creates the document shown here:

Less09.doc Stylesheet

Type	Style Based On	Style Name	Built-In?	In Use?	Description
Char		Default Paragraph Font	Yes	Yes	The font of the underlying paragraph style +
Char	Default Paragraph Font	codeText	No	Yes	Default Paragraph Font + Font: Courier New, Red
Char	Default Paragraph Font	Comment Reference	Yes	Yes	Default Paragraph Font + Font: 8 pt
Char	Default Paragraph Font	Emphasis	Yes	Yes	Default Paragraph Font + Italic
Char	Default Paragraph Font	Endnote Reference	Yes	Yes	Default Paragraph Font + Superscript
Char	Default Paragraph Font	FollowedHyperlink	Yes	Yes	Default Paragraph Font + Underline, Violet
Char	Default Paragraph	Footnote Reference	Yes	Yes	Default Paragraph

TIP Document designers often suggest using the same font for each level of heading in a document. The style "families" in Word, such as the Index, TOC, and Body Text styles, reflect this approach. However, to use the same font for each style in a family of styles—each of the Heading styles, for example—you must redefine each style. You could make this task much simpler by writing a macro that creates a "source style" for each style family and sets the BaseStyle property for each style so that it refers to the source style. For example, this macro could create a Heading 0 style (which is never actually used in the document) and base each Heading style on it.

Detecting Whether a Style Is in Use in a Document

As you can see by comparing the table generated by the StyleMapper macro against the Lesson09 practice document, it seems that every style in the table has its InUse property set to True. In fact, the InUse property really means something like "used in the style sheet" for the document. For example, you could define and use a style called QuoteText to format a quote, and then decide to delete the quoted text. Even though the style isn't really being used in the document, it still exists in the style sheet, and the statement

```
thisInUse = Styles("QuoteText").InUse
```

would return the value True.

One cause of spurious style InUse values is copying a large amount of text from one document to another in one operation. If the copied material is sufficiently complex, Word copies the entire source style sheet into the destination document, including style names that may have no use in the destination document.

Creating the StyleReallyInUse Function

Let's create a function that determines whether a style is actually being used in the document.

 In the StyleProc module and after the FormatStyleTableDoc procedure, enter the following code:

```
Function StyleReallyInUse(styleName)
'Assumes Style(styleName).InUse = True,
'but we don't know whether it's really being used
'in the document yet.
  Set docRange = ActiveDocument.Content
  docRange.Find.ClearFormatting
  docRange.Find.Style = ActiveDocument.Styles(styleName)
```

```
With docRange.Find
  .Text = ""
  .Forward = True
  .Wrap = wdFindContinue
  .Format = True
End With
docRange.Find.Execute
StyleReallyInUse = docRange.Find.Found
End Function
```

This function begins by storing the range of the main body content (that is, all but the headers, footers, endnotes, and so on) in the docRange variable, and then performs the equivalent of setting options in Word's Find dialog box. First, it clears any previous formatting options, and then it specifies that we want to look for instances of the style name stored in the styleName variable that was passed to the function as an argument.

Next, the procedure sets properties of the Find object: we aren't searching for text; we are searching for a format; we're also searching forward in the document, and if the selection isn't at the beginning of the document, we'll start from the location of the selection and then finish from the beginning of the document.

Finally, we use the Execute method on the Find object to start the search. If successful, the Found property of the Find object returns True, which is then returned by the function itself.

Let's test this function by creating a routine that performs a simple search.

Creating the TestStyleReallyInUse procedure

➤ In the StyleProcs module and after the StyleReallyInUse function, enter the following code:

```
Sub TestStyleReallyInUse()
  Dim Message, Title, Default
  Message = "Enter a style name"
  Title = "TestStyleReallyInUse Macro"
  Default = "codeText"

  isInStylesheet = False
  While Not isInStylesheet
    styleName = InputBox(Message, Title, Default)
    'Test for existence of style in stylesheet.
    For Each thisStyle In ActiveDocument.Styles()
      If thisStyle = styleName Then isInStylesheet = True
    Next thisStyle
    If Not isInStylesheet Then
      MsgBox prompt:="Not in stylesheet."
    End If
  Wend
```

```
          If StyleReallyInUse(styleName) Then
        inUseText = ""
      Else
        inUseText = "not"
      End If
      Msg = "Style [" + styleName + "] is " + inUseText + " in use."
      MsgBox Prompt:=Msg, Title:=Title
    End Sub
```

This routine presents an Input dialog box that requests a style name and pro-
poses the codeText style, which we've created in the Less09.doc practice file.
This Input dialog box is presented from within a While...Wend loop that
assumes the style isn't in the style sheet until it's proven to be there by the test
performed in the For...Next loop. If the style name entered in the Input dialog
box wasn't entered correctly, or isn't in the style sheet, the Input dialog is presented again. Finally, the result from the StyleReallyInUse function is used to
set the text that appears in an output message box.

Running the TestStyleReallyInUse macro

1   Switch to Word and click TestStyleReallyInUse from the
    Lesson09Macros menu.

    The macro first presents this dialog box:

2   Click OK to begin the search. Let's use the proposed style name,
    codeText, because the Less09.doc practice file contains a snippet of text
    toward the end of the file formatted in this character style, shown in red
    (unless you've changed the contents of the file).

    After the macro has found the text, it presents this dialog box:

3   Click Goto from the Edit menu; in the Goto dialog box, select the
    codeTextSample bookmark and click Goto.

4   Click Cut from the Edit menu to remove the text from the document.

5   Click TestStyleReallyInUse from the Lesson09Macros menu again to verify that no text having the codeText character style remains in the document.

 TIP   You could use the StyleReallyInUse function in combination with the StyleMapper macro to implement a routine that deletes styles that are unused in the document. You could even create "protected" styles (ones that would not be deleted even if not currently in the document), based on a characteristic such as the suffix *-Prot* added to the style name (for example, *codeTextProt*).

Document Creation and Formatting Through a Macro

Let's consider a more complete example of creating a document and formatting its various parts by writing a set of routines that extracts all the code from the modules contained in the active document and inserts it into a Word document, complete with headings for each module and procedure. The Visual Basic Editor has its own Print command on the File menu, but the output generated isn't formatted well. This macro will do the job better.

Working with code in a Visual Basic procedure doesn't directly pertain to formatting Word documents through changing Word object properties, but to create a document we have to get information from somewhere, and it can be very handy to take a nicely formatted printout with you away from the computer to document, analyze, or debug your code.

To implement this system of macros, we need the following procedures:

- A WriteLine procedure that enters each line of code into the Word document and formats each line in a specified style

- A ModulesToWordDoc procedure for creating a new Word document and managing the extraction of code from the modules in the active document

- A FormatStyles procedure for defining the styles in the listing document

- A FormatDoc procedure for specifying the listing's document-level formats

- A FormatHeader procedure that adds a running head to the document that lists the document name, date of printing, and page number

Prepare the project

1 In the Visual Basic Editor, right-click in the Project Explorer window, click Insert, and then click Module.

   The Visual Basic Editor inserts a new module.

2 In the Properties window, change the name of the module from *Module1* to **MacroDoc**.

3 Click References from the Tools menu, and then click the Microsoft Visual Basic for Applications Extensibility object library in the Available References list box. (The name of this library will probably be truncated in the dialog box.)

4 Click OK in the References dialog box.

We need to add a reference to the Extensibility object library because the objects and methods that let us access code in a module belong to this library, and by adding a reference to it, we can make them available for programming.

Create the WriteLine procedure

▶ In the MacroDoc module, enter the following procedure:

```
Sub WriteLine(thisText, thisStyle)
  'Enter the text.
  Selection.InsertAfter thisText
  'Set the style for the insertion.
  Selection.Style = thisStyle
  'Add a carriage return.
  Selection.InsertAfter vbCr
  'Move insertion point to beginning of next line.
  Selection.Collapse Direction:=wdCollapseEnd
End Sub
```

The WriteLine procedure is similar to statements in other programming languages (WriteLn in Pascal, for example) that take an argument that specifies the text to be output, followed by a carriage return. The procedure also takes an argument for the style of the line, which lets us format text in the Heading 1 or Normal styles, for example.

We make all of this happen by exploiting the Selection object. Starting with the current selection, which we assume to be an insertion point, the macro inserts the text specified in the thisText argument. The macro then applies the style specified in the thisStyle argument and adds a carriage return. Because the InsertAfter method expands the selection to include the text entered, we need to collapse the selection to an insertion point again at the end of the routine. Because the inserted text is a carriage return, the effect is to move the insertion point to the beginning of the next line.

Create the ModulesToWordDoc procedure

Now let's create a routine for entering code in the document.

➤ In the MacroDoc module and after the WriteLine procedure, enter the following code:

```
Sub ModulesToWordDoc()
  Dim procLineCount As Long
  Dim thisLine As Long

  Set sourceDoc = ActiveDocument
  'Create new document--recorded code.
  Documents.Add

  If ActiveWindow.View.SplitSpecial = wdPaneNone Then
    ActiveWindow.ActivePane.View.Type = wdNormalView
  Else
    ActiveWindow.View.Type = wdNormalView
  End If

  'Get each VB component and list it.
  For Each thisComp In sourceDoc.VBProject.VBComponents
    WriteLine thisComp.Name, "Heading 1"
    'If the component is a code module, then scan for "Sub "
    procLineCount = thisComp.CodeModule.CountOfLines

      For thisLine = 1 To procLineCount
    'Identify lines that start with
    'Sub, Function, or Private,
    'in order to add headings.
    findSub = thisComp.CodeModule.Find( _
      Target:="Sub", _
      StartLine:=thisLine, _
      StartColumn:=1, _
      endline:=thisLine, _
      EndColumn:=3, _
      WholeWord:=True)
    findFunction = thisComp.CodeModule.Find( _
      Target:="Function", _
      StartLine:=thisLine, _
      StartColumn:=1, _
      endline:=thisLine, _
      EndColumn:=8, _
      WholeWord:=True)
    findPrivate = thisComp.CodeModule.Find( _
      Target:="Private", _
      StartLine:=thisLine, _
      StartColumn:=1, _
```

207

```
                endline:=thisLine, _
                EndColumn:=7, _
                WholeWord:=True)

        'If the line is the beginning of a procedure,
        'insert a level-2 heading into the listing.
        If findSub Or findFunction Or findPrivate Then
            thisProcName = _
                thisComp.CodeModule.ProcOfLine(thisLine, vbext_pk_Proc)
            WriteLine _
                thisText:=thisProcName, _
                thisStyle:="Heading 2"
        End If
        WriteLine _
            thisText:=thisComp.CodeModule.Lines(thisLine, 1), _
            thisStyle:="Normal"
      Next thisLine
   Next thisComp

   'Set style formats.
   FormatStyles

   'Set document formats.
   FormatDoc

   'Format header for the listing.
   FormatHeader sourceDoc
End Sub
```

The ModulesToWordDoc procedure is the central routine in this system of macros and is one of the more complex in this book, so we'll take it apart piece by piece.

First, the macro saves the name of the active document, so that later statements can access it to extract the code in its attached modules.

Next, the macro creates a new document to hold the code listing. To create this code, we recorded the action of clicking New from the File menu and inserted the recorded code into the procedure.

The next block of code is the core of the procedure, and makes use of the objects, methods, and properties in the Extensibility Library, which offers the VBProject, VBComponents, and CodeModule objects. If we were to translate the structure of this block into plain English (sometimes called *pseudocode*), it might look something like this:

```
For each module in the document named in sourceDoc,
   Print the name of the module in the Heading 1 style.
   Read each line of code in the module.
   If a line starts with Sub, Function, or Private,
      then get the name of the procedure containing the line,
      and print it in the Heading 2 style.
   Print the line of code in the Normal style.
```

The Visual Basic Extensibility library offers three methods that enable us to get at the code in a module. The Find method of the CodeModule object looks at a line of code for the text specified in its Target argument; if it finds the text, the method returns True, which we store in the findSub, findFunction, or findPrivate variables.

If any of these variables is True, we use the ProcOfLine method to determine the name of the procedure containing the line, and then we use the WriteLine routine to enter its name in the new document in the Heading 2 style.

Finally, we use the Lines method of the CodeModule object to get the actual line of code, and we use the WriteLine routine to insert the statement in the listing document in the Normal style.

The remaining three lines of code in the ModulesToWordDoc procedure call three other procedures in turn for defining style formats (FormatStyles), document formats (FormatDoc), and the contents of the header for the listing (FormatHeader). Let's turn to these procedures next.

Create the FormatStyles procedure

➤ In the MacroDoc module and after the ModulesToWordDoc procedure, enter the following code:

```
Sub FormatStyles()
   'Redefine Normal style.
   With ActiveDocument.Styles("Normal")
      .Font.Name = "Courier New"
      .Font.Size = 9
   End With
End Sub
```

This short procedure simply sets the Normal style to 9-point text in the Courier New font; you could add code to set formats for the Heading 1, Heading 2, and Header styles, which are all used in the listing.

Create the FormatDoc procedure

➤ In the MacroDoc module and after the FormatStyles procedure, enter the following code:

```
Sub FormatDoc()
   'Set document formats--recorded and unedited.
   With ActiveDocument.PageSetup
      .LineNumbering.Active = False
      .Orientation = wdOrientPortrait

      'Wide page margins for long VB statements.
      .TopMargin = InchesToPoints(0.75)
      .BottomMargin = InchesToPoints(0.75)
      .LeftMargin = InchesToPoints(1.25)
      .RightMargin = InchesToPoints(1)

      .Gutter = InchesToPoints(0)
      .HeaderDistance = InchesToPoints(0.5)
      .FooterDistance = InchesToPoints(0.5)
      .PageWidth = InchesToPoints(8.5)
      .PageHeight = InchesToPoints(11)
      .FirstPageTray = wdPrinterDefaultBin
      .OtherPagesTray = wdPrinterDefaultBin
      .SectionStart = wdSectionNewPage
      .OddAndEvenPagesHeaderFooter = False
      .DifferentFirstPageHeaderFooter = False
      .VerticalAlignment = wdAlignVerticalTop
      .SuppressEndnotes = False
      .MirrorMargins = False
   End With
End Sub
```

We created this code by recording the act of clicking Page Setup from the File menu and entering values for the margins in the resulting document that are wide enough to permit listing most Visual Basic statements in single lines without wrapping. We left in the code for other document properties such as those for the page dimensions and printer trays, because if not specified they would revert to whatever settings the user had last entered. You may need to alter these settings a little for your own system.

Create the FormatHeader procedure

➤ In the MacroDoc module and after the FormatDoc procedure, enter the following code:

```
Sub FormatHeader(docName)
   'View the header for the document--recorded.
   If ActiveWindow.View.SplitSpecial <> wdPaneNone Then
      ActiveWindow.Panes(2).Close
   End If
   If ActiveWindow.ActivePane.View.Type = wdNormalView _
      Or ActiveWindow.ActivePane.View.Type = wdOutlineView _
      Or ActiveWindow.ActivePane.View.Type = wdMasterView Then
         ActiveWindow.ActivePane.View.Type = wdPageView
   End If
   ActiveWindow.ActivePane.View.SeekView = _
      wdSeekCurrentPageHeader

   'Enter text for the header.
   Selection.TypeText Text:="Code Modules for " + docName
   Selection.TypeText Text:=vbTab & Now
   Selection.TypeText Text:=vbTab & "page "
   Selection.Fields.Add Range:=Selection.Range, Type:=wdFieldPage

   'Define formats for the header.
   With Selection.ParagraphFormat
      With .Borders(wdBorderBottom)
         .LineStyle = wdLineStyleSingle
         .LineWidth = wdLineWidth050pt
         .ColorIndex = wdAuto
      End With
   End With
   Selection.MoveLeft Unit:=wdCharacter, Count:=1
   With Selection.ParagraphFormat
      With .Borders(wdBorderBottom)
         .LineStyle = wdLineStyleSingle
         .LineWidth = wdLineWidth050pt
         .ColorIndex = wdAuto
      End With
   End With
   Selection.MoveUp Unit:=wdLine, Count:=1, Extend:=wdExtend
   Selection.Font.Bold = True
   Selection.Font.Name = "Helvetica"

   'Redefine the Header style from the selection.
   ActiveDocument.Styles("Header").AutomaticallyUpdate = False
End Sub
```

Much of the code in this routine was recorded first and then adapted so that it didn't set formats that weren't important, and to make the edited macro more general-purpose. Recording actions and then commenting out blocks of code that don't directly pertain to the actions you want to enact enables you to develop code more quickly, and helps you to learn Visual Basic as well. To see an earlier version of the entire recorded macro, look in the Less09.doc practice file, at the FormatHeaderOrig procedure at the end of the MacroDoc module.

The main features added to this code are statements that pass the name of the source document to the FormatHeader routine (which is in turn stored in the docName variable and entered in the header with the time and date of the document's creation), and a field that prints the number of each page in the listing.

Finally, we format the header and use the AutomaticallyUpdate property of the Style object to redefine the Header style from the currently selected text.

TIP A useful feature of the Visual Basic Editor isn't found on any menu. Tucked away on the Edit toolbar, the Comment Block and Uncomment Block commands let you perform "brain surgery" on recorded code, so that you can deactivate a series of statements that may or may not be useful for your macro. You can run the macro with the lines commented out and see if the result is what you want, and uncomment them if the results are unsatisfactory.

To use these commands, you can display the Edit toolbar, but perhaps the best strategy is to put them on the shortcut menu for the Code Window. To do this, right-click any toolbar. In the Customize dialog box, click the Toolbars tab and then the Shortcut Menus item. When you do this, the Visual Basic Editor displays a toolbar containing a list of the various classes of shortcut menus. Click Code Windows and then Code Window to display the Code Window menu. In the Customize dialog box, click the Commands tab, click the Edit category, and then scroll down the Commands list to find the Comment Block and Uncomment Block commands. Drag them onto the Code Window menu. Your screen should resemble the following illustration.

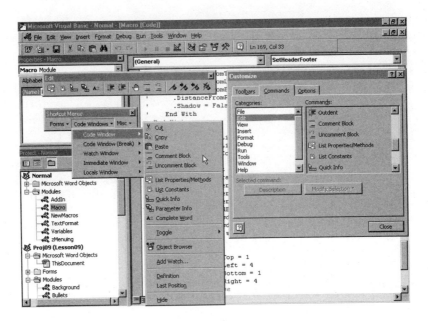

Running the macro

1   Switch back to Word and make sure the window for the Less09.doc practice file is active.

2   Click ModuleToWordDoc from the Lesson09Macros menu.

When you run the macro, Word processes the text in the project and creates a document like that shown here:

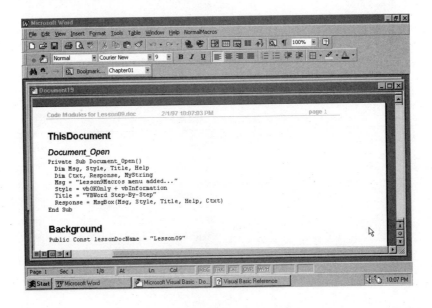

Installing the MacroDoc
module in the Normal template

You can run the ModulesToWordDoc macro as written only when the Less09.doc window is active; doing so lists the macros in the Proj09 project, which isn't very useful. To make the ModulesToWordDoc macro more general-purpose, you can copy the MacroDoc module to the Normal template and make it readily accessible from any document as follows:

1   Switch to the Visual Basic Editor, and then drag the MacroDoc module from the Proj09 project to the Normal project. This creates another copy of the module in the Normal template. (You could then remove the copy of the module in the Proj09 project, but to minimize problems while doing these exercises, we recommend that you leave the project intact.)

2   Implement an interface for running the macro, for example, by adding a button to a toolbar or a command to a menu.

If you want to continue to the next lesson

➤   Keep Word and Word's Visual Basic Editor running, and turn to Lesson 10.

If you want to stop for now

➤   Switch to Word and click Exit from the File menu. If you see a Save dialog box, click Yes.

Lesson Summary

To	Do this
Set paragraphs to a built-in style	Use one of the built-in style constants. For example: `ActiveDocument.Content.Style = wdStyleNormal`
Get information about styles in a style sheet	Use style properties such as the LocalName, BaseStyle, BuiltIn, InUse, or Description properties.
Determine whether a style is in use in a style sheet	Use the InUse property.
Determine whether a style is in use in a document	Use a For...Next loop to check whether a style exists in the style sheet, and then use the Find method to search for actual instances of the style in the document.

For online information about	Do this
Working with Properties	Search for "understanding objects, properties, methods, and events" (Visual Basic Reference)
Working with Word object properties	Search for "Microsoft Word objects" (Microsoft Word Visual Basic)
Styles in Word	Search for "about styles" (Word Help); search for "Style object" (Microsoft Word Visual Basic)
Accessing code modules from Visual Basic	In the Visual Basic Editor, click References from the Tools menu, and select Visual Basic for Applications Extensibility. Open the Object Browser; from the Libraries drop-down list, click VBIDE. For information about Visual Basic Editor objects, click the Help button in the Object Browser.

Preview of the Next Lesson

In the next lesson, "Working with Text and Files," you'll experiment with working with text the old-fashioned way: not as Word objects, but as characters in text strings. You'll also work with files and directories, and you'll learn to read text files without using Word.

Working with Text and Files

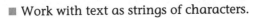

In this lesson you will learn how to:

Estimated time
60 min.

- Work with text as strings of characters.
- Learn about various encoding systems for character sets.
- Use string operators to manipulate text.
- Use Visual Basic commands to interface with text files outside of a Word document.
- Create a system of procedures that automate the process of assembling a series of files into a single document.

In this lesson, you'll explore the fascinating world of processing text and handling files with Visual Basic. The emphasis here won't be as much on using Word objects as on working with strings of characters apart from their appearance and placement in a Word document, in much the same way that programmers thought of text in the days before object-oriented languages. By the end of this lesson, though, you'll have created the largest set of macros in this book, a set which uses a bit of almost everything we've covered.

Start the lesson

1 Start Microsoft Word and open Less10.doc in the practice files folder.

When you open this document, Word adds to the menu bar the Lesson10Macros menu, which lists the macros created in Lesson 10.

2 From the Tools menu, click Macro, and then click Visual Basic Editor.

3 Find and open the Macros module in the Proj10 project.

As you work through the examples in this lesson, you can run your macros by clicking corresponding items on the Lesson10Macros menu.

 NOTE There's another module in the Lesson10 project called Background that contains housekeeping macros we've created for the lesson. You can study or ignore these macros, but don't change them.

Working with Text

When you're dealing with unformatted text itself, you're really dealing with a series, or *string,* of characters. As we discussed in Lesson 7, you can access the characters in a Word document through the Characters collection object, each item of which corresponds to a Range object specifying that character's location in the document.

In this lesson, we'll use the Characters collection as well as other objects (such as the Word object) that help you work with text in a document, but in the context of writing text-processing procedures. We'll mostly focus on considering characters as abstract data rather than as Word objects.

Coding Systems for Character Sets

Perhaps the first thing to learn about working with text is the difference between a character that you see on the screen or on paper and the same character as it is represented internally. So that computer applications can work with text, an encoding scheme is used that associates a binary number with every character or symbol in a document. There are several systems for encoding character sets in use in the world today.

The most common encoding scheme is 7-bit ASCII, which stands for American Standard Code for Information Interchange. In this system, 7 bits of information are associated with each of 127 uppercase and lowercase characters that you would find on any standard typewriter, plus a few characters such as the tab and the carriage return. Even today, nearly all electronic communication in the form of text, such as standard Internet e-mail, uses this encoding scheme. In the 7-bit ASCII system, for example, the letter *A* is associated with the binary code 1000001, which is equivalent to the decimal number 65.

Eight-bit ASCII adds another bit of data (to make one byte), which effectively increases the number of possible symbols that can be encoded to 256. In this system, the so-called "upper ASCII characters" encode symbols such as "curly quotes," bullets such as those at the beginning of the bulleted list at the beginning of this lesson, and additional letters, such as the non-English ø in Tromsø.

The Unicode character standard is a character encoding scheme developed by the International Standards Organization (ISO) that uses 16 bits (or 2 bytes) of data to represent characters, which allows for 65,536 possible symbols that range numerically from -32768 to 32767. Different fonts may use the Unicode encoding scheme to associate a given code with a character that may differ from the version found in a Roman font. For example, each of the following symbols are characters that have a Unicode (and an ASCII) value of 65:

A   ✡   **A**   A   ⊙

You can review these sets of characters when you click Symbol from the Insert menu. When you do this, you'll see the following dialog box:

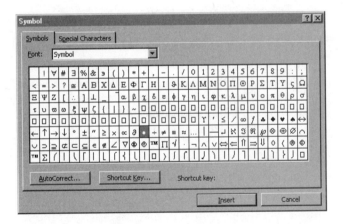

You can insert a symbol based on its appearance in the Insert Symbol dialog box, but there's no way to use Word features alone to determine the character number of a given symbol. To experiment with encoding schemes further, let's create a macro that gives you this information.

Create the GetASCII macro

1   In the Visual Basic Editor, right-click in the Project Explorer window, click Insert, and then click Module.

The Visual Basic Editor inserts a new module.

2   In the Properties window, change the name of the module from *Module1* to **ASCII**.

3   In the ASCII module, enter the following code:

```
Sub GetASCII()
  If Selection.Type = wdSelectionIP Then
    Exit Sub
  Else
    Set thisChar = Selection.Range.Characters.First
  End If

  'Set up and display message box.
  Title = "GetASCII Macro"
  msg1 = "Character: [" + thisChar + "]" + vbCr
  msg2 = "ASCII: " + CStr(Asc(thisChar)) + vbCr
  msg3 = "Unicode:" + CStr(AscW(thisChar))
  msgTot = msg1 + msg2 + msg3
  answer = MsgBox(msgTot, vbInformation, Title)
End Sub
```

The If...Then...Else block at the beginning of this macro attempts to simulate the behavior of many of Word's features (such as the Edit menu's Copy command) which do nothing if nothing is selected in the document. In other words, the instructions are: if the selection is an insertion point, exit the procedure, and if not, store the first character in the selection in the thisChar variable.

The next block of code sets up and presents a MsgBox dialog box that displays the character selected in three forms: the character as a symbol, and its code in the ASCII and Unicode character set standards.

The ASCII character 13, represented in a Word macro by the constant vbCr, results in a paragraph mark when used in a document, but we use it in the dialog box to end a line of text. Visual Basic supports several other constants for working with text:

Constant	ASCII	Meaning	Entered in a Word document by pressing:
vbCr	13	Carriage return	ENTER
vbLf	10	Linefeed	SHIFT+ENTER
vbTab	9	Tab character	TAB
vbCrLf	13, 10	Carriage return plus linefeed	Either ENTER or ENTER + LINEFEED
vbNewLine	13, 10 or 10	Which is entered depends on the platform running the macro.	ENTER (RETURN on some platforms)

Run the GetASCII macro

1   In the Less10.doc practice file, find the row of symbols near the beginning of the document, and select the *A* at the beginning of the row.

2   Click GetASCII from the Lesson10Macros menu.

When you do this, your screen should look like this:

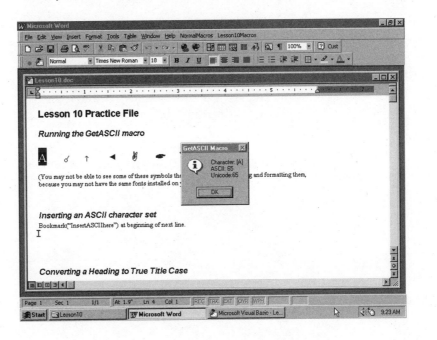

To create these symbols, we entered the letter *A* eight times in the Less10.doc practice file and formatted each instance in various symbol and dingbat fonts.

3 Select the third symbol, which is formatted in the Fences font and looks like an upward-pointing arrow, and click the GetASCII command again.

When you do this, your screen should look like this:

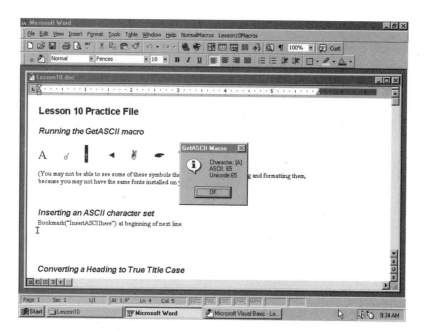

As you can see, even though the symbol is different, the macro reported it as an *A*, having an ASCII value of 65. Finally, to make matters even more confusing, do the following:

4 Select the fifth character in the row, which has been formatted in the Zapf Dingbats font, and run the GetASCII macro.

When you do this, your screen should look something like this:

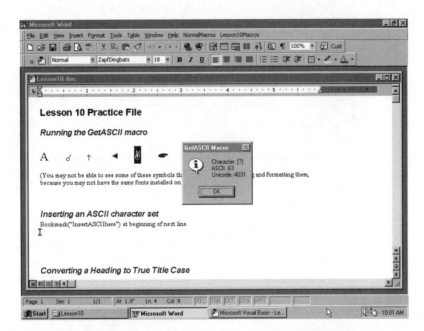

In this case, it seems that nothing matches: the reported character isn't an *A* but a question mark (which does have an ASCII value of 63), and the Unicode value for the character is -4031. This happens because the Visual Basic interface doesn't support the Unicode character set, but it does correctly determine the corresponding code. Therefore, when you're using Word or a Word macro to find and replace symbols in a document, if you're not careful you could end up replacing characters you didn't intend to. For example, you could intend to replace every instance of a dingbat in a document having an ASCII value of 65 with another, and wind up replacing every instance of the letter *A* as well.

5   Finally, try selecting other items in the Less10.doc practice file, such as graphics, section marks, and tab characters, and then running the GetASCII macro to find the codes used for these items.

String Operators and Functions

Visual Basic offers several operators that are analogous to the mathematical operators for working with numbers. We've used the most common string operator many times in this book already—the concatenation operator, +. Sometimes in code you'll see the & symbol, which is nearly equivalent to the + symbol but which forces evaluation of the expression to a character string. Similarly, Visual Basic offers several string functions for taking strings apart in various ways, some of which we'll describe in the rest of this lesson.

Let's investigate working with strings by implementing a macro that improves on one of Word's "formatting" features—the Change Case command on the Format menu. When you click Change Case, you'll see this dialog box:

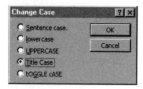

With this feature you can change the selected text to various combinations of uppercase and lowercase letters. One of these options is called Title Case, which capitalizes the first letter in each word in the selection. The problem with Word's Title Case option, typically used when formatting headings, is that it does two things that deviate from standard English style. First, it capitalizes words that, in standard English, aren't usually capitalized: short prepositions (such as *of, to,* and *from*), conjunctions (such as *and* and *but*), and articles (such as *the*). Second, the feature changes to lowercase every character except the first in each word of the selected text, regardless of whether a word uses internal capitalization—like the word *MacArthur*. Therefore, it's usually better not to use this feature and to edit the text in a heading by hand.

Let's implement a more useful version of this feature by creating a macro that does two things. First, we want the macro to look at each word in the selection and, if it appears on a list of exceptions, leave it alone. Second, we want the macro to capitalize only the first character in each word we specify and leave the rest alone.

Create the TrueTitleCase macro

➤ In the ASCII module and after the GetASCII procedure, enter the following code:

```
Sub TrueTitleCase()
  'Create collection for word exception list.
  Dim noTitleCaseWords As New Collection
  With noTitleCaseWords
    .Add "a"
    .Add "an"
    .Add "the"
    .Add "to"
    .Add "of"
    .Add "with"
    .Add "from"
    .Add "this"
    .Add "and"
    .Add "but"
  End With
```

```
'Read each word in the selection into an array.
Dim wordArray(25) As Range
nWords = 0
For Each thisWord In Selection.Words()
  nWords = nWords + 1
  Set wordArray(nWords) = thisWord
Next

'For each word in wordArray
For n = 1 To nWords
  'Get the word, sans ending space, if any.
  trimWord = RTrim(wordArray(n))

  'Check the trimmed word against the collection.
  testResult = False
  For Each testWord In noTitleCaseWords
    If trimWord = testWord Then testResult = True
  Next

  'If it wasn't in the list,
  'capitalize first letter of word.
  If testResult = False Then
    Set initChar = wordArray(n).Characters(1)
    initChar.Text = UCase(initChar)
  End If
Next
'Capitalize first word in selection, regardless.
Set initChar = wordArray(1).Characters(1)
initChar.Text = UCase(initChar)
End Sub
```

The first thing this macro does is define a new Collection object, which for the purposes of this macro is used in much the same way an array would be. User-defined Collection objects offer the Count property for returning the number of items in the collection, the Add method for adding items, the Remove method for removing them, and the Item method for enumerating them. After defining the noTitleCaseWords collection object, we use the Add method to add words that we don't want capitalized to the list.

The next section of the macro defines an array called wordArray, each item in which holds a Range object that corresponds to a Word object in the current selection.

The For...Next loop is the heart of the macro. One quirk of the Words collection object is that each "word" really consists of the word itself and its trailing space character. The RTrim string function takes a string—in this case the text associated with each Word Range object in wordArray—and clips off the space characters on the right end of the word, if any. Therefore, we need to compare the trimmed version of each word in the array against each item in the noTitleCaseWords collection, one by one.

If a particular trimmed word is not found in the collection, testResult is set to False, and we find the Range object corresponding to the first character of the word and use the UCase string function to convert the character to uppercase. Finally, we want to capitalize the first character in the selection (we're assuming here that the selection will always be a sentence or heading), regardless of whether it was found in the exception list.

Run the TrueTitleCase macro

1   Switch to Word and click SelectTitleCaseBookmark from the Lesson10Macros menu to jump to the TitleCase bookmark that was previously defined.

2   Click TrueTitleCase to convert the selected text into title case.

When you do this, your screen should look like this:

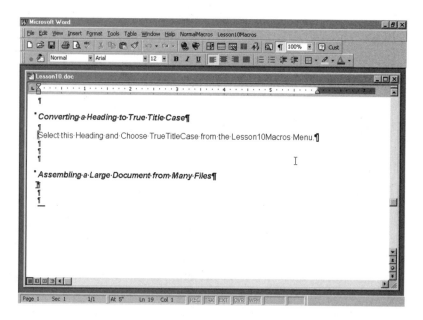

3   If you want to run the TrueTitleCase macro again, run ResetTrueTitleCaseExample on the Lesson10Macros menu, or use the TrueTitleCase macro on other text in the Less10.doc practice file.

Assembling a Large Document from Many Files

When you're working with text documents, a common and rather tedious task is assembling a series of files into one larger package, for example, when you're doing research on some subject and you're saving text files from a variety of sources such as saved e-mail messages, newsgroup articles, Web documents, and personal notes.

One way to implement such a file assembler would entail opening each file as a Word document, selecting the entire contents of each file, and pasting each passage into the destination document. Another way to do this might involve recording Word's Insert File command to insert files into the destination document one file at a time.

For this lesson, however, we'll explore the ability of Visual Basic to read files directly, using its equivalents of classical BASIC statements for performing operations with files, filenames, paths, and directories. Along the way, we'll also use a few more of the string functions to process filenames.

Our system of procedures for combining these files should do the following:

- Let the user specify a source directory containing the files to assemble.

- Create a new work directory and copy the source files into it.

- Read the list of files in the directory into an array.

- Open each text file and insert its contents into a single destination Word document.

We'll call the main macro for the system the CombineFiles procedure, which will call several other routines as needed. First, though, let's get a collection of files with which we can experiment.

Acquire a file set

To test the system, you can use a set of files on your own hard disk, such as a series of saved e-mail message files. Alternatively, you can download files from an information service such as CompuServe or via the Internet.

One interesting source for files results from the efforts of many people to provide electronic texts, or *etexts,* over the Internet. Many of these documents are in the public domain and are made available to anyone who wishes to download them. The following table lists several organizations having Web or FTP sites for the purpose of distributing etexts, from which sites you can download one or more sets of files for this lesson. (Make sure the material you want is in the public domain before you download it.)

Resource	URL
The Electronic Text Center at the University of Virginia	http://www.lib.virginia.edu/etext/ETC.html
Project Gutenberg	http://www.promo.net/pg/ ftp://uiarchive.cso.uiuc.edu/pub/etext/gutenberg/ http://uiarchive.uiuc.edu/ (search engines) gopher://spinaltap.micro.umn.edu:70/11/Gutenberg/
The On-line Books Page	http://www.cs.cmu.edu/books.html
The Eris Project	gopher://gopher.vt.edu:10010/10/33
The ETEXT Archives	http://www.etext.org/
Alex: A catalogue of Electronic Texts on the Internet	gopher://gopher.lib.ncsu.edu:70/11/library/stacks/Alex
The Eden Etext Archive	http://www.cs.rmit.edu.au/etext/
Project Bartleby	http://www.columbia.edu/acis/bartleby
Yahoo's list of electronic literature	http://www.yahoo.com/Arts/Humanities/Literature/Electronic_Literature
Internet Public Library	http://ipl.sils.umich.edu/
Library of Congress Home Page	http://lcweb.loc.gov/homepage/lchp.html
Alive and Free	http://www.c3f.com/alivfree.html

For this exercise we'll access a directory at an FTP site that contains the text of the book *Moby Dick*, by Herman Melville; each of chapter of this book is stored as a separate file. These files were prepared by Professor Eugene F. Irey of the University of Colorado, and are made available by Project Gutenberg, a volunteer effort begun in 1971 by Michael S. Hart, now at Benedictine University in Illinois, to distribute public-domain etexts. The Web site for Project Gutenberg (at http://www.promo.net/pg/) promotes the replication and distribution of public-domain classics and lists approximately 1000 etexts stored at the site.

Create the InsertHyperlink macro

You can download the files for this lesson using a Web browser such as Microsoft Internet Explorer or Netscape Navigator. We want the files at the FTP site specified by the URL (for Universal Resource Locator) ftp://uiarchive.cso.uiuc.edu/pub/etext/gutenberg/etext91/. Just for fun, though, let's automate the process of using a hyperlink to jump to the FTP site so that you can download the files.

1   In the Visual Basic Editor, right-click in the Project Explorer window, click Insert, and then click Module.

The Visual Basic Editor inserts a new module.

2   In the Properties window, change the name of the module from *Module1* to **Internet**.

3   In the Internet module, enter the following code:

```
Sub InsertHyperlink()
  'Go to Internet bookmark in Less10.doc.
  Selection.GoTo _
    What:=wdGoToBookmark, _
    Name:="Internet"
  'Enter a heading, in Heading 3 style.
  Selection.InsertAfter _
    "FTP site for text files"
  Selection.Style = "Heading 3"
  'Add a carriage return.
  Selection.InsertAfter vbCr
  'Move insertion point to beginning of next line.
  Selection.Collapse Direction:=wdCollapseEnd
  Selection.Style = "Normal"

  'Edit ftpServer and ftpPath for the site
  'from which you want to download text files.
  ftpServer = "ftp://uiarchive.cso.uiuc.edu/"
  ftpPath = "pub/etext/gutenberg/etext91/"
  ActiveDocument.Hyperlinks.Add _
    Anchor:=Selection.Range, _
    Address:=ftpServer + ftpPath, _
    SubAddress:=""

  'Jump to location of first hyperlink in document.
  If ActiveDocument.Hyperlinks.Count >= 1 Then
    MsgBox _
      Prompt:=ActiveDocument.Hyperlinks(1).Address, _
      Title:="InsertHyperlink Macro"
    ActiveDocument.Hyperlinks(1).Follow _
      NewWindow:=True
  End If
End Sub
```

This macro jumps to the Internet bookmark in the Less10.doc practice file, inserts a heading in the Heading 3 style, moves the insertion point to the beginning of the next line, and changes back to the Normal style.

Next, the macro defines the ftpServer and ftpPath variables (solely for the purpose of avoiding a line that would otherwise be too long in the code listing). The Add method of the Hyperlink object adds a hyperlink to the Less10 practice file. The Anchor argument of the Add method specifies the location of the hyperlink in the active document. The Address argument specifies a destination URL to which the hyperlink points. In this case, the URL points to an FTP site, but you could also specify any of the following destinations (we've also reproduced this table in the Less10 practice file, which contains active hyperlinks for the listed destinations):

Prefix	Type of URL, and example
ftp://	Opens a window on an FTP site. ftp://uiarchive.cso.uiuc.edu/pub/etext/gutenberg/etext91/ A directory at Project Gutenberg.
http://	Opens a window on a Web page. http://www.halcyon.com/chris/ Chris Kinata's home page.
file://	Opens the file, probably using Word. file://c:/MyDocuments/MyNovel.doc A document on your hard disk (assuming this is a valid path for your system).
gopher://	Connects to a gopher server. gopher://gopher.vt.edu:10010/10/33 The Eris Project gopher server.
mailto://	Sends mail to the specified address. mailto://chris@halcyon.com/ Sends mail to Chris Kinata.
telnet://	Opens a telnet connection (a command-line interface) with a remote computer. telnet://halcyon.com/ (You would replace *halcyon* with the name of your server.)
news://	Opens a window displaying newsgroup articles for the specified newsgroup. news://news.halycon.com/ (You would replace *halcyon* with the name of your server.)

The SubAddress argument specifies a location inside the destination document; in the case of a Web document in the HTML format, this would be an anchor in the HTML document. If the destination document belongs to Word, this would be a bookmark.

Finally, the macro checks for the existence of hyperlinks in the active document using the Count property of the Hyperlinks collection object, presents a message box that displays the name of the URL pointed to in the hyperlink, and uses the Follow method to jump to the destination of the hyperlink itself.

Run the InsertHyperlink macro

1 Switch to Word and run the macro. (If you're using the prepared routine in the Less10 practice file, click InsertHyperlink from the Lesson10Macros menu.)

Word sends a message to Windows to log onto your Internet service provider, launches your browser (such as Microsoft Internet Explorer or Netscape Navigator), and tells it to jump to the specified FTP site. If the logon process doesn't work correctly or your browser doesn't launch as expected, log on manually, start your browser, and run the macro again.

2 In your browser, scroll down the list of files at the FTP site and click moby.zip.

Your browser attempts to download the file, and may present you with a dialog box asking whether you should decompress this .zip file, or save it to disk. If you save the file to disk, use a utility such as WinZip to decompress it, and make sure the extracted files reside in a new directory. (If you don't have WinZip, you can download it from the Web site at www.shareware.com.)

What happens when you click on a hyperlink depends on the URL specified in the hyperlink. If the URL prefix is *http://*, *ftp://*, or *gopher://*, your Web browser will load the file and display a window containing the destination document. If the URL points to a Web address, but no file is specified, your browser will try to open the default documents welcome.html or index.html. If the URL prefix is *file://* and the document is a Word document, Word itself will open the file and display a document window for the file.

If the URL specifies a document rather than a directory, Word may try to open the document regardless of its file type.

Set up the CombineFiles system

1 In the Visual Basic Editor, right-click in the Project Explorer window, click Insert, and then click Module.

The Visual Basic Editor inserts a new module.

2 In the Properties window, change the name of the module from *Module1* to **FileOps**.

3 In the FileOps module, enter the following code:

```
Dim fileList(200) As String      'Max 200 filenames.
Dim maxFileNum As Integer        'Max array index.
Dim sourcePath As String         'Path to source file directory.
Dim destPath As String           'Path to working directory.
Dim baseFilename As String       'Filename without extension.

Sub CombineFiles()
  Selection.GoTo _
    What:=wdGoToBookmark, _
    Name:="AssembleDoc"
  SetupWorkDir
  ReadFileList sourcePath

  Selection.TypeText _
    Text:="_____original file list" + vbCr
  WriteFileListToDoc

  CopyFilesToWorkDir
  ReadFileList destPath

  SortFileList
  Selection.TypeText _
    Text:="_____sorted file list" + vbCr
  WriteFileListToDoc
  AppendFiles

End Sub
```

At the beginning of the module, we define several global variables that we use to store the list of files and the location of the directory containing the source files, and we specify a working directory to which we'll copy the files so that they can be processed without tampering with the originals.

The CombineFiles procedure uses the Less10.doc practice file to record progress in assembling the files in the working directory into one document. The first step in the macro moves the current selection to the AssembleDoc bookmark in the Less10.doc document so that subsequent instructions to record the progress of the macro will be recorded there.

Next, we call the SetupWorkDir procedure, which prompts the user for the location of the source file directory stored in sourcePath and creates a new working directory stored in destPath.

The ReadFileList procedure takes a pathname as an argument and reads the filenames in the specified directory into the fileList array. CombineFiles then enters a tag in the Less10.doc document and calls the WriteFileListToDoc procedure, which inserts a list of each filename into the Less10.doc document.

The CopyFilesToWorkDir procedure copies each file in the file set into the working directory stored in the destPath variable. There's one complication, though: the files in the Moby Dick file set have names in the form *moby.x*, where *x* is the sequential number of the file: *moby.0, moby.1, moby.2,* and so on. The problem with this is that sorting the files based on this format of numeric file extension results in a sequence that begins

```
moby.0
moby.1
moby.10
moby.100
moby.101
...
moby.109
moby.11
moby.110
```

and so on. Clearly, assembling the files in this order will result in a very confusing novel. We need to change the format of the numeric extension from *.x* to *.xxx*, so that the sorted list will look like

```
moby.000
moby.001
moby.002
moby.003
```

and so on. The CopyFilesToWorkDir procedure performs this task, so that the SortFileList routine will be able to sort the fileList array correctly. After fileList has been sorted, another call to the WriteFileListToDoc procedure inserts the filenames into the Less10.doc document so that we can verify the list has been sorted correctly.

Finally, the AppendFiles procedure creates a new document, opens each filename in the series, and appends its contents at the end of the document.

Create the SetupWorkDir procedure

➤ In the FileOps module and after the CombineFiles procedure, enter the following code:

```
Sub SetupWorkDir()
   'Ask user to find the source directory.
   msg1 = "Change to the directory containing the files"
   msg2 = "you want to append, and then click Cancel."
   msgTot = msg1 + vbCr + msg2
   msgStyle = vbYesNo
   msgTitle = "SetupWorkDir Macro"
   answer = MsgBox(msgTot, msgStyle, msgTitle)
   If answer = vbNo Then End
```

233

```
'Do File Open dialog to find name of directory.
dialogAnswer = Dialogs(wdDialogFileOpen).Show
'MsgBox dialogAnswer
sourcePath = CurDir

'Get the parent directory
'by finding last directory in pathname.
lastSlash = Len(sourcePath) - 1
While Mid(sourcePath, lastSlash, 1) <> "\"
  lastSlash = lastSlash - 1
Wend
parentPath = Left(sourcePath, lastSlash)
sourceDir = Mid(sourcePath, lastSlash + 1, 999)
destDir = sourceDir + "2"
destPath = parentPath + destDir + "\"
sourcePath = sourcePath + "\"

'Show msgbox requesting to proceed.
msgT = "Reading files from source path:" + vbCr
msgT = msgT + sourcePath + vbCr + vbCr
msgT = msgT + "Source Directory: " + vbCr
msgT = msgT + sourceDir + vbCr + vbCr
msgT = msgT + "Parent path:" + vbCr
msgT = msgT + parentPath + vbCr + vbCr
msgT = msgT + "To destination path:" + vbCr + destPath
msgStyle = vbYesNo + vbInformation
answer = MsgBox(msgT, msgStyle, msgTitle)
If answer = vbNo Then Exit Sub

'Create working directory within parent directory.
MkDir destPath
End Sub
```

The main idea behind the SetupWorkDir procedure is that we can use Word's standard File Open dialog box to set the current directory to that containing the files we want to combine. The procedure begins by presenting a message box that looks like this:

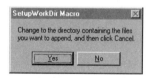

Next, the statement

```
dialogAnswer = Dialogs(wdDialogFileOpen).Show
```

uses the Show method on the Dialogs collection object, which belongs to the Word Application object, to present the Open dialog box, shown here:

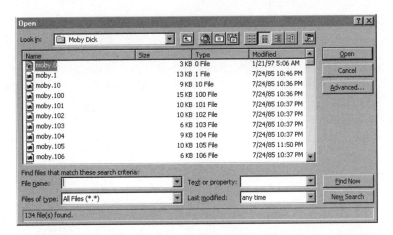

The user opens the directory containing the original files and then clicks Cancel to set the current directory. The complete pathname of the directory is returned by the CurDir Function and stored in the sourcePath variable. On our machine, this pathname looks like

```
C:\!My Documents\Work\VBWSBS\Lesson10\Moby Dick
```

The next task is to take this pathname and extract the path to its parent directory, as well as the name of the source directory without the path, which we use to construct the name of the working directory. The idea here is to determine the location of the last backslash character in the pathname; once we know the position of this character in the string, we can use it to extract both the pathname of the parent directory and the name of the source directory itself. The block of code that does this is a little tricky, so we'll take it apart line by line.

The first statement in this block,

```
lastSlash = Len(sourcePath) - 1
```

uses the Len string function to find the number of characters in the string stored in sourcePath and then backs up one character position.

The While...Wend block,

```
While Mid(sourcePath, lastSlash, 1) <> "\"
   lastSlash = lastSlash - 1
Wend
```

uses the Mid string function to return a single character (the "1" argument) from sourcePath, given the starting position stored in lastSlash. The first value of lastSlash is one less than the length of the string; if that wasn't a backslash character, we subtract one from this position and try it again. After a few iterations, the loop finds the last backslash character in the pathname.

The next two statements,

```
parentPath = Left(sourcePath, lastSlash)
sourceDir = Mid(sourcePath, lastSlash + 1, 999)
```

use the Left and Mid string functions and the character position stored in lastSlash to separate the parent directory, stored in parentPath, from the name of the directory itself, stored in sourceDir.

The last few statements in this block,

```
destDir = sourceDir + "2"
destPath = parentPath + destDir + "\"
sourcePath = sourcePath + "\"
```

construct the name of the working directory by appending the character *2* to the name, and then they construct the full pathname of the destination directory by concatenating the names of the parent directory, the working directory, and a final backslash.

Now that we've taken care of the messy details of determining where we're going to put everything, we present the second message box, which looks like this (if you run the macro on your computer, the pathnames will be different than those shown here):

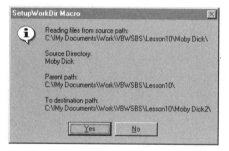

The last statement in the macro uses the ChDir statement to set the current directory to the pathname stored in destPath.

Now that everything is set up, we need to be able to transfer the names of all the files in a specified directory to the fileList array so that we can work with them.

Create the ReadFileList procedure

> In the FileOps module and after the SetupWorkDir procedure, enter the following code:

```
Sub ReadFileList(pathname)
  'Read list of files into filename array.
  ChDir pathname
  thisFile = Dir(pathname)
  fileList(0) = thisFile
  gettingFiles = True
  fileNum = 1
  While gettingFiles
    'Get the next file.
    thisFile = Dir()

    'If no file then thisFile = ""
    If thisFile = "" Then
      gettingFiles = False
    Else
      'Store filename in the array.
      fileList(fileNum) = thisFile
      fileNum = fileNum + 1
    End If
  Wend
  'Reset the max file number.
  maxFileNum = fileNum - 1
End Sub
```

The ReadFileList procedure takes the pathname to look in as an argument for the list of filenames, and the ChDir statement uses this to set the current directory.

The Dir function is a little tricky. It takes a pathname to look in as an argument; the first time you call the Dir function, it returns the name of the first file found in the specified directory, which we store in fileList(0).

Later calls to the Dir function without using an argument return the next filenames in the directory. When there are no more files in the specified directory, Dir returns a null string—in Visual Basic, this is encoded as two quotes with nothing in between. The If...Then...Else block tests for this: if there are no more files, then the macro exits the While...Wend loop; otherwise, it stores the filename in the next available element of the fileList array.

Finally, since maxFileNum is incremented after storing a filename in the fileList array, the macro sets it back one position so that the number of filenames stored in the array is accurate.

Now let's create a routine for printing a list of these filenames in the active document—in this case, the Less10.doc practice file.

237

Create the WriteFileListToDoc procedure

In the FileOps module and after the GetASCII procedure, enter the following code:

```
Sub WriteFileListToDoc()
'For debugging, enter filename
'into the active document.
  For n = 0 To maxFileNum
    Selection.TypeText _
      Text:=CStr(n) + ": " + fileList(n) + vbCr
  Next
End Sub
```

This is a very simple routine that enters every element in the fileList array into the active document, on its own line and preceded by the element's index number in the array.

After you run the CombineFiles macro (we'll get to that in a bit), you can switch to the Less10.doc document and look at the order in which filenames were entered into the fileList array, as shown here:

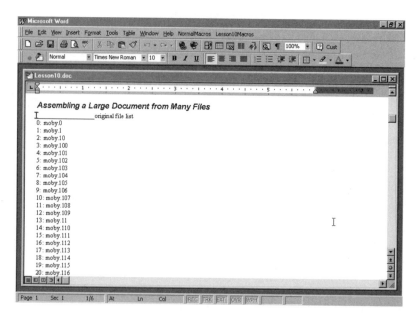

Notice that the files in this list have filenames in the form *moby.x,* where *x* is the sequential number of the file. Obviously, these names will need to be sorted so that we can assemble the files in the correct order. To do this, we'll need to copy

238

all the files in the list from the source directory (stored in sourcePath) to the working directory (stored in destPath). We'll reformat the file extensions at the same time, so that they can be sorted properly later.

Create the CopyFilesToWorkDir procedure

➤ In the FileOps module and after the WriteFileListToDoc procedure, enter the following code:

```
Sub CopyFilesToWorkDir()
  For n = 0 To maxFileNum
    thisFile = fileList(n)
    sourceFilename = sourcePath + thisFile

    'Parse the filename and pad zeroes at left end.
    dotPos = InStr(1, thisFile, ".")
    extension = Mid(thisFile, dotPos + 1, 999)
    baseFilename = Left(thisFile, dotPos - 1)
    While Len(extension) <> 3
      extension = "0" + extension
    Wend

    newFileName = baseFilename + "." + extension
    destFilename = destPath + newFileName
    FileCopy sourceFilename, destFilename
  Next
End Sub
```

The CopyFilesToWorkDir procedure consists only of a For...Next loop that iterates once for every filename in fileList. The core of the routine is in the statement

```
FileCopy sourceFilename, destFilename
```

which copies a file from one place to another, given the full pathname of each file.

The single complication is that we want to pad each file extension with zeros, turning (for example) *moby.1* into *moby.001*, so that we can read the file list in the working directory and sort the names in the fileList array into their proper order.

To do this, we use the InStr string function to determine the location of the "." in the filename, starting from the first character of the filename and continuing to the right. We know there's only one instance of a period character in a filename, so we don't have to worry about finding the correct instance of the desired character, as we did when finding the rightmost backslash character in the SetupWorkDir routine described earlier in this lesson.

Using the position of the period stored in dotPos, we split the filename into the extension and the base filename. Once we have the extension, we use the While...Wend loop to check the number of characters in the extension; if the length of the extension isn't three characters, we need to add another 0.

Finally, we assemble the new destination filename and copy the file from the source directory to the destination directory.

At this point, the CombineFiles routine uses the ReadFileList procedure described earlier to update the fileList array with the new filenames and then calls the SortFileList routine.

Create the SortFileList procedure

➤ In the FileOps module and after the CopyFilesToWorkDir procedure, enter the following code:

```
Sub SortFileList()
'Crude bubble sort technique.
  For m = 1 To maxFileNum
    For n = 1 To maxFileNum - 1
      If fileList(n) > fileList(n + 1) Then
        temp = fileList(n)
        fileList(n) = fileList(n + 1)
        fileList(n + 1) = temp
      End If
    Next
  Next
End Sub
```

This routine implements what programmers call a "bubble-sort" algorithm, in which each pair of items is compared—in this case, the pairs of filenames stored in the fileList array—up to the maximum number of filenames stored in the array. If the first item in the pair is "greater" (that is, follows the second item in alphabetic order), then the two items are swapped, using the temp variable for interim storage.

To take an example, let's assume that the first few entries in the fileList array are

fileList(1)	moby.003
fileList(2)	moby.001
fileList(3)	moby.002

In this case, the first pass through the inner For...Next loop looks at fileList(1) and fileList(2); since *moby.003* is "greater" than *moby.001,* the two items are swapped, which produces the list

fileList(1)   moby.001

fileList(2)   moby.003

fileList(3)   moby.002

In the second pass, fileList(2) is compared with fileList(3); again, since *moby.003* is "greater" than *moby.002,* the two items are swapped. Each iteration through the inner For...Next loop has the effect of moving a single item to its correct order in the list. The outer loop iterates through the list once for every item in the list so that each item finds its proper place. This is possibly the simplest sorting method possible; it's easy to understand, but it sorts lists more slowly than more efficient algorithms.

After the filenames have been sorted, the CombineFiles routine calls the WriteFileListToDoc procedure to list the fileList array in the Less10.doc document, as shown here:

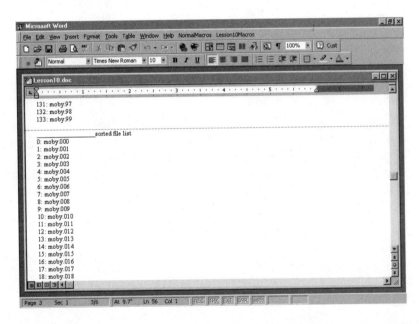

All that remains is to use the sorted fileList to create the collection document for the file set.

Create the AppendFiles procedure

➤ In the FileOps module and after the SortFileList procedure, enter the following code:

```
Sub AppendFiles()
   'Create new doc.
   Documents.Add

   If ActiveWindow.View.SplitSpecial = wdPaneNone Then
      ActiveWindow.ActivePane.View.Type = wdNormalView
   Else
      ActiveWindow.View.Type = wdNormalView
   End If

   'With each file in the array,
   For n = 0 To maxFileNum
     'Open the file.
     Open fileList(n) For Input As #1
     Do While Not EOF(1) ' Loop until end of file.
       thisChar = Input(1, #1) ' Get one character.
       Selection.TypeText Text:=thisChar
     Loop
     Close #1  ' Close file.
   Next
End Sub
```

The first part of this procedure consists of recorded actions in Word to create a new document. The second part consists of two loops. The outer For...Next loop iterates once for every filename in the fileList array; the first task inside this loop is to use an Open statement to open the specified file for input as a sequential text file; the *#1* is a file number assigned to the file that is referenced in the Input file function inside the Do While loop.

The Input function takes two arguments: the first is the number of bytes to read from the file, and the second is the file number of the open file. Each character read is stored in the thisChar variable, and entered in the new document, one character at a time. While there are still characters to read, the EOF file function (EOF stands for *End Of File*) returns False; when there are no more characters to read from the file, the EOF function returns True, and the Do While loop ends. The Close statement closes the file, and the macro moves on to the next file.

Run the CombineFiles procedure

> Switch back to Word, and click the CombineFiles command from the Lesson10Macros menu.

When you do this, the routine presents the dialog boxes shown earlier in this lesson and inserts both the presorted and sorted file lists in the Less10.doc document. Then there's a long pause while the AppendFiles routine inserts the contents of each file into the collection document. When done, the new document should look like this:

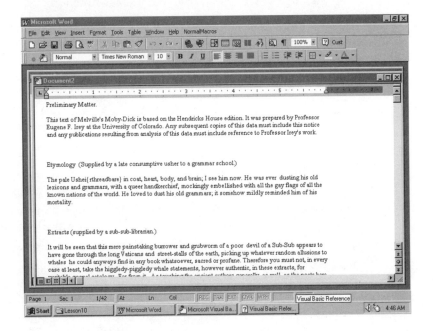

![elephant icon] **TIP** If you wanted to adapt this system of macros so that it didn't renumber and sort the file list, making it more general purpose, you could skip the WriteListToDoc and SortList procedures and one instance of the ReadList procedure. Another idea would be to insert the name of each file as a Level 1 heading before reading in the file and then use Word's Outline View to rearrange the parts of the collection document. Finally, you could also create a UserForm that lets you choose options for combining documents.

If you want to continue to the next lesson

> Keep Word and Word's Visual Basic Editor running, and turn to Lesson 11.

If you want to stop for now

➤ Switch to Word, and click Exit from the File menu. If you see a Save dialog box, click Yes.

Lesson Sumary

To	Do this
Get the ASCII value of a character	Use the Asc function.
Get the Unicode value of a character	Use the AscW function.
Work with the case of each character in the selected text	Use a For Each loop with the Characters collection object. For example: ```For Each thisChar in Selection.Range.Characters() ...your code Next thisChar```
Concatenate two text strings	Use the & or + operator. For example, "Moby " + "Dick" evaluates to *Moby Dick*.
Remove trailing spaces from text	Use the RTrim function. For example, *RTrim("Hello ")* evaluates to *Hello*.
Change a character to uppercase	Use the UCase function. For example, *UCase("a")* evaluates to *A*.
Display a built-in dialog box	Use the Show method on a member of the Dialogs collection. For example, *dialogAnswer = Dialogs(wdDialogFileOpen).Show*.
Find the number of characters in a text string	Use the Len function. For example, *Len("Hello")* evaluates to *5*.
Return a string inside another string	Use the Mid function. For example, *Mid("Hello", 2,1)* evaluates to *e*. Or, use the Left or Right functions; for example, *Right("Hello",2)* evaluates to *lo*.
Find the position of one string in another	Use the InStr function. For example, *InStr(1, "MyVacation.doc",".")* evaluates to *11*.
Open a text file for input	Use the Open statement. For example: ```Open "MyDoc.txt" For Input As #1```
Read one or more characters from a text file	Use the Input function. For example, *Input(1, #1)* returns one character from file #1.
Close a text file	Use the Close statement. For example, *Close #1* closes file #1.

For online information about	On the Visual Basic Help menu, click Contents And Index, click the Contents tab, open Microsoft Word Visual Basic Reference, click the Index tab, and then
String functions	Search for "returning strings from functions"
Creating user-defined collection objects	Search for "collection object"
Working with direct file access	Search for "writing data to files," "Input # statement," or "Open statement"
Displaying Word's built-in dialog boxes	Search for "Dialog Object" or "Dialogs Collection Object"

Preview of the Next Lesson

In the next lesson, you'll learn about using Automation in a Word macro to control another Office application, such as Microsoft Excel or PowerPoint.

Using Microsoft Office Application Objects

Estimated time
50 min.

In this lesson you will learn how to:

- Use Automation to manipulate Microsoft Office application objects.
- Use Excel's Pmt function to compute a loan payment from a Word macro.
- Use Excel's Pivot Table feature to summarize the information in a Word table.
- Open and run a PowerPoint presentation in a Word document.
- Use Word 97 application objects in a Visual Basic 5.0 program.

Throughout this book, you've explored the essential application objects in the Word 97 object model, and you've learned how to manipulate them with properties, methods, and a variety of Visual Basic statements and control structures. In this lesson, you'll expand your programming repertoire by learning how to use the application objects in other Microsoft Office applications. You'll learn how to use Excel 97 and PowerPoint 97 objects in a Word macro, and you'll learn how to use Word 97 objects in a program created for the Visual Basic 5.0 compiler. These skills will help you extend your Visual Basic programming expertise into new areas, and help you build integrated solutions that leverage the strengths of each application in the Microsoft Office application suite.

Automating Microsoft Office Applications

Automation (previously known as OLE Automation) is a Microsoft technology that allows one application to access the commands and features of another application remotely. In plain English, this means that you can use Excel's Pivot Table feature from within a Word macro without spending the time to write the Pivot Table feature yourself or knowing exactly how it goes about its business. Automation lets you expand your existing macros by integrating the best features of other applications without the development costs—you simply access the application objects with the necessary arguments, and let Automation do the rest!

Not all Windows-based applications support Automation, only those that have been specifically designed to make available, or *expose,* their functionality via an object model with recognizable properties, methods, and events. The Windows-based applications that do expose their objects are called *object* or *server* applications, and the programs that use these objects are called *controlling* or *client* applications. Currently, the following Microsoft applications can be used as either object or controlling applications:

- Microsoft Word 97
- Microsoft PowerPoint 97
- Microsoft Access 97, Microsoft Access 95
- Microsoft Excel 97, Microsoft Excel 95, Microsoft Excel 5.0
- Microsoft Outlook 97 (custom forms developed with the VBScript language)
- Microsoft Project 97, Microsoft Project 95
- Microsoft Visual Basic 5.0 Compiler, Microsoft Visual Basic 4.0 Compiler

Each application provides its own Visual Basic programming language, and in many cases, more than one version is supported.

 NOTE Microsoft is currently licensing the Visual Basic for Applications programming language, so you'll soon find other applications for Windows that support object Automation and Visual Basic macros.

Using Automation in Word 97

Creating a Word macro that uses the features of an object application is a straightforward process. First, you need to add a reference to the object library you want to use in your macro, and determine how the commands you want to run translate into the object application's object model. Then you need to complete a few simple programming steps, which include declaring an object variable, using the object's methods and properties, and releasing the object's memory space when you're finished. The following list details the steps you need to follow.

Step 1 Add a reference to the object library you want to use in your macro module by using the References command on the Tools menu. After you activate the object library, you can browse the objects, properties, and methods it exposes by using the Visual Basic Object Browser.

 NOTE The object library for each application that supports Automation is installed automatically when you run the application's setup program. If you plan to distribute your macro, be sure that each computer in your workgroup has a copy of the object application software.

Step 2 Write your Word macro. In the procedure in which you plan to use Automation, create an object variable by using the Dim statement, and then load an Automation object into the object variable by using the CreateObject function. This example creates a PowerPoint object variable:

```
Dim ppt As Object          'use ppt as variable name
Set ppt = CreateObject("Powerpoint.Application.8")
```

Step 3 Use the methods and properties of the Automation object in the procedure, consulting the Help files in the Object Browser or the object application documentation for the proper syntax. These PowerPoint statements display the PowerPoint user interface, open a presentation, and run the slide show:

```
ppt.Visible = True         'open and run presentation
ppt.Presentations.Open  "C:\WordVB\Less11\pptfacts.ppt"
ppt.ActivePresentation.SlideShowSettings.Run
```

Step 4 When you've finished using the object application, release the object variable to conserve memory:

```
Set ppt = Nothing          'release object variable
```

In the following exercise, you'll create a Word macro that uses the Excel 97 Pmt function to calculate loan payments. The macro will be built entirely in Word, using the functionality of Excel via Automation.

Automating Excel from Word

If you've spent much time using Excel, you know that it contains a wealth of functions designed to calculate financial values, mathematical and statistical results, date and time calculations, and much more. Word doesn't provide access to these tools, so most Word users simply switch to Excel or pull out their Hewlett-Packard calculators when complex formulas come up in their documents. Automation solves this problem, however; with a few program statements, you can use any Excel function in a macro. Let's give it a try.

NOTE To complete the following steps, you'll need Excel 97 installed on your computer. (If you have Office 97 installed, you're all set.) You can also use Excel 95 or Excel 5.0 to practice Automation, but since the Excel object model has changed a little between versions, you'll need to make a few modifications to the statements you use. See the Excel Visual Basic online Help for details.

Create the ExcelPMT macro

Complete the following steps to build a macro that computes the monthly payment for a loan using the Excel Pmt function.

TIP You can either create the ExcelPMT macro from scratch now or open the Less11 document in the \WordVB\Less11 folder and run the ExcelPMT macro we created for you.

1   From the Word Tools menu, click Macro, and then click Macros.

2   Type **ExcelPMT** in the Name text box, and then verify that Less11 is selected in the Macros In drop-down list.

3   Click Create.

Word starts the Visual Basic Editor and opens a new macro procedure named ExcelPMT in the Code window.

4   From the Tools menu, click References, and then select the Excel 8.0 Object Library.

The Excel 8.0 Object Library is required for Automation. Your References dialog box will look similar to the following:

The Excel.Sheet object opens Excel and creates a new worksheet object.

5 Now type the following program statements in the Code window:

```
Dim xl As Object                        'create object variable
Dim loanpmt, msg$
If Selection.Type = wdSelectionNormal Then 'if text is selected
    Set xl = CreateObject("Excel.Sheet")   'create Excel object
    loanpmt = xl.Application.WorksheetFunction.Pmt(0.19 / 12, _
    36, Selection.text)                  'call Excel Pmt function

    msg$ = "The monthly payment at 19% interest over 36 months is "
    MsgBox msg$ & Format(Abs(loanpmt), "$#.##") 'show payment
    xl.Application.Quit                  'quit Excel
    Set xl = Nothing                     'release object variable
Else
    MsgBox "No principal amount selected"
End If
```

This macro creates an object variable named xl and uses the CreateObject function to assign the Excel.Sheet object to the variable if a number has been selected in the Word document. (The macro uses the selected number for the principal amount. If no text is selected, the Else statement displays the message *No principal amount selected*.) The macro

251

then calls the Excel Pmt function through the WorksheetFunction object, which is a member of the Excel Application object.

This particular call to the Pmt function specifies a 19 percent annual interest rate (calculated monthly), a 36-month payment term, and a principal amount that has been entered by the user. In this case, Excel runs invisibly "behind the scenes," but you can also make Excel appear and interact with the program, as you'll see in the next macro. After the Pmt function call, the macro displays the calculation results in a message box formatted for currency with the Format function. Normally, Excel displays a negative number for loan payments (because it is money that you pay out), but here we've used the Abs (absolute value) function to make the output a positive number.

Run the macro

Now run the macro to see how Excel Automation works.

View Microsoft Word

1 Click the View Microsoft Word button on the Visual Basic Editor toolbar.

Word displays the Less11 document.

2 Type **$1000**, and then select the amount you just typed, which represents the loan principal. (You may include the dollar sign or spaces in your selection, but don't select the carriage return symbol—it will cause the macro to fail.)

3 Run the ExcelPMT macro.

Word starts Excel via Automation and computes the periodic payments that are required for the loan principal you selected. The result ($36.66) is displayed in a message box:

4 Now move the insertion pointer elsewhere in your document (that is, make no selection), so that you can test the Else statement in the macro.

5 Run ExcelPMT again.

The message *No principal amount selected* is displayed on the screen.

Use the Object Browser to view Excel objects

The previous Automation example worked pretty well when we identified exactly which Excel objects and functions you should use and how you should go about typing them. But what if you want to experiment with a few different Excel objects using Automation? How would you determine which objects, properties, and methods to use? Once again, the solution is the Visual Basic Object Browser, which lets you explore each of the objects in the object library you're connected to. Since you've already established a link to the Excel 8.0 object library, give the Object Browser a try now to learn more about Excel functions.

To use the Object Browser to discover how to use the Excel Rate function, which determines the rate of return for an investment, follow these steps:

1 From the Visual Basic View menu, click Object Browser.

The Object Browser opens in the Visual Basic Editor. As you learned in Lesson 7, the Object Browser contains a Project/Library drop-down list, which you can use to display the object libraries included in your project. It also contains a Search list for creating keyword searches, and a Classes list, which you can use to select a particular object to examine. When you select an object in the Classes list, the methods, properties, and events featured in the object are listed in the Members list.

2 Open the Project/Library list, and then click the Excel Object Library.

A list of the Automation objects exposed by Excel fills the Classes list. By selecting only the Excel Library, you will narrow your search to only Excel objects.

3 Click the Search list, type **rate**, and then press ENTER.

The keyword search produces one entry in the Search list, an Excel worksheet function named Rate.

4   Click Rate in the Search list.

The location of the Rate function in the Excel object model is displayed in the Classes and Members lists, and the syntax for the Rate function is displayed at the bottom of the Object Browser.

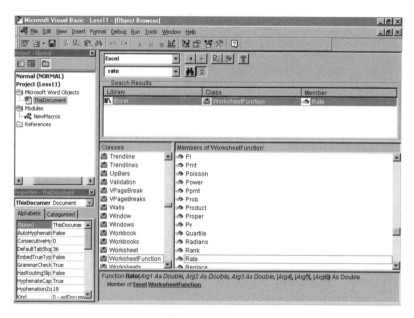

5   Click Help in the Object Browser to display the Excel Help file associated with worksheet functions.

Help

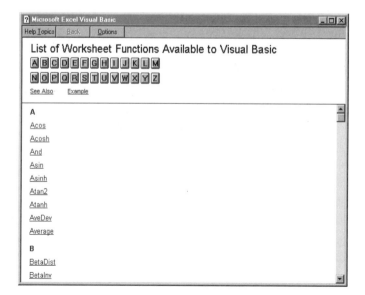

6 Click the R button in the Help file, and then click Rate.

The Help file for the Rate function appears. Rate determines the interest rate returned by an investment when the investment principal, the number of payments, and the total gain are known. It is a close companion to Pmt, and it's useful for determining the "seaworthiness" of a potential investment.

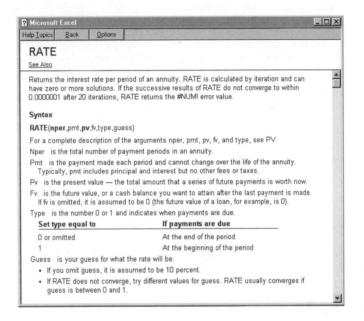

 TIP Most object libraries provide Help files that detail how a particular object, method, or property in the application's object model should be used. It's not always easy to find a quick solution for your Automation goals, because different applications have different object models, and different techniques are often required for working with selected text, copying data, and executing commands. But looking in the object library's Help files is the best way to get started.

7 Review the article on the Rate function, and then close the Help file.

8 Click the Close button in the Object Browser.

You've finished exploring Excel functions. Now let's move on to a more significant Automation example.

Using Excel's Pivot Table Feature

The most sophisticated data management feature in Excel is the Pivot Table command, which allows you to create new views of tabular information by "pivoting" rows into columns and columns into rows. Pivot tables let you customize how the data in a table is represented, and give you the option of including summary information that can be useful in reports and other documents. If you work with tables often in Word, you can write a macro that uses Excel's Pivot Table feature remotely through Automation.

In the next exercise, you'll create a macro that copies a table from Word into Excel and then creates a pivot table. The following illustration shows what the transformation will look like, which you may find helpful should you choose to use the macro in your own work.

Sales Table in Word

Sales Rep	Region	Month	Sale	Description
Anderson, Rhea	South	February	$700	Advance orders, front list
Anderson, Rhea	South	February	$1,400	Educational kits
Anderson, Rhea	South	January	$750	Educational kits
Blickle, Peter	West	February	$600	Advance orders, front list
Blickle, Peter	West	January	$1,100	Misc. backlist books
Blickle, Peter	West	January	$500	Misc. backlist books
Cashel, Seamus	Midwest	January	$1,200	Advance orders, front list
Cashel, Seamus	Midwest	January	$1000	Educational kits
Cashel, Seamus	Midwest	February	$450	Misc. backlist orders
Greif, Jacob	East	January	$1,000	Advance orders, front list
Greif, Jacob	East	January	$250	Advance orders, front list
Greif, Jacob	East	February	$800	Misc. backlist orders

Pivot Table in Excel

	A	B	C	D	E	F
1	Sum of Sale	Sales Rep				
2	Month	Anderson, Rhea	Blickle, Peter	Cashel, Seamus	Greif, Jacob	Grand Total
3	January	750	1600	2200	1250	5800
4	February	2100	600	450	800	3950
5	Grand Total	2850	2200	2650	2050	9750
6						

Create the PivotTable macro

Complete the following steps to build a macro that converts a Word table into an Excel pivot table.

 TIP You can either create the PivotTable macro from scratch now, or you can open the Less11 document in the \WordVB\Less11 folder and run the PivotTable macro we created for you.

---

1   From the Word Tools menu, click Macro, and then click Macros.

2   Type **PivotTable** in the Name text box, and then verify that Less11 is selected in the Macros In list.

3   Click Create.

Word starts the Visual Basic Editor and opens a new macro procedure named PivotTable in the Code window.

4 From the Tools menu, click References, and then verify that the Excel 8.0 Object Library is selected.

The Excel 8.0 Object Library is required to start Excel and create a pivot table. However, you only need to make one object library reference per module, so the one you made in the ExcelPMT exercise will work here, too.

5 Now type the following program statements in the Code window:

```
Dim xl As Object
Dim oTable, myRange, aCell, r, c

If Selection.Information(wdWithInTable) = True Then
    Set oTable = Selection.Tables(1)
    Set xl = CreateObject("Excel.Sheet") 'start Excel
    xl.Application.Visible = True          'show Excel
    r = 0                                  'initialize row count
    Do   'copy each table cell from Word to Excel
        r = r + 1                          'increment row count
        c = 0                              'initialize column count
        For Each aCell In oTable.Rows(r).Cells  'loop through rows
            c = c + 1                      'increment column
            Set myRange = aCell.Range      'get value w/out cell mark
            myRange.MoveEnd Unit:=wdCharacter, Count:=-1
            xl.ActiveSheet.Cells(r, c).Value = _
                Format(myRange, "#.#")     'copy cell to worksheet
        Next aCell
    Loop Until r = oTable.Rows.Count       'loop once for each row
    'Finally, create pivot table in Excel with Pivot Table wizard
    xl.Application.Dialogs(xlDialogPivotTableWizard).Show
    'Then save worksheet for later use
    xl.Application.Dialogs(xlDialogSaveAs).Show
    Set xl = Nothing                       'release object variable
Else
    MsgBox "Insertion point not in a table"
End If
```

The most involved part of this macro is copying the selected Word table to a new Excel worksheet using Visual Basic program code. Unfortunately, Word and Excel use a slightly different table format in their macro languages, so you can't copy the selected Word table to Excel directly or use it as a remote data source for the Pivot Table wizard. Instead, you need to copy the Word table to Excel one cell at a time and then run the Pivot Table wizard after the new worksheet is in place. Fortunately, the Do and For...Each loops you learned about in Lesson 3 make this an easy task. The loops in this routine use an object variable named oTable to hold the current Word table, and an object variable named aCell to hold the current table cell. The For...Each loop locates each cell in the table with the r (row) and c (column) variables, and the myRange object is used to remove the end-of-cell mark from each cell in the Word table before it gets copied. If you don't remove these end-of-cell marks from the table, they will appear in Excel and cause problems with the Pivot Table command.

After the macro copies each cell in the table over to Excel, it opens the Pivot Table wizard dialog box by using the Dialogs object and the Show method. Then, to stop the macro from quitting and discarding the new pivot table, the macro opens the Save As dialog box to let you save the worksheet to disk. Pivot tables are quite malleable, so you'll probably want to retrieve the new table now and then when you want to extract different information, or choose a different view.

Run the macro

Now run the macro to see how Word creates an Excel pivot table for you.

View Microsoft Word

1 Click the View Microsoft Word button on the Visual Basic Editor toolbar.

Word displays the Less11 document.

2 Click a cell in the Sales Rep table, and then run the PivotTable macro.

Word starts Excel with the CreateObject function, opens a new worksheet, and then copies each cell in the table to Excel. Word then runs the Pivot Table wizard, which displays the following dialog box:

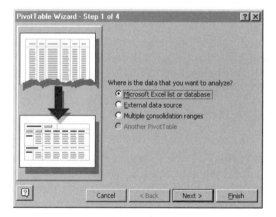

3 Click Next to select your new Excel worksheet as the source for the pivot table, and then click Next again to accept the default cell range recommended by the wizard.

Excel displays the third screen of the wizard, which asks you to organize the fields and calculations in your pivot table. You'll see a grid that looks a bit like a worksheet, with blank areas for rows, columns, and data. The column headings in your table will appear as movable buttons on the right side of the dialog box.

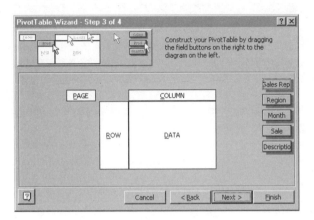

4 Define the initial layout of your pivot table by dragging column headings (or fields) from the right side of the dialog box into the Row, Column, and Data areas. Drag the Month heading to the Row area, drag the Sales Rep heading to the Column area, and drag the Sale heading to the Data area.

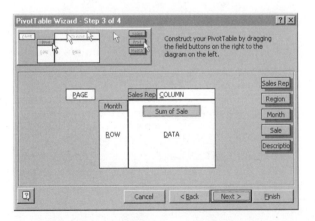

Fields placed in the Row area will become rows in the new table, fields placed in the Columns area will become columns, and fields placed in the Data area will be added together with the Sum function. Of course, the great thing about pivot tables is that you're not locked into this initial arrangement at all—you can create new combinations of rows, columns, and data at any time!

5 Click Next to display the final screen of the Pivot Table wizard, and then click Finish to accept the default location for the table.

Excel creates your pivot table in a new worksheet, and then prompts you to save it to disk.

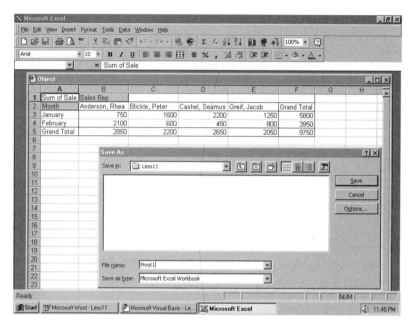

6 Specify the \WordVB\Less11 folder, type the name **Pivot1**, and then click Save.

Excel saves the pivot table and then quits, returning you to your Word document.

TIP To run the Pivot Table wizard again in Excel, start Excel and open the Pivot1 workbook, and then choose the PivotTable Report command from the Excel Data menu. The wizard will present the same series of dialog box screens that you saw in this exercise, and you'll be able to customize the pivot table to fit your new requirements.

Automating PowerPoint from Word

PowerPoint is Microsoft's state-of-the-art presentation software application, which allows you to create slide shows, multimedia presentations, kiosk displays, custom Web pages, and much more. PowerPoint 97 now includes the Visual Basic for Applications macro language, so you can write PowerPoint macros that automate how your slides are created and presented. In addition—and this is exciting for us—you can now use Automation to control PowerPoint from Microsoft Word or another controlling application.

Automating PowerPoint from Word is similar to automating Excel—simply create a link to the PowerPoint object library with the References command, create a PowerPoint object variable with the CreateObject function, and use the variable to run PowerPoint commands. In the following exercise, you'll build a simple macro that opens and runs a PowerPoint presentation right from your Word document.

Create the RunPresentation macro

The PowerPoint 97 application object is called Powerpoint. Application.8.

Complete the following steps to build a macro that starts PowerPoint 97, opens a presentation, and runs it.

 TIP You can either create the RunPresentation macro from scratch now, or you can open the Less11 document in the \WordVB\Less11 folder and run the RunPresentation macro we created for you.

---

1 From the Word Tools menu, click Macro, and then click Macros.

2 Type **RunPresentation** in the Name text box, and then verify that Less11 is selected in the Macros In list.

3 Click Create.

Word starts the Visual Basic Editor and opens a new macro procedure named RunPresentation in the Code window.

4 From the Tools menu, click References, and then select the PowerPoint 8.0 Object Library.

261

The PowerPoint 8.0 Object Library is required for Automation. Your References dialog box will look similar to the following:

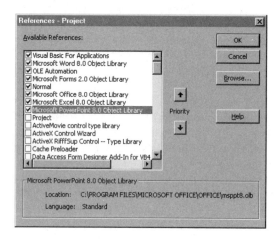

5 Now type the following program statements in the Code window:

```
Dim ppt As Object        'create object variable

Dim reply
reply = MsgBox("Run PowerPoint Facts presentation?", vbYesNo)
If reply = vbYes Then
    MsgBox ("Press spacebar to move from slide to slide.")
    Set ppt = CreateObject("Powerpoint.Application.8")
    ppt.Visible = True   'open and run presentation
    ppt.Presentations.Open "C:\WordVB\Less11\pptfacts.ppt"
    ppt.ActivePresentation.SlideShowSettings.Run
    Set ppt = Nothing    'release object variable
End If
```

This macro creates an object variable named ppt for the PowerPoint application object and then asks whether to run a PowerPoint presentation called PowerPoint Facts. If the user clicks Yes, the macro assigns the Powerpoint.Application.8 object to the ppt variable with the CreateObject function, displays the PowerPoint application with the Visible property, and opens the presentation file pptfacts.ppt with the Open method. The macro then runs the presentation with the Run method, and you can move from slide to slide by pressing the SPACEBAR.

Run the macro

Now run the macro to see how a PowerPoint presentation is automated from Word.

View Microsoft Word

1 Click the View Microsoft Word button on the Visual Basic Editor toolbar.

Word displays the Less11 document.

2 Start the RunPresentation macro.

Word asks you if you want to run the PowerPoint Facts presentation with a message box.

3 Click Yes, and then click OK when you are instructed to press the SPACEBAR during the slide show.

Word starts the PowerPoint presentation, and loads the first slide. (The background photograph comes from the Microsoft Windows 95 launch, and features Bill Gates and Jay Leno.)

4 Examine each slide in the presentation, pressing SPACEBAR to move from one to the next.

5 When you've finished reviewing the slide show, click the Close button on the PowerPoint title bar to quit the application and return to Word.

Congratulations! You've learned how to control two essential Office applications from a Word macro!

Controlling Word Objects from Visual Basic 5.0

As a final, optional exercise, we thought you might enjoy seeing how Word 97 itself is called from another controlling application through Automation. Throughout this book, you have used Word's programmable objects from within a Word macro, but you can also access them through the macro language of another controlling application, such as Excel, PowerPoint, Access, Project, or the Visual Basic compiler. In this lesson, you'll learn how to call Word from the Visual Basic 5.0 Programming System, a software development tool or *compiler* that you can use to create stand-alone executable (.exe) files that run under Windows 95 and Windows NT. If you've enjoyed writing Word macros in this book and you want to learn more, Visual Basic 5.0 is the next logical step.

NOTE Visual Basic 5.0 Learning Edition, Professional Edition, or Enterprise Edition is required to run the following demonstration program. If you don't have this compiler, simply follow along without running the program—you may find the information useful down the road.

The Word Application Object

Word 97 exposes its functionality to controlling applications through an object named Word.Application, an Automation interface very similar to the one used in Excel, PowerPoint, and the remaining Office 97 applications. The following exercise shows you how to use Word to check the spelling and grammar of sentences that you type in a Visual Basic text box. This is an especially handy feature in a Visual Basic program, because creating a spelling checker from scratch would be an extremely time-consuming endeavor. Not only would you need to create an electronic dictionary containing thousands of words, but you'd also need to create a parsing tool that analyzed the grammatical structure of each sentence. However, using Automation and Microsoft Word, you can check your spelling with just a few program statements!

Use Word via Automation

If you have the Visual Basic 5.0 compiler handy, here's what you do to automate a Word object:

1   Start the Visual Basic compiler by clicking the Start button, pointing to Programs, pointing to Microsoft Visual Basic 5.0, and then clicking the Visual Basic 5.0 program icon.

2   Click the Existing tab in the New Project dialog box, browse to the C:\WordVB\Less11 folder, and double-click Spelling.vbp.

> **TIP** Visual Basic programs are stored in project (.vbp) files, and typically include several supporting files (.frm, .bas, and so on). To make it easy for you, we've enclosed all the files you need for this program in the \WordVB\Less11 folder.

3 If the Spelling.frm form is not visible, select the Spelling form in the Project Explorer, and then click the View Object button. You'll see the user interface for the Visual Basic program, as shown in the following illustration:

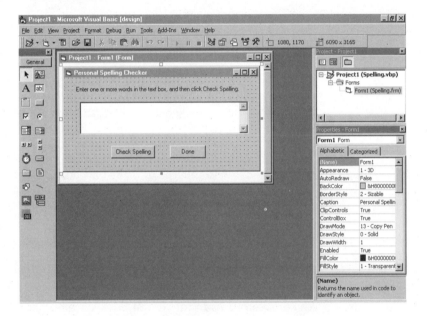

A Visual Basic form is similar to a UserForm in Word; it just has more features and design options. This particular form contains a multiline text box object, capable of holding one or more lines of text, a label, and two command buttons.

4 From the Project menu, click References, and scroll to the reference to the Microsoft Word 8.0 Object Library.

This object library reference creates a link between Visual Basic and Word 97. It is required for each Visual Basic project you create that uses Word Automation.

5 Click OK to close the References dialog box.

6 Double-click the Check Spelling button to see the program code that controls the Word Automation.

You'll see the following program statements:

```
Private Sub Command1_Click()
Dim wd As Object      'create Word object variable
Set wd = CreateObject("Word.Application")
wd.Visible = False    'hide Word
wd.Documents.Add      'open a new document
wd.Selection.Text = Text1.Text   'copy text box to document
wd.ActiveDocument.CheckSpelling  'run spell/grammar check
Text1.Text = wd.Selection.Text   'copy results back
wd.ActiveDocument.Close  SaveChanges:=wdDoNotSaveChanges
wd.Quit               'quit Word

Set wd = Nothing      'release object variable
End Sub
```

As you learned earlier in the lesson, you Automate another application's objects by creating an object variable, using the variable to call the program's objects, properties, and methods, and then releasing the object to conserve memory. In this particular Automation routine, we hide the Word user interface, open a new document, copy text to the new document, run the spelling and grammar checker, and copy any corrections back to the Visual Basic text box. After the event procedure checks the spelling, it closes the active document and then quits Word. The whole process looks a little familiar, doesn't it?

Run the program

Start

1   Click the Start button on the Visual Basic toolbar to run the Spelling program.

    The program runs in the Visual Basic development environment.

2   Type the following phrase into the text box: **workingg with objectss**.

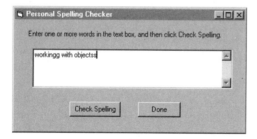

3   Click Check Spelling to check the structure and readability of the sentence by using Word's combined spelling and grammar checker.

Visual Basic starts Word and checks the sentence. After a moment, a dialog box appears identifying the first of two spelling errors, as shown in the following illustration:

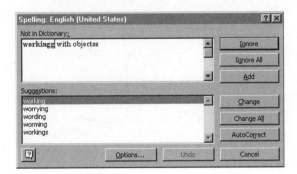

4   When you've finished making changes, click OK to close the spelling checker.

Word quits, and your Visual Basic program reappears, with the suggested changes made in the text box. With just a few lines of code, you used Word 97 from within a Visual Basic program. Not bad!

5   Click Done to quit the program.

The program quits, and the development environment reappears.

6   From the Visual Basic File menu, click Exit. If you are prompted to save any of your changes to the Spelling project, click Yes.

You're done using Visual Basic in this lesson.

One Step Further: What Next?

Congratulations! You've completed the entire Word Visual Basic programming course. We encourage you to continue your learning by exploring topics of interest to you in the Word Visual Basic online Help, and by using any of the following programming resources provided by Microsoft Press:

■   For a comprehensive reference to the Visual Basic for Applications macro language in *all* Microsoft Office 97 applications, purchase *Microsoft Office 97/Visual Basic Language Reference* (Microsoft Press, 1997), ISBN 1-57231-339-0. This is the official Microsoft programmer's reference for creating macros in Office 97, with some useful information for Word Visual Basic developers.

- To explore writing applications for Windows 95 and Windows NT with the Visual Basic 5.0 compiler, we recommend *Microsoft Visual Basic 5.0 Step by Step*, by Michael Halvorson (Microsoft Press, 1997), ISBN 1-57231-435-4. This book describes how to write general-purpose utilities such as games, clocks, text editors, bitmap browsers, database applications, and integrated applications that leverage Office 97.

- To apply your new programming skills to Excel macros, we recommend *Microsoft Excel 97/Visual Basic Step by Step*, by Reed Jacobson (Microsoft Press, 1997), ISBN 1-57231-318-8. Learn how to create a loan payment calculator, build an Enterprise Information System, construct a database report generator, and much more.

- To extend your Visual Basic expertise into database programming, try *Microsoft Access 97/Visual Basic Step by Step*, by Evan Callahan (Microsoft Press, 1997), ISBN 1-57231-319-6. Learn how to use wizards, filters, functions, navigation tools, and custom reports with Visual Basic macros.

 TIP You can order Microsoft Press books toll free in the United States by calling 1-800-MSPRESS. For the complete listing of Microsoft Press books, connect to the Microsoft Press web page using the address http://www.microsoft.com/mspress/.

Lesson Summary

To	Do this
Select an object library	From the Tools menu, click References. Select the check box next to the desired application or applications.
View application objects that support Automation	From the View menu, click the Object Browser command. Select the objects you want to examine in the Project/Library list.

Create an object variable in a program	Use the Dim and Set statements. For example:
	 `Dim ppt As Object`
	 `Set ppt = _`
	 `    CreateObject("Powerpoint.Application.8")`

Access application features by using Automation	Create an object variable, and then reference the methods or properties of the object. For example: `ppt.ActivePresentation.SlideShowSettings.Run`
Release the memory used by an object variable	Use the Set statement and the keyword Nothing with the variable name. For example: `Set ppt = Nothing`

For online information about	From the Visual Basic Help menu, click Contents And Index, and then
Excel objects	Click Contents, open Microsoft Excel Visual Basic Reference, double-click Getting Started With Visual Basic, and then double-click Excel Objects.
PowerPoint objects	Click Contents, open Microsoft PowerPoint Visual Basic Reference, double-click Microsoft PowerPoint Visual Basic Reference, and then double-click Microsoft PowerPoint Objects.
The Object Browser	Click Index, type **Object Browser**, and press ENTER. Double-click the Object Browser topic.
Programming application objects	Click Index, type **OLE Automation objects, creating**, and press ENTER. Double-click the CreateObject Function topic.

Index

SPECIAL CHARACTERS

& (ampersand), in front of menu commands, 95
_ (line continuation character), 69
+ operator (addition), 47, 51
+ operator (concatenation), 223
/ operator (division), 47, 51
= operator (equal to), 56
^ operator (exponentiation), 47, 51
> operator (greater than), 56
> = operator (greater than or equal to), 56
\ operator (integer division), 47, 51
< operator (less than), 56
< = operator (less than or equal to), 56
* operator (multiplication), 47, 51
- operator (negation), 51
< > operator (not equal to), 56
& operator (string concatenation), 47, 223
- operator (subtraction), 47, 51

A

access keys, for menu commands, 95
ActiveWindow object, 29
AddBookmarkCombo procedure, 178, 179–181
addition operator (+), 47, 51
Add method, 45
And logical operator, 62
App_DocumentChange routine, 178, 180, 183, 184
AppendFiles procedure, 233, 242–243
Application objects, 157–159
arguments, 41
    defined, 38
arrays, 36
ASCII characters, 218–219
    GetASCII macro, 220–223
AutoClose macro, 136
AutoExec macro, 136
AutoExit macro, 136
auto macros, 135–141
    creating a log file using the Close event, 138–141
    disabling, 136

B

BaseStyle property, 202
BaseStyle property of Style object, 196
BookmarkChoice routine, 178, 181, 184
Bookmark combo box, 179–181
bookmarks, 162–163
    defined, 178
    navigating with, 178–184
        AddBookmarkCombo procedure, 179–181
        application-level event handler, 182–183
        BookmarkChoice routine, 181
        moving modules to the Normal template, 179
        registering the event handler, 183–184
        testing the navigation system, 184
Boolean data type, storage size and range of, 36
Boolean expressions, 56
bounds checking, 68
Browser buttons, navigating using, 174–177
browsing objects, 174–175
BuiltIn property of Style object, 197
ButtonClicked variable, 41, 42
Button Editor, 90–91
buttons, toolbar
    adding, 89–92
    running macros with, 5
ButtonStyle argument, 41, 42
Byte data type, storage size and range of, 36

Automation, 248–256

Automation, 248–256
    applications that support, 248
    in Word 97, 249
    of Excel, from Word, 248, 250–260
    of PowerPoint, from Word, 261–263
    of Word application objects, from Visual
        Basic 5.0, 264
AutoNew macro, 136–138
AutoOpen macro, 136
AutoTable macro, 67–70

C

capitalization, TrueTitleCase macro for, 224–226
Case clauses, 63
Case Else clauses, 64
CenterHeading macro, 30–34, 37
Change Case command, 224

Index

Index

Learn to build high-performance *Windows* and *Internet* applications with *Visual Basic*!

MICROSOFT® VISUAL BASIC, DELUXE LEARNING EDITION, is a comprehensive training kit that will teach you how to put Microsoft Visual Basic to work building high-performance Windows and Internet applications. The kit contains the complete version of Visual Basic 5.0, Learning Edition, and is the easiest way to learn to use it. You choose the training that fits your own learning style—easy-to-follow, interactive, computer-based training with multimedia lessons and exercises, or your choice of two outstanding Visual Basic programming guidebooks.

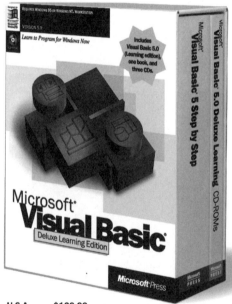

U.S.A.	**$129.99**
U.K.	£121.99 [V.A.T. included]
Canada	$174.99
ISBN 1-57231-551-2	

Microsoft®*Press*

Take productivity in stride.

Microsoft Press® *Step by Step* books provide quick and easy self-paced training that will help you learn to use the powerful word processor, spreadsheet, database, desktop information manager, and presentation applications of Microsoft Office 97, both individually and together. Prepared by the professional trainers at Catapult, Inc., and Perspection, Inc., these books present easy-to-follow lessons with clear objectives, real-world business examples, and numerous screen shots and illustrations. Each book contains approximately eight hours of instruction. Put Microsoft's Office 97 applications to work today, *Step by Step*.

Microsoft® Excel 97 Step by Step
U.S.A. **$29.95**   ($39.95 Canada)
ISBN 1-57231-314-5

Microsoft® Word 97 Step by Step
U.S.A. **$29.95**   ($39.95 Canada)
ISBN 1-57231-313-7

**Microsoft® PowerPoint® 97
Step by Step**
U.S.A. **$29.95**   ($39.95 Canada)
ISBN 1-57231-315-3

Microsoft® Outlook™ 97 Step by Step
U.S.A. **$29.99**   ($39.99 Canada)
ISBN 1-57231-382-X

Microsoft® Access 97 Step by Step
U.S.A. **$29.95**   ($39.95 Canada)
ISBN 1-57231-316-1

**Microsoft® Office 97 Integration
Step by Step**
U.S.A. **$29.95**   ($39.95 Canada)
ISBN 1-57231-317-X

Microsoft Press® products are available worldwide wherever quality computer books are sold. For more information, contact your book retailer, computer reseller, or local Microsoft Sales Office.

To locate your nearest source for Microsoft Press products, reach us at mspress.microsoft.com, or call 1-800-MSPRESS in the U.S. (in Canada: 1-800-667-1115 or 416-293-8464).

To order Microsoft Press products, call 1-800-MSPRESS in the U.S. (in Canada: 1-800-667-1115 or 416-293-8464).

Prices and availability dates are subject to change.

Microsoft®Press

Create ActiveX™ controls and Internet-enabled applications— fast!

MICROSOFT® VISUAL BASIC® 5.0 DEVELOPER'S WORKSHOP, Fourth Edition, is a one-of-a-kind book-and-software package that gives you the recipes to build powerful, full-featured graphical applications for Windows® 95 and Windows NT® This book demonstrates everything from creating a screen saver to building ActiveX controls that can be used in a Web page. You'll learn by example how to:

- Build 32-bit applications for Windows 95 and Windows NT
- Develop reusable objects to enhance your productivity
- Extend the language by calling Windows API functions
- Take advantage of ActiveX technologies
- Access data on an Internet server
- Install applications over the Internet

Create full-featured Windows 95 and Windows NT–based applications faster than ever before with MICROSOFT VISUAL BASIC 5.0 DEVELOPER'S WORKSHOP!

U.S.A.	**$44.99**
U.K.	£41.99 [V.A.T. included]
Canada	$60.99
ISBN	1-57231-436-2

Microsoft®Press

Keep things **running** smoothly

around **the Office.**

These are *the* answer books for business users of Microsoft Office 97 applications. They are packed with everything from quick, clear instructions for new users to comprehensive answers for power users. The Microsoft Press® *Running* series features authoritative handbooks you'll keep by your computer and use every day.

Running Microsoft® Excel 97
Mark Dodge, Chris Kinata, and Craig Stinson
U.S.A. $39.95 ($53.95 Canada)
ISBN 1-57231-321-8

Running Microsoft® Word 97
Russell Borland
U.S.A. $39.95 ($53.95 Canada)
ISBN 1-57231-320-X

Running Microsoft® PowerPoint® 97
Stephen W. Sagman
U.S.A. $29.95 ($39.95 Canada)
ISBN 1-57231-324-2

Running Microsoft® Access 97
John L. Viescas
U.S.A. $39.95 ($53.95 Canada)
ISBN 1-57231-323-4

Running Microsoft® Office 97
Michael Halvorson and Michael Young
U.S.A. $39.95 ($53.95 Canada)
ISBN 1-57231-322-6

Microsoft *Press*

Authoritative information.
Impressive results.

Covers Microsoft Office 97 for Windows 95, Windows NT, and the Apple Macintosh

MICROSOFT PROFESSIONAL EDITIONS

Master the Powerful Development Platform Within the World's Most Popular Office Suite

Microsoft Office 97 Visual Basic Programmer's Guide

Microsoft Press

U.S.A.	**$34.99**
U.K.	£32.49
Canada	$46.99
ISBN 1-57231-340-4	

With this guide and a basic knowledge of Microsoft® Visual Basic® for Applications or any Microsoft Office programming language, you'll learn to do everything from automating individual tasks to creating full-fledged custom applications. You'll explore Microsoft Visual Basic for Applications version 5.0, the common programming language shared by applications in Microsoft Office 97. And always, you'll get the authoritative, inside story from the people who actually developed Microsoft Office 97.

Microsoft®*Press*

IMPORTANT—READ CAREFULLY BEFORE OPENING SOFTWARE PACKET(S). By opening the sealed packet(s) containing the software, you indicate your acceptance of the following Microsoft License Agreement.

MICROSOFT LICENSE AGREEMENT

(Book Companion CD)

This is a legal agreement between you (either an individual or an entity) and Microsoft Corporation. By opening the sealed software packet(s) you are agreeing to be bound by the terms of this agreement. If you do not agree to the terms of this agreement, promptly return the unopened software packet(s) and any accompanying written materials to the place you obtained them for a full refund.

MICROSOFT SOFTWARE LICENSE

1. GRANT OF LICENSE. Microsoft grants to you the right to use one copy of the Microsoft software program included with this book (the "SOFTWARE") on a single terminal connected to a single computer. The SOFTWARE is in "use" on a computer when it is loaded into the temporary memory (i.e., RAM) or installed into the permanent memory (e.g., hard disk, CD-ROM, or other storage device) of that computer. You may not network the SOFTWARE or otherwise use it on more than one computer or computer terminal at the same time.

2. COPYRIGHT. The SOFTWARE is owned by Microsoft or its suppliers and is protected by United States copyright laws and international treaty provisions. Therefore, you must treat the SOFTWARE like any other copyrighted material (e.g., a book or musical recording) except that you may either (a) make one copy of the SOFTWARE solely for backup or archival purposes, or (b) transfer the SOFTWARE to a single hard disk provided you keep the original solely for backup or archival purposes. You may not copy the written materials accompanying the SOFTWARE.

3. OTHER RESTRICTIONS. You may not rent or lease the SOFTWARE, but you may transfer the SOFTWARE and accompanying written materials on a permanent basis provided you retain no copies and the recipient agrees to the terms of this Agreement. You may not reverse engineer, decompile, or disassemble the SOFTWARE. If the SOFTWARE is an update or has been updated, any transfer must include the most recent update and all prior versions.

4. DUAL MEDIA SOFTWARE. If the SOFTWARE package contains more than one kind of disk (3.5", 5.25", and CD-ROM), then you may use only the disks appropriate for your single-user computer. You may not use the other disks on another computer or loan, rent, lease, or transfer them to another user except as part of the permanent transfer (as provided above) of all SOFTWARE and written materials.

5. SAMPLE CODE. If the SOFTWARE includes Sample Code, then Microsoft grants you a royalty-free right to reproduce and distribute the sample code of the SOFTWARE provided that you: (a) distribute the sample code only in conjunction with and as a part of your software product; (b) do not use Microsoft's or its authors' names, logos, or trademarks to market your software product; (c) include the copyright notice that appears on the SOFTWARE on your product label and as a part of the sign-on message for your software product; and (d) agree to indemnify, hold harmless, and defend Microsoft and its authors from and against any claims or lawsuits, including attorneys' fees, that arise or result from the use or distribution of your software product.

DISCLAIMER OF WARRANTY

The SOFTWARE (including instructions for its use) is provided "AS IS" WITHOUT WARRANTY OF ANY KIND. MICROSOFT FURTHER DISCLAIMS ALL IMPLIED WARRANTIES INCLUDING WITHOUT LIMITATION ANY IMPLIED WARRANTIES OF MERCHANTABILITY OR OF FITNESS FOR A PARTICULAR PURPOSE. THE ENTIRE RISK ARISING OUT OF THE USE OR PERFORMANCE OF THE SOFTWARE AND DOCUMENTATION REMAINS WITH YOU.

IN NO EVENT SHALL MICROSOFT, ITS AUTHORS, OR ANYONE ELSE INVOLVED IN THE CREATION, PRODUCTION, OR DELIVERY OF THE SOFTWARE BE LIABLE FOR ANY DAMAGES WHATSOEVER (INCLUDING, WITHOUT LIMITATION, DAMAGES FOR LOSS OF BUSINESS PROFITS, BUSINESS INTERRUPTION, LOSS OF BUSINESS INFORMATION, OR OTHER PECUNIARY LOSS) ARISING OUT OF THE USE OF OR INABILITY TO USE THE SOFTWARE OR DOCUMENTATION, EVEN IF MICROSOFT HAS BEEN ADVISED OF THE POSSIBILITY OF SUCH DAMAGES. BECAUSE SOME STATES/COUNTRIES DO NOT ALLOW THE EXCLUSION OR LIMITATION OF LIABILITY FOR CONSEQUENTIAL OR INCIDENTAL DAMAGES, THE ABOVE LIMITATION MAY NOT APPLY TO YOU.

U.S. GOVERNMENT RESTRICTED RIGHTS

The SOFTWARE and documentation are provided with RESTRICTED RIGHTS. Use, duplication, or disclosure by the Government is subject to restrictions as set forth in subparagraph (c)(1)(ii) of The Rights in Technical Data and Computer Software clause at DFARS 252.227-7013 or subparagraphs (c)(1) and (2) of the Commercial Computer Software — Restricted Rights 48 CFR 52.227-19, as applicable. Manufacturer is Microsoft Corporation, One Microsoft Way, Redmond, WA 98052-6399.

If you acquired this product in the United States, this Agreement is governed by the laws of the State of Washington. Should you have any questions concerning this Agreement, or if you desire to contact Microsoft Press for any reason, please write: Microsoft Press, One Microsoft Way, Redmond, WA 98052-6399.

The Step by Step
Practice Files CD-ROM

The enclosed CD-ROM contains timesaving, ready-to-use practice files that complement the lessons in this book. To use the practice files, you'll need Microsoft Word 97 (version 8) or Microsoft Office 97 and either the Microsoft Windows 95 operating system or version 3.51 Service Pack 5 or later of the Microsoft Windows NT operating system.

Most of the *Step by Step* lessons use practice files from the disk. Before you begin the *Step by Step* lessons, read the "Installing and Using the Practice Files" section of the book. There you'll find a description of each practice file and easy instructions for installing the files on your computer's hard disk.

Please take a few moments to read the license agreement on the previous page before using the enclosed disk.

Register your Microsoft Press® book today, and let us know what you think.

At Microsoft Press, we listen to our customers. We update our books as new releases of software are issued, and we'd like you to tell us the kinds of additional information you'd find most useful in these updates. Your feedback will be considered when we prepare a future edition; plus, when you become a registered owner, you will get Microsoft Press catalogs and exclusive offers on specially priced books.

Thanks!

I used this book as

- ● A way to learn the software
- ● A reference when I needed it
- ● A way to find out about advanced features
- ● Other_____

I purchased this book from

- ● A bookstore
- ● A software store
- ● A direct mail offer
- ● Other_____

I consider myself

- ● A beginner or an occasional computer user
- ● An intermediate-level user with a pretty good grasp of the basics
- ● An advanced user who helps and provides solutions for others
- ● Other_____

I will buy the next edition of the book when it's updated

- ● Definitely
- ● Probably
- ● I will not buy the next edition

The next edition of this book should include the following additional information:

1 •_____

2 •_____

3 •_____

The most useful things about this book are_____

This book would be more helpful if_____

My general impressions of this book are_____

May we contact you regarding your comments?　● Yes　● No

Would you like to receive a Microsoft Press catalog regularly?　● Yes　● No

Name_____

Company (if applicable)_____

Address_____

City_____State_____Zip_____

Daytime phone number (optional) (_____)_____

NO POSTAGE
NECESSARY
IF MAILED
IN THE
UNITED STATES

BUSINESS REPLY MAIL
FIRST-CLASS MAIL   PERMIT NO. 53   BOTHELL, WA

POSTAGE WILL BE PAID BY ADDRESSEE

MICROSOFT PRESS
MICROSOFT® WORD 97/ VISUAL BASIC®
STEP BY STEP
PO BOX 3019
BOTHELL WA 98041-9946